Arkansas Mischief

Arkansas Mischief

The Birth of a National Scandal

JIM McDOUGAL
and
Curtis Wilkie

A JOHN MACRAE BOOK
Henry Holt and Company, Inc.
New York

Henry Holt and Company, Inc.
Publishers since 1866
115 West 18th Street
New York, New York 10011

Henry Holt® is a registered trademark of
Henry Holt and Company, Inc.

5-8-07   25.00

Library of Congress Cataloging-in-Publication data are available.

ISBN 0-8050-5808-7

Henry Holt books are available for special
promotions and premiums. For details contact:
Director, Special Markets.

First Edition 1998

Designed by Paula R. Szafranski

Printed in the United States of America
All first editions are printed on acid-free paper. ∞

1   3   5   7   9   10   8   6   4   2

To Claudia Riley, for her care and strength.

To Carter, Leighton, and Stuart, for their support.

Oh! Didn't he ramble, ramble?
He rambled all around, in and out the town.
Oh! Didn't he ramble, ramble?
He rambled 'til the butchers cut him down.

—*From the Dixieland jazz standard*
"Oh! Didn't He Ramble"
Attributed to Will Handy, 1902

Acknowledgments

On behalf of Jim McDougal, I'd like to thank: Claudia Riley, Chris Vlasto, Sam Boyce, Ernie and Elaine Dumas, John Ferguson and the staff of the Arkansas History Commission, Richard Ford, Bill Simmons, Parker Westbrook, Marion Elizabeth Rodgers, Jack Files, Gary Bunch, Russ Perrymore, Michele Manon, Lloyd Grove, Caroline Teasdale, Cal Ledbetter, Kane Webb, Roy Reed, Hal Moody, Michael Isikoff, Jeff Gerth, Jason Berry, Warren Clark, Marilyn Latham, Alma Williams, Tom Oliphant, Sean Mullin, and my colleagues at the *Boston Globe*.

For their help and professionalism, especially during the days following Jim's death, special thanks to our agent, Deborah Grosvenor, and our editors at Henry Holt, John Macrae and Rachel Klauber-Speiden.

C.W.

Preface

When Jim McDougal's agent called to ask if I might collaborate with McDougal on his memoirs, I wasn't really interested. He had the image of an eccentric with a credibility problem, I told her. Eventually, she persuaded me to visit him at his Arkadelphia home a few days before he was to enter prison. Instead of meeting a crazy, embittered man, I found a charming raconteur. Jim had a wealth of funny Arkansas stories and a philosophical attitude about his impending imprisonment.

Obviously, I knew we were fellow southerners, but I discovered we were born within a month of one another, each an only child in a household of Scots-Irish parents. We liked books and history and appreciated the quirky rhythms of southern politics. More importantly, I decided he was believable. (Journalists who covered the Whitewater case say he was a very reliable source.) Before I left Jim that first day, a friendship was formed.

Jim was fatalistic. He had a premonition that he would die in prison, and he was eager to tell the full story of his involvement in the Whitewater case in the context of his colorful career in Arkansas politics.

After I agreed to work with him, we began a long series of exchanges. He called from prison early every morning to talk for twenty to thirty minutes. There were at least a hundred of these conversations. To deal with matters too sensitive to discuss over the monitored telephone, I visited him seven times in prison.

Shortly after he was confined at the Federal Medical Center in Lexington, Kentucky, he called to report that doctors wanted to operate on a blocked artery. He felt it was unnecessary and didn't want to undergo surgery. He added a mordant note: "The conspiracy boys could sure have fun if I died on the operating table." Jim asked me to alert some of his friends in the Whitewater press corps to make inquiries about his condition at the prison. After several newspapers, news magazines, and networks expressed interest in his health, the prison authorities chose to forgo surgery. Jim was relieved.

Following his transfer to a facility in Fort Worth, there was a break in our talks. Several days later, he called to say he had been held in "solitary confinement"—the authorities called it "administrative detention"; inmates called it "the hole"—because he was unable to produce a urine sample during a spot check for drugs. Jim said his plumbing refused to work on demand because of the nitroglycerine, lithium, and other strong medications he took to alleviate his serious illnesses. He asked me to call an intermediary who would relay his plight to the office of Kenneth Starr, the independent counsel. After agreeing to cooperate in the investigation of President Clinton, Jim had little choice but to look to Starr's office for protection. Jim wanted to avoid disciplinary actions. He hoped he could be paroled as soon as late April 1998.

Occasionally during our daily talks, he said he felt tired or ill, but he continued to call religiously. He went through the first draft of the book in the fall and made a few changes. On reflection, he said, he wanted to tone down some of the profanity. Otherwise he felt the manuscript captured his voice.

Where it was possible, the quotes in the book were taken from transcripts, periodicals, and court documents. In some cases, the quotes were reconstructed from Jim's account and confirmed with the individuals involved. In a few cases, I had to rely on Jim's memory. The research undertaken convinces me of the truth of his account.

We completed our project in mid-February. It was no longer necessary for us to talk each day, but I asked him to stay in touch, to call every few days.

I last talked with him in late February. He was going over the final draft of the manuscript and seemed in a good mood. There was one discouraging note. He had attended a preliminary parole hearing that had not seemed to go well. His hopes for a spring release seemed dim, but he kept up his spirits.

He called again on March 4. I was not at home, and he left a light-hearted message on my answering device, promising to call in a day or two. I never heard from him again. Because Jim was physically unable to urinate on demand once again, he was restricted to "administrative detention" and was in solitary when he was stricken on the morning of March 8. Minutes after the authorities rushed him to a hospital, Jim McDougal was pronounced dead. It was the sixth anniversary of Jim's first appearance on the front page of the *New York Times*—the day the original Whitewater story was published.

On Friday, March 13, Jim was buried in the family plot of his dear friends, the Rileys, in Arkadelphia. There was no McDougal family left to mourn him. Claudia Riley arranged for a jazz band to play at the graveside service. A gray overcast robbed the sun of its warmth as a hundred or so of Jim's friends and a half dozen television camera crews departed the cemetery; only his inexpensive coffin and a few sprays of flowers were left. Jim's life had ended, just as he spent much of it, alone.

Curtis Wilkie
March 14, 1998

Arkansas Mischief

Prologue

Before I acquired a number—185 25 009 from the Federal Bureau of Prisons—I had a name and reputation in Arkansas: Jim McDougal, known at various times as a prodigy, playboy, political insider, and successful capitalist. Once I was a friend and adviser to the mighty in the state. Now the newspapers call me the "Promoter" and the "Godfather of Whitewater."

For many years, I worked with the most prominent figures in Arkansas and became associated in business with some of them: a senator, J. William Fulbright; a governor, Jim Guy Tucker; and, of course, Bill Clinton. We prospered. I developed land, controlled banks, made millions of dollars. But my fortune is lost, and the whirl that my wife, Susan, and I enjoyed within the circles of power in Arkansas is over. Susan and I are divorced. She is imprisoned in California; I am an inmate at the Federal Medical Center prison in Fort Worth. We have had no contact for more than a year.

Over the past year and a half since my conviction in the Whitewater case, I've had time to reflect on my fate; I've come to understand how Arkansas politics and its intimate connections consumed my life. In many ways, as I said in an interview just before entering the penitentiary, I was merely the latest victim of the Clinton tornado, joining a long list of associates who were used by Bill and Hillary Clinton and then pitched aside when their usefulness was over.

Perhaps it's an indication of my own grandiloquence, but I feel like a character in a Shakespearean tragedy. The cast, after all, includes the leader of a great country, a man at once lovable, cunning, and deeply flawed. God forgive me, but his wife reminds me a bit of Lady Macbeth. Together, the Clintons emerged from their own little kingdom in Arkansas to become the most powerful couple on earth, yet they have diminished themselves through a string of unnecessary lies and broken promises. Along the way, they destroyed erstwhile friends and are haunted to this day by their ghosts.

I grew up in an era when Arkansas was represented by honorable men: Fulbright, John McClellan, and Wilbur Mills. Though they were imperfect, their word was bond; they followed a traditional code of political conduct that seemed to disappear with the nickel bottle of Coca-Cola. Their generation gave way to a new breed of leaders, articulate, bold, and, most importantly, telegenic. Clinton and Tucker were exemplars of the modern school of Arkansas politics, overachievers determined to get ahead regardless of the cost. With them, deals were too often consummated with a wink instead of a firm handshake. They were my contemporaries, and I was a con artist in their company. But I finally grew weary of their phony piety, and after I blew the whistle on them, the case developed into a national scandal.

The Arkansas story that spilled into Whitewater is long and complex. Many of its characters are dead now. Clinton hangs on at the White House. Tucker was driven from the governor's office. Some of the lesser known went to jail. The Whitewater ledger is a book of victims, with only a few villains. It is an account of ambitious young men climbing from rural obscurity, of business and greed and politics intersecting in a small southern state, of friendships breaking apart and lives ruined.

With the turn of a new year, 1998, I feel optimistic and relatively healthy. At a hearing when I was sentenced, a doctor testified I had the body of a seventy-six-year-old man. I was fifty-six at the time, a manic-depressive on medication and suffering from blocked arteries. Today, I'm lifting weights. Oddly enough, I'm exposed to more sunlight in prison than I saw in seclusion in Arkansas. I hope to be released soon, but if I don't win parole it won't be the end of the world.

Since I spent much of this decade dealing with lawyers and journalists, I like to say that I've improved my associations by joining the criminal class. As Dostoyevsky wrote, prison is life in miniature, where one learns to cope with a strange environment. Inside our fenced facility, on a windswept hill on the eastern edge of Fort Worth, several hundred men from different backgrounds—blacks, Latinos, and whites with vocations as electricians, accountants, plumbers, and politicians—co-exist in a highly structured setting.

From the day the gates closed behind me, I have been struck by the courtesy and compassion of my fellow inmates. As I'm walking down the corridor, a man in prison khakis holds a door open for me. Rising from our communal dinner table, a departing inmate says, "If you gentlemen will excuse me . . ." Strong men volunteer to push wheelchairs for the older inmates. There is a civility here that the outside world lacks, and I trust these men more than many of my old associates.

After my divorce, my mother's death, and the solitude of a one-bedroom home in the out-of-the-way town of Arkadelphia, Arkansas, I've warmed to the social exchange. During each day, we are permitted a period to sit and talk, like students in a college dormitory. Invariably, the discussions turn to the experiences that brought us here. The older guys are often bank robbers, driven to desperate action by debt. Recalling the times when they brandished weapons, they express remorse for terrifying women tellers. Others are doing time for more mundane offenses, embezzlement or cheating on their taxes. Regardless of the nature of their convictions, everyone has a story.

Appearance here is very important. To make their stories more compelling, some of my new friends aggrandize their crimes, inflating the size of their thefts and the danger of the moment. Surprisingly, a large number of the inmates describe themselves as victims and insist upon their innocence.

I no longer make such a claim. Convicted on eighteen counts of fraud, I admit my guilt. Mine is the most notorious case in the prison, yet I find I'm able to laugh at certain episodes as I relate my story. I like to close my tales by invoking a line from an old country-and-western song, "I'm sick, sober, and sorry."

Yet I don't feel terribly penitent. I prefer to think of myself as a good pirate in the tradition of southern populists, quick to bend the law to defy the establishment.

It's therapeutic to talk about the case, to tell about some details for the first time. Things become clearer. I recognize my behavior as contradictory at times, and remember I am, after all, manic-depressive. I'm also irreverent. H. L. Mencken once said he liked to throw dead cats into the sanctuary. So do I. But I try not to exaggerate; there's no need to do so. It's a good story, as large and misunderstood as the state of Arkansas.

1

For much of this century, Arkansas has been ridiculed as America's Dogpatch, a poor, rural home for yokels, a place where hounds amble along dirt roads, chickens peck for bugs in the yard, and well-to-do families flaunt Sears washing machines on their front porches. Perennially, we are at the bottom of every economic indicator, fighting Mississippi for forty-ninth place. Our population is less than any southern state, and our land area the slightest of any state on the continent west of the Mississippi River. No airline uses Arkansas as a hub. The federal interstate highway system bypasses much of the state. Even the name of our capital begins with the word "little."

At the state university in Fayetteville, a menacing boar from the Ozarks—the razorback hog—was adopted as a symbol of the school. A hog call became Arkansas's war cry. At sporting events, the student body still rises as one, hands fluttering skyward, to issue the blood-curdling refrain: "Whooooooooo, pig! Soooo-ey!"

In the days when radio was the main form of home entertainment, Arkansas was a frequent butt of humor. We were the target of gentle yarns spun by a native son, the comedian Bob Burns. A popular voice in the 1930s, Burns talked of his barefoot relatives. Arkansas was the source of cracker-barrel philosophy broadcast by Lum and Abner, who held court at their Jot 'Em Down Store in the mythical Arkansas village of Pine Ridge. Sponsored each week by Horlick's Malted Milk, Lum and Abner created a world of bucolic characters, peopled by the likes of kindly Grandpappy Spears.

Sometimes, the Arkansas jokes took malevolent form. H. L. Mencken, the iconoclastic columnist for the *Baltimore Sun* papers, mocked Arkansas mercilessly in the 1930s. "Only on the records of lynchings and open-air baptisms is the state near the top," he wrote. Mencken described Arkansas as "the worst American state" and wondered "why so many of its farmers are miserable, exploited, chronically half-starved share-croppers without reserves and without hope." The state senate responded by passing resolutions calling for Mencken to be deported from the United States. The Arkansas chapter of the Knights of the Ku Klux Klan was not so diplomatic; it denounced Mencken as a "moral pervert."

Arkansas was still reeling from the Great Depression when the cartoonist Al Capp created *Li'l Abner*, a comic strip set in Dogpatch and featuring such curious characters as pipe-smoking Mammy Yokum; Daisy Mae, a backwoods beauty in tattered dress; and Li'l Abner himself—well-intentioned but slow-witted, a mountain manchild bursting out of his overalls. Arkansas was assumed to be the locale, and entrepreneurs later encouraged the parody by developing a Dogpatch, USA, theme park in the Ozarks near Harrison.

Not to be outdone by this secular attraction, Gerald L. K. Smith, an evangelical, rabble-rousing anti-Semite—Mencken called him "the champion boob bumper of all epochs"—chose another Ozark town, Eureka Springs, to build a glistening white statue of Jesus, seven stories high, overlooking the site for Smith's ersatz Oberammergau passion play, a drama blaming the Jews for the crucifixion of the savior. Down the road, Smith purveyed a line of Christian trinkets at his Christ Only Art Gallery.

Strains of Protestant fundamentalism ran through the state like mighty rivers. The Southern Baptists have always been the strongest denomination. Frowning upon the legalization of alcohol and the mingling of races, the Baptists dictated the mores of numerous Arkansas communities for years, keeping them dry and segregated. The hardshell arbiters of Arkansas society were reinforced by the Church of Christ, a faith holding even sterner views of earthly pleasures. In towns under the watch of the Church of Christ, musical instruments were considered tools of the devil and dancing illicit. During the Cold War period, Harding College, a Church of Christ institution in Searcy, sponsored a "National Education Program" to spread warnings of communist peril lurking in the civil rights movement and among the ranks of peace demonstrators.

Despite our image as a state full of right-wing yahoos, Arkansas had its flirtations on the other side of the political spectrum. In Mena, a west Arkansas town near the Oklahoma border, Commonwealth College cropped up in the 1920s like a red wildflower in a field of cotton. The school was steeped in socialist doctrine and produced a number of graduates who served as labor organizers and foot soldiers for the Loyalist cause in the Spanish Civil War.

One of the school's leaders was Claude Williams, a renegade Presbyterian minister. Williams said his faith in Jesus led him to convictions contrary to the Arkansas norm. "I cannot believe in race prejudice or class antagonism and exploitation," he declared, and he kept on his office wall pictures of his heroes: Jesus, Lenin, and Eugene V. Debs. When Williams intervened in a farmworkers dispute involving the death of a black laborer, he was beaten so badly by a vigilante mob that he moved to other pursuits. Commonwealth was finally shut down by the authorities in 1940 on the grounds that the school was subversive.

One of Commonwealth's most famous alumni, Orval E. Faubus, would deny his enrollment at the school after he became a major figure in Arkansas politics. Though he disavowed it, Faubus carried leftist baggage in his background. His father, Sam Faubus, was an exuberant prophet who roamed the northwestern corner of the state on behalf of socialism during the early years of the century. When Sam Faubus named his son Orval, he chose Eugene for his middle name in homage to Eugene Debs, leader of the Socialist Party of America.

Populist movements flourished in pockets of the state. A radical farmers organization, the Brothers of Freedom, enlisted forty thousand members in Arkansas at the height of its power in the 1880s. They were the precursors of the Southern Tenant Farmers Union, a group started in northeastern Arkansas in 1934 but beaten down within a few years by the powerful landowners of the region.

At the beginning of the twentieth century, Arkansas elected colorful populist Jeff Davis governor. Davis railed against the establishment, denouncing the banking interests in Little Rock as "high-collared roosters" who dressed in "collars so high they can't see the sun except at high noon." Davis's enemies fought insult with invective. The *Helena World*, a conservative newspaper in a Mississippi River Delta town, dismissed Davis as a crude aberration out of the hills, "a carrot-headed, red-faced, loud-mouthed, strong-limbed, ox-driving mountaineer lawyer, and a friend of the fellow who brews forty-rod bug-juice."

We may have been a poor state, but we were rich with personalities.

In 1940, the year I was born, Arkansas's per capita income was only 42 percent of the national average; 78 percent of our people lived either on farms or in towns with populations of less than 2,500. We had fewer white-collar workers than almost any other state.

We were an agrarian society, perhaps not too far removed from the caricatures of Mencken and Capp. Along the Mississippi River, in the eastern part of the state, cotton planters reigned over duchies in the Delta. The fertility of the land was the envy of the agricultural world. The dark alluvial soil produced bumper crops and a less admirable by-product—an Old South feudal system where wealthy landowners ruled sharecroppers and itinerant farm workers living in peonage to the plantation.

But our Delta, a relentlessly flat 150-mile corridor between Jonesboro and Lake Village, occupies only a sliver of the state. The topography of Arkansas—and the way of life—shifts dramatically away from the river. The ground begins to rise near my little home-town of Bradford to meet the foothills and mountains of the Ozarks, where the land is as mean as a miser.

When I was growing up, the region served as the home of the hill people, the small farmers who, each planting season, engaged in battles with the elements without the benefit of armies of Delta field hands. They lived in reclusive communities, loyal to family and church and suspicious of strangers.

From the time the state was founded in 1836, a dichotomy has existed between the Delta planter class and the populist hill folk. The differences have been played out in regional rivalries and clashes in the state legislature, but there is a third distinctive ele-ment in the state's demographics.

As the Ozarks fall away to the rolling countryside in the southern part of the state, the terrain is dominated by vast stretches of timberland. Here, lumber replaces cotton and soybeans as the cash crop, and local society bears little resemblance to either the Delta or the Ozarks.

Below the Ouachita mountain range, citizens seem estranged from the rest of the state, carrying grudges based on a belief that their region is systematically shortchanged in Little Rock when pub-lic funds are parceled out for highways and other projects. The people feel a closer kinship to the wildcatters of Tulsa and the small ranchers of Tyler, Texas.

Wedged between Tennessee and Mississippi to the east and Texas and Oklahoma to the west, our state is neither southern nor western. Though Arkansas belonged to the Confederacy, we have little of the "moonlight and magnolias" mystique that characterizes our neighbors who still worship the Lost Cause. In places like Texarkana, words are more likely to be pronounced with an east Texas twang than with the softer southern accent heard across the river from Memphis. And in the Ozarks, forms of Elizabethan English can still be heard, spoken in cadences so odd and countrified they sound as though they belong on the stage of the Grand Ole Opry.

Local boosters like to call Arkansas the Wonder State. It's no wonder we sometimes suffer from an inferiority complex and an identity crisis.

Arkansas politics reflected our geography. We were part of the eleven-state monolith once known as the "Solid South," a bloc that could be counted upon to deliver its electoral votes every four years to the Democratic nominee for president. Allegiance to the Democratic Party was an outgrowth of the Reconstruction and lingering resentment against the Republican administrations for imposing severe hardship on the Confederate states following the Civil War. Once the northern rulers and their local sympathizers, known contemptuously as "carpetbaggers and scalawags," were routed, southerners regained control of their governments. Across the region, voters became fierce Democrats—but for few reasons that would attract them to the national Democratic Party today. It was a reaction against the party of Lincoln, and these early Southern Democrats moved vigorously to disenfranchise black voters and resegregate the races. Their hegemony would last for most of the twentieth century.

Arkansas became a Democratic stronghold, yet we were different from the rest of Dixie. Our politics were not as poisoned by race as the states with large concentrations of black residents. Alabama, Georgia, Mississippi, and South Carolina spawned generations of demagogues, leaders who evoked fears of a black uprising and a new Reconstruction. Although many claimed to be populists, they perverted the ideology by pitting poor whites against poor blacks. In elections where blacks were unable to vote, racists such as Theodore G. Bilbo thrived in Mississippi during the first half of the century, and a modern generation of segregationists, personified by George C. Wallace of Alabama, kept up the resistance to black rights. In Arkansas, we had only one modern champion of segregation, Faubus; others who coveted Faubus's mantle were unsuccessful.

Compared to the rest of the South, Arkansas has always had a relatively small black population (less than 16 percent in the 1990 census). As a result, Arkansas escaped much of the racial turmoil of the midcentury.

Rather than suppressing the potential power of blacks at the ballot box, Arkansas plantation owners actually encouraged their employees to register to vote. The system produced impressive results in the counties of east Arkansas; like eastern Europe under dictatorship, 100 percent of the votes went to the candidate of the establishment in many precincts. Landowners doubled as political bosses. They paid the poll taxes for their employees, told their workers how to vote, and ensured a heavy turnout on election days. The *Arkansas Gazette* reported in 1948: "Plantation owners in the Delta counties usually control the votes of their many tenants who cast their ballots in boxes set up in the owners' commissaries."

In Arkansas, the poll tax—eventually outlawed as election reforms were forced on the South—actually served as a device to discourage poor whites from voting. Fearing an uprising by populist interests, embodied in what was known as the "sawmill vote," the establishment laid obstacles in their path by maintaining the tax.

We had democracy in Arkansas, but it was run by an oligarchy. In an assessment of Arkansas in his famous 1947 travelogue of the nation, *Inside U.S.A.*, John Gunther listed the powers in Arkansas: Delta planters, the Baptist Church, the timber empires, and the Arkansas Power & Light Co. I would have added the railroads, and the statewide associations of sheriffs and county judges.

◆ ◆ ◆

I grew up with the legend of an Arkansas political machine, as though some grand master in Little Rock orchestrated events. In fact, the Arkansas machine could never compare with the big-city political operations fueled with patronage and dependent on military-like discipline, where loyalty flowed from block worker to precinct captain to ward chairman to party boss. Organized labor, an important component in Democratic politics, was practically non-existent in Arkansas until after World War II. In Arkansas, the party was a confederation of county organizations, controlled by local leaders watching out for the interests of the establishment and banding together behind favorite candidates.

Sheriff Marlin Hawkins of Conway County became one of the most famous practitioners of Arkansas machine politics. It was said Hawkins could deliver the precise number of votes needed to swing any election in his county. He ran the place for years. A charming man who started his career as a social worker, Hawkins befriended the population of the county, which was practically all white, in the hills north of Little Rock. Hawkins had one eye. He smiled often as his carrot and used law enforcement as his stick. By passing out favors judiciously, he amassed a reliable following. Hawkins savored his reputation as a kingmaker and when he wrote his memoirs, he entitled the book, not entirely facetiously, *How I Stole Elections*.

Yell County, in the Ouachita forests west of Conway, also had a reputation as a machine county, controlled by Sheriff Earl Ladd, a respected figure in criminal justice circles around the state. On the other hand, Garland County was run for years by the redoubtable mayor of Hot Springs, Leo P. McLaughlin, renowned for stuffing ballot boxes and tolerating illegal casinos in his city. In White County, my home, the power brokers were the Abbington brothers from Beebe; A. P. Mills of Kensett, the father of Congressman Wilbur Mills; and Truman Baker, a well-connected auto dealer in Searcy.

The local leaders were adept at the art of quid pro quo and often used roads as a bargaining tool. A construction project to blacktop a rural road meant jobs, and highway improvements enhanced the quality of life in the area. Politicians who could deliver road contracts were assured the support of the county bosses, who, in turn, convinced voters to back these chosen candidates because "community interests" were at stake. The understandings usually produced lopsided electoral results, and added to the appearance of a machine.

But alliances shifted from election to election. As Neal R. Pierce wrote in his chapter on Arkansas in *The Deep South States of America* in 1974, "Because the conservatives controlled Arkansas so completely, its politics clear into the 1940s were characterized by a fluid factionalism in which virtually no serious issues were discussed."

Arkansas Democrats had a tradition that no one served more than two consecutive two-year terms as governor. When Carl Bailey tried to defy the unwritten rule in 1940, he was beaten. There was an expression I often heard while growing up: "He needs to move on, he's had his two terms." We had a succession of new governors every four years during my boyhood: Bailey, Homer Adkins, Ben Laney, Sid McMath. Francis Cherry served only two years before he was ousted in 1954 by Faubus, who broke tradition by winning six straight terms.

While big-city machines tended to suppress new faces, forcing ambitious young politicians to earn their stripes by working their way up from minor posts, the Arkansas system was wide open to fresh blood. Little-known candidates could be transformed into leaders overnight in a state where politics were highly personalized and divided by the Delta, the hills, and the forests.

In *Southern Politics*, V. O. Key's study of the region in 1949, the author found that "in Arkansas, more than in almost any other Southern state, social and economic issues of significance to the people have lain ignored in the confusion and paralysis of disorganized factional politics." Arkansas politicians, Key said, drew "their strength in particular areas in terms of their relations with local leaders rather than from the fact that their policy positions conflicted or agreed with local interests."

During this period, when county leaders were switching from one politician to another with astonishing regularity in races on the state level, Arkansas's political stability was concentrated in our congressional delegation. Enjoying a devotion Arkansas rarely extended to local officeholders, the same senators and congressmen were returned to Washington, election after election. I believe there was a genuine desire by the Arkansas electorate to send our very best leaders to Washington and to keep them there, to show the nation we were not all a bunch of hillbillies, hunkered around the campfire chewing on raw meat. Outrageous clowns might occupy some county offices in Arkansas, but on the national level, our leaders were serious, thoughtful men who were a match for anyone in Congress. Coming from a state with no Republican opposition, they were able to build longevity in an era when seniority was the most formidable weapon in Congress. And I think they, too, were acutely aware of Arkansas's unflattering reputation, and worked hard to bring prestige to the state.

As Irish New Yorkers once boasted that their city wore its flamboyant mayor, Jimmy Walker, like a rose in its lapel, Arkansas's congressional delegation brightened our state like boutonnieres.

Long before Clinton went to the White House, Arkansas exercised big muscle in Washington. When I became politically active, our small, disadvantaged state seemed to control Congress. Besides Fulbright, who became chairman of the Senate Foreign Relations Committee, we were blessed with John L. McClellan, who headed several panels during his career and wound up chairman of the Senate Appropriations Committee. In the House, Wilbur Mills, head of the House Ways and Means Committee in the days before the strengths of chairmen were diluted by reform, was arguably more powerful than the Speaker. At the same time, Oren Harris served as chairman of the House Interstate and Foreign Commerce Committee. We boasted four chairmen, and the rest of our congressmen held key assignments on other committees.

Back home in Arkansas, we took pride in Fulbright's erudition and McClellan's investigation of the mob. We experienced vicarious pleasure when Mills outwitted the wise guys; we marveled that he wrote the tax laws for the country. Our men in Washington were the stars in our little universe, and their names commanded respect wherever politics was a topic.

Tammany clubhouses and precinct headquarters were foreign to Arkansas. Our general stores served as our political forums, places where farmers gathered to buy goods, engage in conversation, and pass judgment on current events. The dialogue may not have sparkled with the sophistication of a Georgetown salon, but the discussions were earnest. In the days before television brought faraway athletic contests into our living rooms, politics was our sport. We spoke of our elected officials with familiarity—not only the county judges, but United States senators, too. There was a sense at the general store that John McClellan was just as likely to walk in as the local justice of the peace.

It was an intimate political culture, where promising newcomers could make valuable connections and establish names for themselves quickly. The last generation born into these times was the one including Bill Clinton and me. The system enabled me, an unknown fellow from the little town of Bradford, to wield uncommon clout in Arkansas when I was still in my twenties, and it made possible Clinton's meteoric rise. But in the years since Clinton and I broke into politics, the system has undergone dramatic change, and the homespun world we grew up in has been lost forever.

2

M y earliest memories come from the store: chattering customers in denim coveralls washed pale, the murmur broken by radio static, the comforting aroma of cottonseed. My life evolved around Middleton & McDougal Feed Store, a family business offering me a perspective on the hard times of rural Arkansas as well as a refuge from it. The Great Depression may have been broken by the New Deal in parts of the country, but Arkansas still suffered in the 1940s. There was little industry in the area, and wages were low for the few fortunate to have regular jobs.

I will never forget the faces of the farmers, desperate with worry, who made up most of the workforce in White County. They toiled in an unforgiving hill country, where the soil was worn from years of indiscriminate planting, and they faced a constant struggle to make ends meet. Our store, which sold farm supplies in the little town of Bradford, was a center of commerce for them and a cozy place for me. The store's "Middleton" was a relative I called Uncle Bert, a gentle old man who raised my mother from the time she was eleven. The "McDougal" was my father, Leo.

Uncle Bert had lost his sight as a young man. His car overturned and battery acid leached into his face before he could be pulled from the wreck. In spite of his handicap, Uncle Bert knew every corner of the drafty old building. When he bought it earlier in the century it was a municipal structure, and he wired his wife to boast, "I just bought Bradford's city hall." Actually, it was a tin warehouse, so airy one could back a truck into it. Uncle Bert moved easily around the counters, the bins of seed and beans, the racks of merchandise, and a stove flanked by two benches where folks sat to pass time.

Customers thought he had mystical powers because he could differentiate between one-, five-, and ten-dollar bills when counting out change; they didn't realize he folded each denomination differently. I was no more than four years old when my parents began to post me at the store daily to make sure no one stole from the till or tried to cheat Uncle Bert. Money was stored in a little office where we kept the "cash drawer." We were businessmen and spoke of the "cash drawer" with the same reverence a rabbi might reserve for the ark of the covenant.

Uncle Bert cherished my company. I was christened James Bert McDougal; my middle name was his. He liked me to sit in his lap, and he would run his fingers over the contours of my face to learn how I looked. He was the only member of my family who ever showed much affection. My family couldn't articulate love. They would do anything for you, but they couldn't get words of endearment out of their mouths. There was no hugging among the men of my family. Never. The only embraces I recall involved relatives from Milwaukee, who had not visited in ten years, and even then, only the women embraced.

My parents were reserved, reflecting the abstemious lifestyle our ancestors brought from Scotland six generations earlier. Meals at home were eaten mostly in silence. My father, a reticent man, responded to our questions with replies of one syllable. The McDougals would never be confused with those Mediterranean families who turned dinner into a time of celebration. We finished eating in minutes. For us, dinner was a biological necessity, not a social occasion.

Although my father was a religious man, he never gave thanks before a meal. He thought it was a Pharisee habit. Perhaps, too, he concluded there was little that warranted thanks. We ate leftovers. Being "Scotch," my mother wasted nothing. Mashed potatoes, cooked on Sunday, were served until the dish was exhausted. Often, we ate potatoes till Thursday.

My mother was never demonstrative. The only time she slapped me was the occasion I had the temerity to call her "Mama." She thought it was a country way of talking. I was expected to call her "Mother." Father was "Daddy," never "Pop" or "the old man." Slang was unacceptable in our household. My family abhorred the idioms of the poor, lest we be lumped as white trash ourselves. I was told that proper English and an educated manner of speaking would enable me to rise above the uncultured ways of White County.

Before Wal-Mart, an Arkansas invention, and television revolutionized the way we shop and spend our leisure time, Bradford was a picture of small-town life, a typical Arkansas hill town, seventy miles northeast of Little Rock. Our population was only 720, but our movie theater, cafes, and stores were an outpost of civilization for the surrounding countryside. Established by the Missouri Pacific Railroad, which settled several White County towns with immigrant workers in the 1800s, Bradford was laid out to railroad specifications. The Bradford settlers were Scots-Irish; a few miles down the line in Russell, the railroad workers came from Germany. My mother's family moved into the region around 1820, and the McDougals followed a decade later, long before the railroad arrived, fitting into the Celtic, Protestant composition of the area.

The McDougals were descended from one of Scotland's largest clans and came to America after choosing the wrong side during one of the many eighteenth-century wars on the British Isles. My branch of the family eventually pushed west to Arkansas, part of the wave of Scots-Irish pioneers who cleared the frontier and settled the South and the western lands beyond.

Bradford was founded at the edge of the Ozark foothills, where the lowland of the Delta gains elevation. A dusty thoroughfare lined with groceries, a drugstore, clothing shops, and the five-and-dime store, our Main Street sloped up one of the hillsides. Middleton & McDougal was around the corner on Front Street, facing the railroad tracks. Streets running parallel to the tracks in railroad towns were usually named Front and considered prime location.

We had a procession of regular customers, farmers whose families dwelled on the edge of poverty, raising livestock and growing vegetables for subsistence while eking out a profit from the strawberry crops they picked in the hillsides. Each spring, dozens of wagons and trucks, overflowing with crates of strawberries, lined the street outside our store, waiting for freight trains to ship the produce to distant markets. If strawberries were plentiful, the crop provided seasonal relief from the farmers' fear of foreclosure. We did business with a few progressive farmers who grew cotton and soybeans in the rich White River bottom, but most of our trade came from the hill people.

Squeezed by the Depression, many of the poorer farmers gave up and moved from Arkansas, abandoning the land they had cleared. When they left, forests reclaimed the ground like a primeval force. While the rest of the country was growing, Arkansas was losing population. There was such a rush from Arkansas during my childhood that we lost nearly a million people—a migration that cost the state two congressional seats.

As merchants, my family was not so hard-pressed. We knew there would always be food on our table, and we recognized that many of our neighbors were so destitute they would be delighted with leftovers. As a result, my family assumed a sense of noblesse oblige, and their sympathies affected my own business and political beliefs as I grew older.

The bank in Bradford was reluctant to loan money to the struggling farmers, so my father helped his customers by extending credit. He kept a box of tickets listing each debtor and the amount owed. Some of the debtors fled in the 1930s, but eventually returned. With guilty expressions, they came by the store to repay their debts. My father found their ticket in his musty box, and his old customers always seemed to know how much they owed.

The Middleton & McDougal store exuded a certain warmth, and farmers would often linger, long after they had made their purchases. We had one customer whom I liked especially, a lively conversationalist with a good sense of humor. Although I had not yet started school, he treated me like an adult. One day, after bantering with me, he drove away from the store with a truckload of cottonseed meal. Seconds later, the peace of Bradford was shattered by the sound of a violent collision. Running to the window, I looked out and beheld a world turned yellow. An express train, barreling through Bradford, had hit the truck, killed the man, and dusted the town with a yellow pall from the cottonseed meal.

We mourned our friend and concentrated our anger on the railroad. Trains seemed to race through town with impunity. There were no warning lights, no bells, no barriers along the tracks. An elderly couple had been killed earlier at the Bradford crossing, yet nothing had been done to ensure our safety. To us, the railroads represented an aloof, higher power that ran roughshod over our little town. Owned by millionaires in faraway places, the railroad companies had always been a target of the populists in Arkansas, along with other symbols of the establishment, the banks and the utilities.

People in Bradford seethed not only at the railroad companies, but at other big, faceless institutions, such as the national insurance companies. It seemed that everyone in town, even my parents, found it acceptable for one of the townspeople to burn down their own home in order to beat the insurance company.

I came by my own populism naturally. It is as much a product of my early environment as my business sense and my love of reading.

My populism was grounded in my parents' religious beliefs. Devout Baptists who neither drank, smoked, nor cursed, they felt that oppressing the poor was sinful and believed that the fortunate had a moral obligation to help others.

In those days, it was not unusual to see tramps walking along the railroad tracks. When they reached town, the vagabonds knocked on doors to seek handouts. My parents gave out plates of food, and the hobos would sit on our doorstep to eat. Sometimes, they were invited to sit at the table with us. Their visits became so regular that my father said, "I think we have a mark on the house." Yet he never stopped feeding them.

As I prepared to enter the first grade at the Bradford school, my mother gave me a lecture, warning me not to say anything if I saw a classmate wearing a shirt that had been mine. She gave away clothes I outgrew or no longer needed. She also told me I should neither laugh nor make any comment about a child wearing a shirt or a dress made from flour sacks. In those days, feed and flour companies stamped patterns on their cloth sacks because they knew poor farmers recycled the material for clothing.

I became aware of the sensitivities of my playmates. After I put a dime in the collection plate in my beginners Sunday school class, I noticed my friends had only given a penny each. When I asked my mother about the disparity, she explained that ten cents was a proper tithe for me because I made a dollar a week at the store. But after discussing the situation with my father, they agreed I should limit my Sunday school contribution to a penny to avoid the appearance of showing off. Each week, my parents changed my dime into a nickel and five pennies. I gave one cent at Sunday school and the remaining nine cents went into the adults' collection plate at the church services following Sunday school.

Though our lives were not without our own troubles, my family was among the fortunate of Bradford. Grandfather James Edward

McDougal, for whom I was given my first name, was a burgher of Bradford by the time I was born. A widower, he was one of White County's more prosperous farmers and lived in a big two-story house with twin porches looking out on his orchards. He owned five hundred acres, with hundreds of pear trees on one side of a long driveway leading to his house. Smaller peach, apple, and cherry trees flourished on the other side of the drive. My grandfather raised prize hogs and grew cotton in the bottomlands created by the White River. He was sociable and well-connected. Some evenings, he hired entertainers and invited friends to join him on his porch to watch magicians or gospel singers perform on the lawn.

Grandfather McDougal was on good terms with our congressman, Wilbur Mills, and I was told that Mr. Mills, as I always called him, had been baptized in the art of political compromise by the elder Jim McDougal. When Mr. Mills started out in politics in the 1930s, he was something of a joke. Overweight, he was known as "Little Wilbur" around Kensett, his hometown. Kensett was in the country, a few miles outside our county seat of Searcy. Even though he held a degree from Harvard Law School, Mr. Mills had little business acumen. After he nearly bankrupted his father's store by offering credit to poor risks while his father was traveling out of the country, it was said the father—one of the most important men in White County—returned and arranged Mr. Mills's election as county judge in order to get him out of the store.

One of Mr. Mills's duties as judge was to obtain the right-of-way for roads. At the time, Highway 67 was under construction between Little Rock and St. Louis, and plans for the route took it through my grandfather's pear orchard. Folks at the courthouse laughed at Mr. Mills. They told him: "I can't wait till you get up to Jim McDougal's pear orchard, Wilbur. That's where your highway's going to stop."

Mr. Mills was determined not to make a fool of himself. He made a personal visit to my grandfather's place and accepted an invitation for supper. Over the dinner table, my grandfather warmed to Mr. Mills and his quiet approach. Though my grandfather preferred to keep the land, he would not obstruct progress. He suggested they compare notes. After dinner, my grandfather and Mr. Mills moved to the parlor and began calculating. Mr. Mills figured that forty-five years remained in the life of the trees in the highway's path. My grandfather computed the annual yield of the trees. They multiplied the annual yield by forty-five and came up with a number. Mr. Mills agreed to pay that amount, my grandfather accepted, and a bond was established between the Millses and the McDougals.

Grandfather McDougal was an imposing figure and an important ally for politicians in White County. Known as a man of great rectitude, he dominated Sunday services at the Baptist church by openly correcting the preacher on biblical quotations or points of doctrine.

My father, Leo McDougal, was a serious, phlegmatic man. He never bothered to carry a Bible to church, like other worshipers. When I asked him why, he told me, "I'll know if the preacher makes a mistake." He was a pious man with a good head for business. Though my father was not a big man, he grew muscular because he worked with little help during the war years. While I watched, he moved hundred-pound sacks of feed by himself.

In 1947, my grandfather thought he was going to die, and he turned over his property and business interests to his two sons, my Uncle Willie and my father. Although the McDougal brothers were friendly, family relations were strained by tension between Uncle Willie's wife and my mother. The two women never got along. My mother considered my aunt a gossip with a vicious tongue. When I was born, I was told, Uncle Willie's wife made the requisite visit to inspect the newest member of the family and told my mother, "Why Lorene, he looks just like a little rat." My mother never spoke to her again.

My father wound up managing the estate in Bradford while Uncle Willie and his wife moved out West. He sold half the property and sent the proceeds to Uncle Willie, who lost the money investing in a contracting business in Yuma, Arizona. Although Grandfather thought he was on his deathbed in 1947, he lasted another ten years. When he finally died, my father had to send Uncle Willie five hundred dollars to come to the funeral. My mother scolded my father for making the subsidy, but the story of their link to Uncle Willie had an ironic ending.

After divorcing his wife, Uncle Willie moved to northern California. Working as an oiler on the construction of a dam—a project that lasted many years—he earned union wages, made lots of overtime pay, and saved practically all his money. He lived in a spartan house trailer, about eight feet wide and forty feet long, and invested in a one-thousand-dollar U.S. savings bond every month. After he died, we discovered a bank box full of bonds. He left everything to my parents, and the bequest helped keep them on Easy Street for the rest of their lives.

Though our family lived in comfort, we were shadowed by demons. Grandfather would sink into deep, inexplicable depressions, and emerge from that state into rushes of manic activity.

Once, as I was riding down the street with him shortly after the end of World War II, he spotted a veteran with no legs sitting against the outer wall of the post office. "These men are heroes, and they have no place to go," my grandfather exclaimed, stopping the car. He began a conversation with the veteran, who explained that he had taken to the street because his in-laws were tired of him lying around the house. When Grandfather McDougal asked if he wanted his own home, the veteran said he had seen a house he liked but was unable to afford it. On the spot, my grandfather wrote him a check to buy the house. It didn't cost a great deal, maybe two thousand dollars, but the veteran was stunned by the gesture. He offered to make out a note to my grandfather. "I don't want a note," Grandfather told him. "Just pay me back when you get the money."

Alcoholism troubled my mother's family. My maternal grandmother was the daughter of a wealthy landowner and legislator from Griffithville, in the lower part of White County. Unfortunately, she chose John Purvis as her husband, an inveterate gambler who drank himself to death before he was forty. He left his widow penniless with six children under the age of thirteen. Two of those children—my uncles—would wind up as alcoholics, as I did. My mother, Lorene, who disdained drink, was rescued when Uncle Bert and his wife, Viola—my grandmother's sister whom I called Aunt Ola—brought her to Bradford to live with them.

My mother was a lovely young woman, with dark hair and a fine complexion, and she quickly attracted my father's interest. In the tradition of small-town mergers, after they married my father became Uncle Bert's business partner. I was an only child. Although World War II brought further austerity to White County, memories of my early years are generally pleasant. At first, we lived in the small house where I was born. For about a year, near the end of the war, we lived on my grandfather's farm. Then my father bought a large two-story house with several lots and extensive outbuildings near the family store.

My father didn't seek stature, but he inherited my grandfather's influence in Bradford. Townspeople looked to him for advice. We had a neighbor, David Hamby, a blacksmith beset with a form of dyslexia. He wrote backward, his handwriting illegible until you held it up to a mirror, when it appeared perfect. Hamby's unusual style was featured in Ripley's *Believe It or Not*, but it caused him problems doing business in Bradford. He relied on my father for assistance with written material.

When the government began to issue ration stamps at the beginning of the war, David filled out a form for gasoline. The officials were unable to read his handwriting properly and concluded that David needed to drive 135,000 miles a year on business. In fact, David drove about 2,000 miles a year, so he certainly had an abundance of stamps. He offered the surplus to my father, but Daddy was so patriotic that we made expeditions to Little Rock by train, in cars grimy with soot and crowded with soldiers and wartime travelers.

When he was thirty-six Daddy was called to the military. On the day he went for his physical I stayed at Uncle Bert's house. When my father returned that night, I ran excitedly to the door and asked, "Where's your gun?" I expected he would appear in uniform with a rifle. I was disappointed when I was told he had failed the physical.

Though the war ended in 1945, rationing and hardship continued into the following year, when I entered the first grade. The two-story white brick school building accommodated all twelve grades and served not only the town of Bradford, but nearby farm communities. The first grade was located on the ground floor, near the main entrance, and as pupils progressed through the years they worked their way upstairs, where the high school classes were held. When I arrived on the first day, I beheld a scene out of Dickens, with seventy children squirming over chairs and desks in one small room. Most of my classmates came in from the country, many of them riding ten to fifteen miles in a school bus.

I adapted to elementary school life. The Bradford school was so overcrowded and understaffed that the second and third grades were combined, with more than a hundred of us in the same room. A lone teacher gave instructions to the second-grade class for a while, then turned to the other group. Finishing my assignments quickly, I was usually misbehaving by the time the teacher resumed studies for my class. She implored my parents to pass me into the third grade. "I've got to keep him busy," she said. "He's driving me crazy." Thus, I telescoped two years of schooling into one.

My education often took place outside the classroom. Although many Arkansas blacks lived in the Delta farmland east of town, Bradford was an all-white community. I remember being astonished by the first black people I ever saw, when I was a child riding with my father and Aunt Ola to Newport, a nearby metropolis of ten thousand. "Look," I blurted. "Niggers!" Aunt Ola slapped my face and admonished me. I was never to use that word again, she said. It was the language of the poor white trash.

On our trips to Newport, eighteen miles away, I encountered another curiosity: Jewish shopkeepers. Jews were totally alien to Bradford, where practically everyone belonged to the Baptist Church or the Church of Christ. It was not until my senior year that a Catholic moved to Bradford. He was a teacher named Pushkarsky, and his students treated him like a rare bird, taking him home to dinner so their parents could meet a living, breathing Polish Catholic. Bradford was incredibly insular, yet my family developed a special affinity with the Jews of Newport. We were fellow merchants and people who respected education. Willie Morris, the Mississippian who gained fame as a writer and editor of *Harper's* magazine in New York, was correct when he said that Jews and southerners are attracted to one another because they are tribes living outside the American mainstream.

In 1948, I lost my closest companion. Uncle Bert died, and I threw up for days, becoming so sick I couldn't attend the funeral. My family took me to the church, but I didn't get out of the car. I just lay on the seat, weak with grief.

After Uncle Bert's death, my father assumed complete control of the store and took Aunt Ola into our household. He built a new house and supervised the entire project. By Bradford's humble standards, it was a mansion with eleven rooms and three baths, a considerable luxury in the little town. He selected every piece of hardwood for the floors and personally directed the carpenters and craftsmen every day for nine months. My father wanted a customized masonry style and rejected the concrete blocks ordinarily used for construction, ordering a machine that produced the desirable blocks. After he bought some property in Newport, a poor piece of land where he was warned he probably wouldn't be able to build, Daddy moved the machine there, produced the blocks, and succeeded in erecting a warehouse.

During this frenzy of activity, he sold the feed store's inventory.

It was not until later that I realized he was in a manic phase. When these projects were completed, he crashed into depression. Back then, it was called a nervous breakdown. For nine months my father did nothing. He would rise in the morning and putter about the house for a bit, then spend the afternoon in bed. A funereal gloom enveloped our household.

When my father arose from this troubled state, he bought a grocery store, a furniture store, another grocery store, and then a variety store. He purchased an old cotton gin and retooled the machinery to grind corn to make feed for cattle. It was a pattern of business expansion and acquisition that I would follow twenty years later.

Leo McDougal was the big businessman in town, and even as a child I tried to emulate his enterprise. When I was eleven, I watched construction crews laying a pipeline near our home and noticed they discarded the heavy steel bands that were used to lash stacks of pipes onto the railcars. I knew that scrap iron had value; like most boys who grew up in the war period when metal was scarce, I saved old tin cans and sold the waste for a few cents. I asked the foreman of the pipeline crew if I could have the steel bands, and he seemed glad to give me the task of clearing the right of way for him.

I learned how to cuss trying to wrap the steel bands. It was a bit like the tedious work of winding a clock spring; just as soon as you think you've got it finished, the coiled metal flies out of place. I enlisted one of my cousins to help me, luring him with some kind of profit-sharing scheme. We dragged these heavy steel bands over to my house, about two hundred feet from the railroad site, and piled them in the front yard. The stack of metal grew until it became difficult to see the house from the street. My father encouraged the venture; he took one of his trucks from the mill and put his employees to work loading the steel bands to drive the salvage to Newport for sale. We made several hundred dollars—big money for a little boy in 1951.

◆ ◆ ◆

In the years before television came to Arkansas, we listened to the radio religiously, at home and the store. I was frightened by the sinister sound of the creaking door introducing the show *Inner Sanctum,* and thrilled to the heroics of *The FBI in Peace and War.* Buster Brown was a Saturday-morning staple.

Fascinated by radio and the emerging medium of television, I appealed to my parents to let me enroll in a Little Rock radio and television trade school in the summer of 1953. Instead of being protective of his only child, my father thought it a logical development for a boy who had been working in the family store for years. I boarded with friends of an aunt, and every morning I'd take a bus to the school, where I was the youngest student. The place was full of girls studying to become secretaries, and they got a kick out of flirting with the newcomer. The male students were older, mostly Korean War veterans studying on the G.I. Bill and not taking their lessons very seriously. After I had been there about three days, I tried an experiment from the workbook and one of the guys complained, "For God's sake, son, slow down. We've been here a year and we're not that far along yet."

The next year, my parents purchased our first television set and we were treated to a snowy signal from a station in Memphis. My favorite show was the one hosted by Groucho Marx; excited, I yelled out the answers to questions on his quiz show. *This Is Your Life,* with the startled guest, was also the rage at that time.

With a friend I exploited my knowledge of radios with an oscillator, obtained by one of my cousins through a magazine advertisement. Using the contraption, we found it possible to talk over a distance of three hundred feet. Deciding to expand our capability, we built an amplifier and strung the wire to a makeshift antenna a quarter mile away. Soon we were broadcasting to the whole town, playing records, relaying BBC programs from a shortwave radio, interrupted by our own commentary. We didn't have a wide audience, but our fledgling radio operation was blamed for the poor television reception in town. Apparently someone called the Federal Communications Commission, and an agent was dispatched to Bradford to silence us. It was my first experience with a bureaucrat.

When I was old enough to drive, I sought entertainment outside Bradford. Newport, a Sodom to many folks, was the only exciting place nearby. It was a "wet" town, filled with honky-tonks. Bradford, on the other hand, had purged itself of beer joints shortly after the end of World War II. Weary of the spectacle of young veterans spending their unemployment checks on booze and brawling in the streets, the town had voted dry. My family belonged to the temperance coalition. Before Bradford went dry, we had to walk past a couple of the beer joints on our way to weeknight church services, and I remember my Aunt Ola wrinkling her nose in disgust.

Newport was in Jackson County, where the more tolerant culture of the Delta prevailed. Thirsty visitors from the hill counties would flock to Newport on Saturday nights. The town was wide open. When I was a teenager, I saw Elvis Presley perform at Porky's Rooftop in Newport. I had begun drinking by the time I was fifteen, tiptoeing past my sleeping parents to my bedroom on nights I caroused. Even though I was underage, I looked "older"—I thought it a great attribute to look eighteen when I was fifteen—and I never had any trouble purchasing alcohol. My friends and I would drink six-packs of Country Club "shorties" before we'd enter the nightclubs so we wouldn't have to pay for expensive beers inside.

Newport had two theaters. After the Bradford theater closed its doors forever, my friends and I began taking the bus on Sunday afternoons to Bald Knob, ten miles away. For a dollar, it was possible to pay the bus fare, buy a ticket to the movie, and enjoy a box of popcorn.

By the time I reached high school, I was fascinated by the emerging rock 'n' roll singers: Jerry Lee Lewis, Chuck Berry, Little Richard. I wasn't that impressed by Elvis; I thought he was a crooner, like Frank Sinatra. But my first girlfriend, Sandra Taylor, loved

Elvis. Her hair was cut and styled in his fashion. She liked Pat Boone, too, and wore Oxford shirts, light-blue jeans, and white bucks, patterned after Boone's clean-cut clothes. After we had been dating for a while, she told me: "I love you more than Pat Boone and Elvis Presley put together." A supreme compliment.

There was only one sour note during my high school years. John Webb, a martinet with a military background, had been hired as superintendent of the Bradford school, and he treated students like conscripts. When I was in the eleventh grade, Harding College invited prospective students to an open house. With my father's approval, I joined several of my classmates on a day trip to Searcy. Webb was furious that we had not asked his permission. He suspended us and then canceled our long-awaited junior class outing.

I had never seen my father so angry. He immediately hired an out-of-town attorney, who determined it was possible to transfer property tax assessments away from the school district. My father then enlisted the support of other parents and took the grievance to the school board, which happened to have several friends and relatives of the McDougal family as members. He told the board: Either Webb goes or we take our properties off the tax rolls of the school district. The school board recognized the severity of the threat, which would have been calamitous for a poor district. Webb was fired. To my knowledge that was the only time my father had a fight with anybody, but it was a good one. As Thomas Jackson, the Confederate general they called "Stonewall," once said after the enemy had been routed, "We slept on the field" where the battle had been fought.

My family showed little interest in politics. Dinner-table commentary included such observations as, "That Roosevelt's having a good year," followed by a nod in response. We were part of the phenomenon known in the South as "Yellow Dog Democrats," those who would vote for a yellow dog before a Republican. Grandfather

McDougal reluctantly departed from the custom in 1928, voting for Herbert Hoover over the Catholic Al Smith. My family said he voted for Hoover because he worried about the pope, but by the time Hoover completed his term, Grandfather was worried about getting enough to eat.

Politics intrigued me when I discovered that the 1948 race for governor offered better entertainment than the movies. James "Uncle Mac" MacKrell, a Baptist minister best known for his radio show, *Bible Lovers Revival*, kicked off his campaign rallies with hymns sung by a gospel quartet, then segued into pitches for his candidacy and a brand of flour he sold on the side. Spider Rowland, a columnist for the *Arkansas Gazette*, made the observation that Uncle Mac was "a most unusual character, for which many people are grateful."

My father's good friend Red Floyd took us to hear Uncle Mac, his favorite candidate, at a church in the Jackson County hamlet of Grand Glaise. We joined a throng so immense that one section of the church floor collapsed. Uncle Mac whipped up crowds wherever he traveled, and at the conclusion of the Grand Glaise rally he stood by the door, thanking his followers and watching them drop campaign contributions of nickels, quarters, and dollar bills into a collection plate. As a successful businessman in Bradford, Mr. Floyd could afford a grander contribution. He tossed in a five-dollar bill. Uncle Mac immediately plucked the bill out of the plate and stuffed it in his pocket.

Roused from political lethargy that year, my family gave their support to Sid McMath, a reform candidate from Hot Springs. McMath had been a war hero, and after coming home he led a G.I. movement to cleanse his city of corruption. Hot Springs was infamous during this period. Al Capone had vacationed there, and after Capone passed from the scene other Chicago gangsters continued to take the waters at Hot Springs. Hotels doubled as gambling halls, and hookers plied their trade. Running on a reform ticket, McMath had been elected prosecutor in 1946. He ousted a tainted regime at City Hall, chased the mob out of town, and set his sights on the governor's office.

When McMath's campaign rolled into Bradford, it seemed the circus had finally come to town. His people set up carousels in front of our store. If children tired of the merry-go-round, a barker offered rides on Shetland ponies or held us spellbound with rope tricks.

I was only eight, but I soon understood the significance of my family's support for McMath. My father and his first cousin Francis Mason, the mayor of Bradford, lined up behind McMath because he agreed to build a blacktop road on a back-country route between Bradford and Denmark. The road was critical to Bradford's designs to become a commercial center. We competed with other towns for the country trade, and unless we could open access to Denmark, the people there would take their business to Bald Knob. McMath won a big majority in Bradford on his way to election. After he failed to fulfill his promise to blacktop the road promptly, my father and his cousin Francis traveled to Little Rock to remind McMath of the agreement. They had barely returned home before a state crew materialized in White County, squirting oil on the dusty road and preparing to lay down the asphalt.

While the Arkansas candidates introduced me to politics, other figures outside the state soon captured my interest. Once I went home after school with a boy named Ivan Ransom, whose family had a small library. I found *Every Man a King* (but no man shall wear the crown) by Huey P. Long, the populist governor and senator from Louisiana. Long had challenged Rockefeller's great Standard Oil Co. trust and the financial establishment in New Orleans before he was assassinated in 1935. I loved the passages in the book in which he expressed his "legal and political opposition to the vested interests." He battled corporate influence in state agencies. "What a fight lay ahead!" Long wrote. "Always my cases in court were on the side of the small man—the underdog." I could almost hear his bombastic redundancy: "I had never taken a suit against a poor man and have not done so to this day."

I learned that Long, as governor, taxed the rich to pay for bridges and roads in remote places where the poor people lived, and he provided free books for the public schools. I became so engrossed in Huey Long's book that the Ransoms gave it to me. It articulated everything I wanted to say when I heard Uncle Bert, my father, and the farmers discussing the oil oligarchy and corporate power.

Convinced we were in the thrall of Wall Street, the farmers suspected brokers and grain speculators, the commodity traders, of manipulating prices. While they sweated in the fields and worried over the weather, they believed the men pushing paper contracts in New York and Chicago were the only beneficiaries.

My family considered the stock market the equivalent of a Las Vegas casino. Dabbling in stocks was gambling, we thought, and dealing in farm-commodity futures was gambling on the backs of the farmers. We had money in the bank, but we didn't buy stocks or speculate in commodities. My father traded in corn; in fact, he made a lot of money from corn, but he never bought grain futures. He always made sure he took physical possession of the corn when he paid for it.

As my understanding of business and politics improved, I sought to learn more and became a voracious reader. Someone gave me all twelve volumes of *The World's Great Orations*, edited by William Jennings Bryan. I memorized Bryan's call to arms against the financial forces at the 1896 Democratic convention, and I can still recite his ringing peroration today: "You shall not press down upon the brow of labor this crown of thorns. You shall not crucify mankind on a cross of gold." Little wonder that I later said politics was entertainment.

Enchanted by the language in the anthology, from the wisdom of Cicero to the political oratory of the early twentieth century, I was also stirred by the defiant words of Wolfe Tone, the Irish patriot, moments before the British hanged him. Some of his most moving phrases seemed to come from the scaffold.

I collected recordings of great addresses, the rousing rhetoric of the labor leader John L. Lewis and the sainted Franklin D. Roosevelt. I became a student of speech making, and developed a speaking style influenced by the passionate voice of Bryan and the working-class harangues of Lewis. I listened to radio speeches at the national political conventions. During the 1952 Democratic convention, I sided with Estes Kefauver, because he was a southern senator from Tennessee and I liked his flamboyant style. Disappointed when he failed to get the nomination, I was further dismayed a decade later when I went to Washington and saw that Kefauver had become a shuffling drunk.

In 1956, I was electrified by the Democratic keynote address by Frank Clement, the governor of Tennessee, who talked of our golfing President Eisenhower's "long fairways of indifference" and punctuated each declaration with the cry, "How long, America, shall these things endure?"

My interest in the convention was whetted by a running debate I had with Mutt Goad, the hamburger-stand operator. As the only outspoken Republican partisan in town, Mutt turned his cafe into a pressure cooker of politics. Along with his hamburgers, he dispensed opinions from behind the counter, whose eight stools were usually filled. Nestled next to the counter lay an ice-cream freezer and a glass candy case. The place buzzed with talk. In 1936, Mutt had bet a local man named Callas that Alf Landon would triumph over Roosevelt. I was told that the loser was to pull the winner in a little red wagon across eighteen miles of gravel road from Bradford to Newport. Mutt, of course, had to take the mule's role after the election, but he made Mr. Callas—a tall, wiry man—keep his seat in the wagon for long, uncomfortable stretches. Mutt kept a clipping from the *Kansas City Star*, a photograph of their triumphant arrival in Newport, on the wall of his cafe, and he never gave up his enmity toward Roosevelt.

He called one of the more pitiful items on his menu a "Roosevelt pie." It was a concoction of moist Southern dressing, padded with chili made from livers and gizzards and other undesirable innards he ground up at my father's store. He poured the stuff over three slices of white bread to make the "pie." Although Mutt gave the dish a derisive name, his customers wolfed down Roosevelt pies as quickly as he prepared them. His other specialty involved a secret relish for his hamburgers, and its smell mingled with the smoky fumes sent up from the sizzling meat on the grill.

Mutt had been sanctioned by FDR's Office of Price Administration for adding too much bread to his hamburger meat. After they informed him he couldn't call the item a hamburger, he labeled the combination a "breadburger" and charged only five cents for it.

Mutt loathed the Democratic Party so much that when the Roosevelt dime was minted, he tried to put it out of local circulation. Since he charged ten cents for his genuine hamburgers, most customers paid with a dime. If it was an FDR dime, Mutt would throw it in a jar. After he saved four thousand dollars in FDR dimes, he realized the U.S. Mint could produce dimes faster than he could fry hamburgers. He used his forty thousand dimes to buy a house. Instead of counting them, Mutt determined how much a pound of dimes was worth and brought the coins to our store to be weighed. I always thought every town should have one Republican, just as every town seemed to have one village idiot and one town drunk.

Despite our political differences, I liked Mutt immensely. He was a big fellow with a high forehead and a quick smile who always wore a clean dress shirt with its sleeves rolled up. He had the trustworthy handshake of a wrestler; his grip was strengthened by years of scooping ice cream. Our discussions were good-natured, and I followed the proceedings at the Democratic convention closely to gather material for our daily arguments.

When Adlai Stevenson claimed the nomination again in 1956, I became his most enthusiastic supporter in Bradford. I requested campaign literature from the Democratic Party and was sent boxes of Stevenson material. When I saw the Stevenson brochures were marked "postage paid," I took them to the postmaster, Herb Whitley, a Democratic holdover not yet replaced by the Republican administration. He agreed they could be mailed without stamps to every house in town. I supplemented the free delivery with personal appeals. With the zeal of a Mormon missionary, I proselytized on Stevenson's behalf. One day, as I paid a return visit to the Ramsey house in hopes of nailing down their votes, I heard Mrs. Ramsey moan to her husband: "Oh, my God, here comes that Jimmy McDougal again."

During the fall campaign, Stevenson scheduled a speaking engagement in Little Rock, and I was frantic to see my hero. The logistics were not easy, but my father arranged my ride to Little Rock with a traveling salesman, and he gave me the fare for a bus trip home.

I saw Stevenson, heard him speak, and was transfixed. He was eloquent, above anything I had ever seen or heard in Arkansas. Afterward, I waited outside, hoping for another look at the candidate. There was a stir in the crowd in the street, and suddenly there was Stevenson, riding in an open convertible. The car was moving slowly, and he reached out to shake hands with his followers. As the car passed, the tips of his fingers touched my palm. I was charged with the power of politics.

3

Throughout my youth, Arkansas seemed to drift in the backwater, rarely warranting interest outside our borders. Events meriting banner headlines in the *Arkansas Gazette* were consigned to the back pages of the *New York Times* or ignored altogether. Our elections escaped attention. Even acts of God, tornadoes and drought, attracted scant notice. Seasons passed without a mention of Arkansas in *Time* magazine.

Then in the fall of 1957 a crisis developed in Little Rock like a sudden fever, and Arkansas became a focal point for the nation. A federal judge ordered the desegregation of Little Rock's Central High School; Governor Orval E. Faubus defied the decree, and the case grew into the first major confrontation between a southern state and the federal government since the U.S. Supreme Court struck down school segregation three years earlier.

Faubus had been elected governor in 1954—the year of the *Brown v. Board of Education* decision—as a critic of the Arkansas Power & Light Co. and an advocate of welfare recipients. He weathered revelations that he had attended Commonwealth College, the socialist school, by claiming he never attended classes, and upset the incumbent, Francis A. Cherry. By Arkansas standards, Faubus appeared moderately liberal, a bona fide descendant of earlier hillbilly populists who made their mark in state politics.

If racial integration, once an unthinkable alternative to the southern way of life, was to be forced on Arkansas, it seemed Faubus would be equipped to handle the transition calmly. But in 1956, he was challenged for re-election by Jim Johnson, a fiery segregationist from the lumber country of southern Arkansas, and the experience changed the course of Arkansas politics. Johnson was the darling of the White County Citizens Council crowd, an organization formed to resist the Brown decision; while Johnson thundered against the Supreme Court, he accused Faubus of showing sympathy toward blacks. A Citizens Council publication, *Arkansas Faith*, falsely branded Faubus as a member of the NAACP and denounced him as a politician "who would trade your daughter for a mess of nigger votes." It was an ugly campaign. Faubus called the *Arkansas Faith* "one of the vilest, most dissolute, neopornographic publications it has ever been my disgust to see," and he attacked Johnson's "hate-filled mouthings of intolerance."

Faubus prevailed, but he recognized the need to outflank Johnson before the next election in 1958, when he planned to flout tradition and run for a third term. The governor's chance came on Labor Day 1957, hours before the new school year was to begin with integrated classes. As the Citizens Council fanned rumors of an insurrection to keep Central High School white, Faubus responded with a televised address in which he informed the state he was sending the National Guard to the school to ensure peace and to prevent any change in the status quo.

For the first time in memory, the world was watching Arkansas when the small group of black students arrived at the school the next morning. With shouts of "Lynch them!" from an organized crowd in the streets reverberating against the facade of the school, the students were turned back by the guardsmen. Segregationists were said to be taking up their hunting rifles, mobilizing in the countryside outside the capital, and dozens of FBI agents and hundreds of reporters converged on Little Rock. The drama played on front pages from Peking to Prague. Faubus found himself in direct conflict with President Dwight Eisenhower, and discovered that his defiance had made him an overnight hero throughout the South.

The situation festered for a couple of weeks. After negotiations between Faubus and Eisenhower failed to resolve the dispute, a federal judge issued an injunction blocking the governor's deployment of the National Guard. With his strategy checkmated, Faubus went off to a Southern Governors Conference at Sea Island, Georgia, and the black students returned to Central High.

On September 23, three weeks after Faubus's televised vow to block desegregation, another angry crowd of about a thousand white demonstrators milled in front of the school building, moaning in disbelief after learning that the black students had been admitted through a side door. The mob turned on a couple of black reporters from northern publications. Amid cries of encouragement to kill the visitors, white goons beat and kicked the journalists. Then the crowd attempted to break through a police line set up at the front entrance of the school. Policemen fought back with billy clubs. Turmoil spilled up and down the street. With the breakdown of order, frightened authorities hustled the black students out of the school before noon.

That was enough for Eisenhower. The next day he federalized the National Guard, taking the unit out of Faubus's hands. The president then dispatched one thousand paratroopers to Little Rock from the 101st Airborne Division stationed at Fort Campbell, Kentucky.

Faubus called it an "occupation," and thousands of Arkansans were infuriated by Eisenhower's action, comparing it to the Reconstruction era. Racial incidents flared inside the school for the rest of the year, yet eight of the nine students managed to stick it out.

The law of the land was upheld, but the governor who attempted to thwart the legal decrees was vindicated by popular vote.

Faubus's putative opponent, Jim Johnson, decided to opt for a seat on the state supreme court, and Faubus swept all seventy-five counties in Arkansas, becoming the first man since the turn of the century to win a third term.

While the Little Rock incident assured Faubus of an advantage in state politics for years to come, it doomed the career of Congressman Brooks Hays, a political progressive and delightful storyteller. Hays had tried to mediate a settlement of the Central High School controversy, and his peacemaking efforts cost him his seat. After Hays was smeared by a write-in campaign by Dale Alford, depicting the gentle congressman as an out-of-touch integrationist, voters turned Hays out of office in the next election. He had served in Congress for sixteen years, and it was the first instance in my memory when Arkansas stripped one of its representatives of the seniority that gave our state disproportionate influence in Washington.

Even though I followed the events, the story seemed somewhat remote. I was a freshman at the University of Arkansas in Fayetteville, an Ozark city in the northwest corner of the state, removed from the capital by two hundred miles of bad highway. The university was already marginally integrated, and there was little objection in Fayetteville to the idea of desegregation. Many members of the faculty were openly critical of Faubus's tactics.

But in most places around the state, resentment simmered over the paratroopers in our capital. Arkansans did not like to be strong-armed. My reaction was similar to that of my family and most of my friends. Since I'd grown up in an all-white town, my feelings about race were not fully evolved. I felt it proper to integrate the schools of Arkansas to ensure equal rights, yet I found the use of force repellent. My parents and I disapproved of Washington sending the Army to Little Rock.

From the millennium, the McDougals have distrusted central authority. Our ancestors never knuckled under to the king. Like the rest of the Scots-Irish who settled the South, we came from rebellious stock. In *Albion's Seed: Four British Folkways in America*, the historian David Hackett Fischer wrote of the southern backcountry tribes: "Their humble origins did not create the spirit of subordination which others expected of 'lower ranks.'" That independence, that resistance to outside authority, lies at the core of the southern embrace of states' rights, I believe, and it reflected my family's feelings. Moreover, we were loyal Democrats and considered the troops a tool of a Republican administration—which made their presence even more oppressive. At the time, Faubus's grandstanding didn't really bother me.

I was more concerned with my own affairs. Because I'd skipped a grade in elementary school, I had just celebrated my seventeenth birthday when I arrived at Fayetteville and was a year younger than my classmates. I majored in political science and soon found myself making the sort of lifelong connections in Fayetteville I had seen my father and grandfather cultivate in Bradford.

I was enrolled in the only university in the state; most of the worthy young men and women who could afford to attend the University of Arkansas flocked to Fayetteville. After graduation, the school's student body became part of a network important for anyone thinking of going into politics. Influential citizens in every town in the state shared a Fayetteville connection.

When my parents accompanied me to the campus to inspect the university shortly before I graduated from high school, we were taken on tour by Jim Blair, a law student from Springdale, a town just north of Fayetteville. A big fellow with bluff manners, Blair seemed headed for the big time in Arkansas. His curriculum vitae already oozed with credentials. He had served as president of the university's student body, he was about to graduate from law school, and he belonged to Acacia, a popular fraternity with ties to the Masonic order. Yet for some reason, I was uncomfortable with Blair from that first encounter. I thought him unctuous and glib.

After I enrolled at the university, I, too, joined Acacia. I became great pals with Joe Hamilton, an impish fellow who would soon be elected to the legislature, and his twin brother, Henry. Two other fraternity brothers, the Hale boys, Milas and David, carried strong family ties to the Democratic Party. Outside Acacia, my closest friends were members of a group trying to rejuvenate the Young Democrats (YD) organization in Arkansas. My roommate, Reynolds Griffith, introduced me to the movement and took me to YD meetings.

I preferred politics to the Razorback mania that broke out each fall over the nationally ranked Arkansas football team. Although I had been pressed into duty as a guard—a position where I could do little harm—on Bradford High School's football squad, I was never interested in sports. The Young Democrats became my extracurricular activity. At our meetings, I cemented a friendship with the Hamilton twins that would last the rest of their lives. They were a couple of years older, but we were political compatriots—partisan Democrats with strong populist views. While my views were formed by my exposure to the poor farmers of White County, the Hamilton boys were shaped by their own background. Abandoned by their parents at birth, diagnosed with congenital heart problems and expected to live only a few days, the twins were adopted by a social worker, a spinster who instilled in them a strong belief in the nobility of the poor.

Drawing upon my practical experience as the self-appointed, teenage "chairman" of the Stevenson campaign in Bradford, I plunged into the Young Democrats activities. The move to revitalize the organization had the backing of Governor Faubus, who had decided he could control the YD and use its membership to extend his power in the state.

During my weekend visits home in my freshman year, I began organizing the Young Democrats in White County. It was natural that I pay calls on the political leaders. A powerful local figure was Truman Baker. Even Faubus deferred to him. Mr. Baker and Faubus had served together on the state highway commission during the McMath administration and survived an investigation into payoffs in connection with highway contracts that led to McMath's defeat in 1952. Mr. Baker had grown up in Rosebud, and there was a joke that he'd paved so many roads into the tiny town that there was no ground left to plow.

Mr. Baker belonged to Faubus's inner circle. A major contributor and fund-raiser, he collected campaign money for Faubus from an assortment of interests around the state. It was said that when Faubus first decided to run for governor in 1954, Mr. Baker, appalled by the hillbilly candidate's apparel, bought Faubus new clothes. Mr. Baker had great influence with Faubus; he was like a clever duke giving advice to the king.

By the time I met Mr. Baker, he was a successful Chevrolet dealer in Searcy; sales at his agency thrived because of his political connections. You could bet there were plenty of Chevys in the state fleet. And our congressman Wilbur Mills was always equipped with a new Chevrolet. Mr. Baker was a big man with a florid face, and he looked the part of a county boss. He smoked cigars and enjoyed political bonhomie, but he never specialized in nuts-and-bolts organization. Realizing my interest in that sort of thing, he started leaving the details to me. I traveled around the county, talking with the party committeemen in the various townships. Though I had no formal title, I acted as Mr. Baker's field man, helping him keep the local Democratic troops happy and taking constituent problems involving the federal government to Mr. Mills's office to solve.

Mr. Baker enlisted my help in the Faubus re-election campaign of 1958. It didn't require great effort; the governor's stand against the federal government made him invulnerable that year. But the experience gave me a firsthand look at the inside of the White County machine, and it was a bit like going behind the curtain with the Wizard of Oz. Mr. Baker gave me a stack of cards with the names of the lieutenants in the so-called machine. Only one person from Bradford was on the list—the new school superintendent, a man totally apolitical. None of the people I knew in Bradford as good Democrats were included on the master sheets.

It was apparent the political field was open to a young man with initiative. Though my father didn't share my zest for politics, he gamely went along with one of my ideas, which was to encourage John Pearce, a young man recently discharged from the Navy, to run for one of our district seats in the state legislature. Pearce was a long shot. I served as Pearce's campaign manager; my father loaned him two hundred dollars to buy a suit and print campaign cards. Our candidate's only other political asset was a 1954 Plymouth we painted with the words "John Pearce for Representative." As a fledgling kingmaker, in an old-fashioned, grassroots campaign, I helped drum up enough support to place Pearce a respectable third in a five-man race.

In command of a bloc of votes, we were approached by Ralph Underhill, one of the two candidates who made it into the runoff. Underhill had been in the legislature during the Depression and was remembered as something of a radical populist. He was from Beebe, on the other side of the county, and weird enough to have come from the other side of the moon. Underhill would mash out burning cigarettes with his fingers, then later wipe his hands across his face; the black ash accentuated his ferocious countenance. He had the look of an anarchist. Jobless, Underhill made his living by entering contests and winning prize money. To improve his odds, my friends and I allowed him to use our names. His home was a shack, but once he won a beautiful Ford Thunderbird in a contest sponsored by the manufacturer of Karo syrup, a key ingredient in pecan pies. As a result, one of my buddies dubbed him the Karo Kid.

Underhill was oblivious to ridicule and determined to win back a legislative seat. If the Pearce-McDougal combine agreed to throw our support to him, Underhill said, he promised to get me appointed assistant reading clerk in the state House of Representatives, a job that would give me the opportunity to meet the movers and shakers of Arkansas. As might be expected of any backcountry kingmaker, I endorsed Underhill with alacrity and encouraged Pearce's supporters to do the same. Underhill won, and he kept his vow. Prior to the legislative session, he traveled around the state to meet with various members of the Efficiency Committee, which controlled patronage in the Arkansas House. He assured them he wasn't as radical as he used to be, and he persuaded them to appoint me. There was one other part of the deal: I had to use part of my new eighty-four-dollar-a-week legislative salary to pay back my father the two hundred dollars he had given to Pearce.

At the age of eighteen, I was off to Little Rock to see the wonders of the Arkansas legislature in session. In addition to reading bills and handling the electric voting machine, I was responsible for operating the microphone. If a member stood up, I needed to know the proper microphone number. To prepare for my job I stayed up far into the night before the legislature convened. Using a Farm Bureau handbook to match the names with the faces of all one hundred members of the House, I would study their seating locations and memorize their microphone numbers. Then I went to sleep, dreaming of the grand adventure awaiting me in the morning.

I soon discovered that the real work didn't take place at the capitol. The focus of activity was the Marion Hotel in downtown Little Rock, a den of legislators, lobbyists, and lawyers, a confluence of business and political interests. Each January of every odd-numbered year, legislators would pour in from the provinces, from places like Pocahontas and Marked Tree, to enjoy the splendor of the state capital. Some of them were relatively sophisticated lawyers, others were poor and unschooled. Worldly by Arkansas standards and flush with expense accounts, the lobbyists waited to greet them. Deals that might be struck casually in the hotel corridors would be sealed over cocktails at night.

The Marion has been demolished, replaced by the Excelsior Hotel, a modern tower of glass and red brick where Bill Clinton is said to have sought sexual favors from Paula Corbin Jones. But in its day, the Marion was one of the most splendid fixtures in Arkansas—a stately place, seven stories high, and resting on the south bank of the Arkansas River. It was the scene of conventions, Rotary Club meetings, and, when the legislature was in session, nightly bacchanals.

I would not have wanted my mother and father to have seen me there. I never saw any money change hands to buy votes, but there was enough raucous social exchange to trouble any self-respecting Baptist, with an enormous amount of drinking and scores of attractive girls. Jobs were scarce, and only the most beautiful young women were hired as secretaries at the capitol. Their presence at the nightly shindigs was largely cosmetic, however. This was the chaste 1950s, and the sexual revolution had not made its way to Arkansas. I doubt there was much sexual congress at the Marion; that kind of behavior took place across the street at the Capital Hotel, a derelict flophouse where, it was said, one could take a room, inform the elevator operator of one's desire, and enjoy a visit within minutes.

The Capital is now the most fashionable hotel in Little Rock, but forty years ago, the Marion Hotel still held the glamour of the Gilded Age. Cigar smoke curled to the high ceiling of the lobby, an ornate room with four marble pillars and a fish pond fed by a fountain. Lawmakers huddled with lobbyists, while old men, retired from state government, lounged in leather chairs, watching, nostalgically, the game they once played. The Marion was segregated. The only blacks were uniformed bellboys, ready to run messages or fetch ice, and waiters in starched white jackets sweeping through the dining rooms with trays of steaks and chops covered with silver hoods, all under the watchful eye of the hotel manager, Mr. Ben Shelley.

Serious eating took place in the Green Room, where images of magnolia blossoms were woven into a green carpet. Red damask draperies decorated the windows; tables were covered with white linen and set with fine silver and crystal. Yet for all this finery, the most popular spot in the Marion was downstairs in the lower lobby, in the Gar Hole, a dark bar rank with the smell of barbecue and stale beer.

The Baptist Church dictated morals for Arkansas, forcing the state to practice a curious system of semi-prohibition. The state was still divided between wet counties and dry counties; wet-county blue laws stipulated that only beer could be sold across the bar. Whiskey could be purchased in liquor stores and discreetly brought into hotels and restaurants, a practice known as brown bagging. When the legislature came to town, the blue laws were circumvented. At least three lobbyists kept private bars operating in suites day and night, handing out complimentary bottles of liquor. Ike Murray, a former attorney general who had gone on to represent the wholesale beer industry, regularly dispensed bottles of Budweiser and top-of-the-shelf brands of liquor from his crowded hotel suite.

In the basement bar, a lone gar, a primitive, alligator-snouted bottom-feeding fish, patrolled the water tank. George Poulos, the manager of the Gar Hole, ran an efficient operation and took care of any legislator who drank too much.

Conveniently located next door in the lower lobby was a barbershop specializing in soothing the pain of hangovers. The place reeked of pomade and bay rum and its mirrors were fogged by steam, but it was a popular gathering spot by midmorning, when legislators stumbled in to get shaves, hot towel packs, and facial massages.

My room, which I had to myself, was one of the "subterranean rooms." Instead of ascending from the lobby in an elevator like others, I walked downstairs. The room, which looked out on an air shaft, commanded four dollars a night; I thought it quite grand.

It was easy to cut expenses. Constant parties offered buffet tables groaning with cold cuts and canapés. In the dining rooms, lobbyists would invariably take care of the bill. We ate breakfast in the coffee shop, and a Cotton Belt railroad lobbyist with the euphonious name of Charles Coalburner walked through the room every morning, passing each table and picking up checks.

Mr. Coalburner was a dignified man. Short, rotund, and well dressed, he didn't chomp cigars, slap backs, or guffaw at dirty jokes. Once he took me to an elegant dinner in the Green Room with Mr. Bellingrath, a wealthy fellow from Pine Bluff reputed to be a major Coca-Cola stockholder. Considering myself bright beyond my years, I informed Mr. Bellingrath that the Coca-Cola company wasted its money on advertising. I thought Coca-Cola, a proud southern product, was God-given. "You don't have to advertise Coke," I told Mr. Bellingrath. "Nobody's ever going to catch up with Coca-Cola." I advised him that Pepsi, the chief competition, was "despised" in the South. I was dreadfully wrong, of course, but there I was, eighteen years old, telling a corporate magnate what to do. Mr. Coalburner may have been embarrassed, but he picked up my check nevertheless.

Mr. Coalburner's generosity was typical of the powerful lobbyists who worked for the utilities, the building contractors, and the railroads. The lobbyist for the bus companies was a beneficent figure, too. The Arkansas constitution of 1874 specifically outlawed the practice of giving free railway passes to members of the legislature, but made no mention of that twentieth-century vehicle the bus. So all the legislators received bus passes. After my friend from the university, Joe Hamilton, was elected to the legislature, he turned over his bus pass to me and I used it to ride around the state for years.

Joe was an irreverent House member. On strolls through the chamber, he flipped the chair backs to jar elderly legislators and mussed the hair of colleagues striving for a groomed appearance. Joe delighted in introducing one legislator as "Mr. Baker, the president and chairman of the board of the Baker Shoe Company of Jasper, Arkansas." The fellow would beam at public mention of his title, even though his empire consisted of one shoe store with an inventory worth about fifteen hundred dollars. Baker was one of the legislators we categorized as "Boskys." In Arkansas, *bosky* is a term for a verdant, overgrown backwoods.

◆ ◆ ◆

Arkansas being a small state, dominated at the time by one party, its legislative sessions were not textbook examples of how a bill becomes law. Partisan interests were drawn along geographical rather than party lines. Some legislators were hopelessly parochial, bound to the biggest businesses of their home district. Others owed their allegiance to big corporations doling out campaign contributions and favors. Temporary alliances were forged rapidly and broken just as quickly. Legislators with no more than grade school education operated with the skills of Machiavelli, or so it seemed, obtaining valuable concessions for votes rendered. No one bothered to assume the pose of a disinterested servant of the commonweal. The Arkansas legislators looked out for themselves and their friends, and if their interests failed to coincide with the state's best interests, then it was too bad. In my first encounter with government in Arkansas, I saw democracy in the raw. It worked, in its own way, but sometimes it was comic and petty.

Sessions at the capitol were usually formalities to complete the business transacted earlier at the Marion. Deals required no floor debate. But one issue could not be settled over cocktails. Arkansas State College in Jonesboro was clamoring to be certified as a university, and only the legislature had the prerogative to make the designation. The campus at Fayetteville, protective of its prestige as the state's only university, opposed the plan, setting off a battle between the schools' alumni associations as well as a struggle between the interests of the Delta and the hills. The legislature was bitterly divided, and epic fights ensued for years. The matter was not resolved until 1967, and it required a parlay involving votes from central Arkansas for the Jonesboro school to win distinction as a university. Legislators from the Little Rock area, who wanted the University of Arkansas to establish a branch in the capital, agreed to support Arkansas State's bid if the Delta's legislative faction would accede to the merger of the University of Arkansas with an existing school in Little Rock.

Most House business was not so lofty. Many measures were, in effect, local bills that triggered no debate. Although local bills were forbidden by the state constitution, hometown representatives got around the prohibition by writing the bills to apply, for example, to any county with a population between 18,100 and 18,500, a description fitting only the representative's home county.

Other bills were drawn up at the behest of special interests, and certain legislators were expected to carry the ball for them. Bill Thompson of Poinsett County was considered the railroads' most reliable man in the legislature. Following the submission of a hostile bill requiring the railroad companies to put tops on motorized carts ferrying their maintenance men up and down the tracks, Thompson rose in indignation. "Why do you think our jeeps didn't have tops in World War II?" Thompson asked, and then answered his question: "So the men could get out of them safely." To require a top for the railroad carts, he bellowed, "would turn them into death traps."

Lowell Whittington, a young legislator and a good friend of mine, acted as point man for Weideker Winery, an enterprise in his Franklin County district. The company supplied him with truckloads of wine, and he stacked the tribute in his room, from the floor to the ceiling. The place looked like a cavern, with cases of wine on both sides of his bed. Lowell distributed bottles to his fellow legislators, though few drank wine. They used it to tip the bellboys delivering setups for stronger drink.

Some legislation was downright capricious. Joe and I concocted a bill to benefit the only Republican in the House, Dewey Massey, a pleasant, unsophisticated fellow from Searcy County who spoke the Elizabethan English of the hills and had no formal education. Though a successful businessman with the wherewithal to afford nice clothes, Dewey favored the tacky neckties the state handed out to legislators. The ties were decorated with an outline of Arkansas and an artificial diamond. They were god-awful, but the "Bosky" legislators wore them because they were free. Dewey was completely unpretentious. Joe and I loved the guy. We drew up a bill designating him "minority leader," instructing the state director of finance to prepare him a special license plate and provide him office space. It passed unanimously. Dewey was very happy to become the official leader of the Republican minority of one—himself.

Other bills were vindictive, such as a measure submitted by Roy Riales to regulate the cost of telephone calls in hotels. Roy was a crafty guy and a leader in the state Senate. He never made much money, and he stayed in one of the Marion's subterranean rooms. Annoyed that the hotel was charging fifteen cents for each call placed from his room—the call box in the lobby cost only a dime— Roy introduced a bill making it illegal for hotels to charge more than the call boxes. The measure would have meant a considerable loss to Southwest Hotels, the company that owned the Marion and three other hotels in town. Miraculously, Roy was elevated from the lower level into luxurious accommodations, and the bills, his and the hotel's, disappeared.

My work at the legislative sessions in 1959 and 1961 took place at a time when Governor Faubus was reaching for greater control. His chief liaison to the legislature was Bill Smith, an influential Little Rock lawyer who took off from his practice during the two-month session to handle Faubus's affairs at the Marion and the State House. Smith was a formidable man who orchestrated many victories for the governor. He roamed the House floor freely, moving up and down the aisles, telling members how to vote. He would say, "Give me a vote, give me a vote." Once he approached Hamilton and told him: "Give me a vote, Joe."

"Screw you, Bill," Joe replied. The members, most of whom fell in line behind Faubus on any issue, were startled.

Joe prided himself on his hillbilly cunning. He wasn't unwilling to make an alliance with Faubus; he simply wanted to work out his own terms. As populists, Joe and Faubus shared a distrust of the railroads, and Joe took advantage of the governor's bias in one

case. After a railroad company shut down operations on a line running from Little Rock to Missouri, through the heart of Joe's district, he took steps to restore service on the line. Disregarding Joe's
efforts, the company began to dismantle the rails, selling them for
salvage and destroying the infrastructure of the system. Joe and
Faubus teamed up to win passage of an incredibly high tax on the
removal of rails. They knew it was a confiscatory tax that wouldn't
stand up in court, but they also knew it would torment the railroad
for years before it could be overturned, and they took great satisfaction from the company's dilemma.

The House was full of colorful characters, and sometimes the
sessions turned unruly. One man who dominated debate was Paul
Van Dalsem, a crude but canny representative from Perry County,
the least-populated district in the state. As chairman of the Efficiency Committee, which had hired me, Van Dalsem expected deference. One day he called me to the podium, where he was
presiding, and growled: "You think I'm a buffoon, don't you, boy?"
In fact, I did, though I didn't tell him. He winked and whispered a
secret: "The way I control this thing is to keep it in total chaos."
Then he whipped from his pocket a linen napkin from the Marion
Hotel and blew his nose.

Van Dalsem would scream and yell and throw the chamber into
pandemonium. His partner in disorder was a fellow from Bradley
County named Carroll Hollensworth. Acting as though he were constantly cranked on speed, Hollensworth smoked cigarettes so fast
they burned like dynamite fuses. But he knew the House rules backward and forward and could tie the place in knots by invoking
parliamentary procedure.

Hollensworth was one of those country fellows said to be as
dumb as a fox. Though he represented a rural county, he held a law
degree and could match wits with anyone. Once, according to another legislative tale, an ambitious young attorney came to Hollensworth's law office to solicit a contribution for the local bar
association's annual party. Hollensworth gave him a check for

twenty-five dollars, and on the "For" line he wrote "liquor." He suspected the young lawyer would challenge him for his House seat someday. Sure enough, the next year the fellow filed as a candidate. Hollensworth produced the canceled check and ran a photo of it in a local newspaper ad, explaining that "the poor, pathetic fellow came by and I just had to loan him the money to buy some whiskey." Hollensworth beat him like a drum.

As a political neophyte, I came to understand that the perception of power can be as important as real power. Assigned to a desk below the Speaker, I could see into corners of the chamber shielded from the Speaker's view by bright decorative lights. When I spotted members in the wings waving their arms and begging to be heard, I called out their names so the Speaker would recognize them. My helpfulness to the backbenchers earned me goodwill.

My reputation was enhanced when I inadvertently aided my friend Lowell Whittington in his challenge to the Faubus administration. Lowell introduced a bill to add county back roads to the state highway system, a boondoggle that would force the state to maintain the roads. Faubus opposed it, but the bill had strong support from rural areas. The vote was nip and tuck, and I clumsily jammed the voting machine while trying to print out the roll call. Lowell's measure appeared to be stuck at fifty votes, one less than necessary for passage. But the legislators were forced to vote again because of my foul-up, and in the next round Lowell's bill got fifty-one votes. Most members assumed I'd delayed the final tally so he could line up one more vote. The legislators appreciated a clever tactic. Though I had been a klutz, they were convinced I was a magician. It was beyond belief that Faubus could be beaten on this issue.

Like any effective governor, Faubus maintained control of the legislature by trading favors. One of the most sought-after items was a season's pass to the racetrack at Hot Springs. The governor's liaison, Bill Smith, lavished passes on friendly legislators. Some members felt it was prestigious to have these passes, and they gathered as many as possible to give to their constituents. There was a downside to the scheme. Some legislators were so pestered by requests for passes from their followers that they introduced bills to make them illegal. The legislation never passed. The biggest event of each session was "Legislative Day" at Hot Springs, when all the members and aides, accompanied by their spouses, would pile onto buses (provided by the bus lobby), partake of a portable bar (provided by the liquor lobby) set up in the back of the bus, and spend a day at the races, compliments of the racetrack.

Like the railroad and utility moguls, the racetrack owners knew how to preserve a sacred cow.

4

B y 1960, Orval Faubus was at the height of his power. The son of socialist tub-thumper Sam Faubus had traveled a long, winding path out of Greasy Creek, the tiny Madison County village in the Ozarks where he was born. From his early days as a migrant worker, he'd managed to win election as circuit clerk; he'd then served in World War II before purchasing the Madison County *Record* in 1947. His snappy, progressive editorials convinced the reformist governor, Sid McMath, to bring him to Little Rock to run the state highway program. After McMath's successor, Francis Cherry, proved too cozy with the Arkansas Power & Light Co., the audacious Faubus used his brief experience in state government as a launching pad to run against Cherry. In *Gothic Politics in the Deep South*, Robert Sherrill summed up Faubus's drive: "Faubus has the kind of stubbornness that serves impoverished, untutored hillbillies as the great evolutionary gene needed to pull them out of the mud and onto the sunlit shore of civilization."

Faubus's triumph ratified the belief that any shrewd dark horse could win in our state. Public office was not automatically handed to the sons of wealth and authority; Arkansas offered a place for poor boys, and the legendary product of Ozark poverty was moving to establish his own personal dynasty, running for re-election to a fourth term as governor. Faubus still enjoyed popularity from the Central High School affair, and he had consolidated his control over the state's fulcrums of power.

Surrounded by a cadre of trusted friends and advisers who kept his campaign treasury filled, he prepared for the 1960 race. Truman Baker, the White County power and my early political benefactor, knew how to call his IOUs with Faubus. When Mr. Baker wanted to expand his auto agency, he bought the National Guard armory in Searcy from the state at his price and converted the building into office space.

Mr. Baker understood the value of connections, and I believe he appreciated my own youthful ambitions. Within a year of my start as an eager Young Democrat, working as Mr. Baker's operative in our home county, I had become acquainted with politicians from every corner of the state. Mr. Baker tapped me as chairman of the Youth for Faubus division of the governor's 1960 re-election campaign. Given one of the four offices in Faubus's headquarters in Little Rock, I felt puffed by an air of importance even though the governor never bothered to visit.

The governor had four weak opponents in the Democratic primary, the only venue for decisive political battles in the days before the Republican Party gained a foothold in Arkansas. Nevertheless, the Faubus organization set about its tasks as though embroiled in a real contest. One of my assignments involved a full-page newspaper advertisement in which I assembled the names, school affiliations, and favorable testimony of a number of Faubus's student followers who applauded his efforts to raise the standard of living among the poor. His programs impressed me because I had seen their impact in White County after he'd managed to divert federal funds to increase state benefits for the poor and elderly. Knowing that many of the older, white recipients were too proud to accept something called welfare, Faubus referred to the benefit as an "old-age pension."

Faubus's manipulation of the Little Rock school desegregation may have been one of the most cynical acts in the history of Arkansas politics, but his administrations were responsible for progress. Our schools and highways improved, and the state felt its first stirrings of economic development. I still considered myself an idealist, believing the best instincts of human nature would prevail, despite my experiences in the House. Taking heart from the positive side of Faubus, I relished speaking for him. With an oratorical style blending the flourish of Franklin Roosevelt and the fire of the evangelist Billy Sunday, I came into demand as a speaker, representing the governor at events around the state.

One Saturday night, Mr. Baker loaned me a car from his Chevrolet agency to drive to his hometown of Rosebud, on the other side of White County. After my speech, I picked up some beer and drove home. With one hand on the steering wheel, the other clutching a can of beer, I knocked an ember from my cigarette, starting a fire on the front seat. Thinking I could simply pour beer on the cushion and extinguish the fire, I soaked the trouble spot while polishing off the rest of the six-pack. Arriving home in Bradford after midnight, I crept to bed past my sleeping parents. At dawn, we awakened to the sound of sirens. Smoke billowed from the auto. The seat had been eaten overnight by a slow-burning fire that had destroyed the interior of Mr. Baker's brand-new Chevrolet. I had to remove the remains of the front seat and sit on a wooden pear crate to drive the wreckage back to Searcy. Before I left I telephoned Mr. Baker. "I'm afraid I've had an accident," I said. I considered my plight, then added, "Let me rephrase that: I've had a catastrophe." He told me that if anyone asked about the accident, I should say that I was thinking of buying the car and had taken it on a trial run. He didn't have to tell me that this was for insurance purposes. Ever the politician, Mr. Baker closed our conversation by saying, "I heard you made a good speech over in Rosebud."

◆ ◆ ◆

Mr. Baker never needed to hold a public office or a position in the Democratic Party leadership to exert influence. He maintained control by putting his loyalists in those jobs. Following the primary, where Faubus easily won renomination as governor, the White County Democrats met to certify the votes and select delegates for the state convention. Mr. Baker feared the results from some of the ballot boxes might be challenged because the Faubus margins were so huge. Wanting a trusted hand in charge of the county convention and knowing I was well versed in parliamentary procedure, Mr. Baker asked me to preside. After the convention concluded without a hitch, Mr. Baker saw to it that I became vice chairman of the White County delegation to the state Democratic convention in Little Rock later that summer.

As Mr. Baker had chosen to go pheasant hunting, Wilbur Mills was the most prominent member of our delegation. I had a plan for the convention: to challenge a Faubus man for our district seat on the state Democratic executive committee.

My rival was Dan Felton, a member of a well-known family of east Arkansas planters. They owned the town of Felton and dominated Lee County. Dan Felton served as our district's incumbent on the executive committee, and his name was on the Faubus slate for reelection at the convention. I don't think he knew he would have opposition. Since his home base was the smallest of the five counties in our judicial district, I quietly made inroads in the other four counties.

Without Mr. Baker to object, I lined up support in White County. I also won the backing of Clarke Kinney, a legislator from St. Francis County. Kinney was a bit older than I—he had been an officer in World War II and Korea—but he looked youthful, and we had become friends during my work in the House. Drawing upon other legislative connections, I obtained commitments from Woodruff County delegates, whose home lay across the White River from Bradford, and I sought support among the delegation from Phillips County in the Mississippi River Delta.

The election of an executive committee member was not a big deal to most delegates, but it meant a lot to me. Organizing supporters before Felton knew what was happening, I won decisively.

A good loser, Felton forgave my coup and we eventually became friends and political allies. But I still worried about repercussions from the Faubus crowd. Before Clarke Kinney and I reached the Gar Hole, we ran into Wilbur Mills, heading back to the auditorium for the convention's main business session. There was a possibility that Faubus delegates could try to overturn my election on the grounds that I was a few weeks shy of my twentieth birthday and ineligible to vote.

Mr. Mills had already heard the news. "Did you beat Dan Felton?" he asked me, increduously.

"Yessir, I did."

"Well, I'll take care of it," Mr. Mills said.

The only person who raised an objection was my government professor at the university, Dr. Henry Alexander. Several days after the convention, I saw him at a legislative weekend in Fayetteville, and he delivered a brief lecture. I might think I was a big shot, he said, but in fact I was merely a de facto member of the executive committee instead of a full-fledged de jure member because of my age. I think he was joking, but I wasn't certain.

Dr. Alexander had a good-humored way of humbling his students. One day in class a fellow asked Dr. Alexander if he ever gave pop tests. "The day I give a pop test is the day I come clambering over the transom," Dr. Alexander said. Sure enough, a few days later, we looked up and Dr. Alexander was climbing through the transom to spring a pop test.

I did not return to the university for the fall semester. Buoyed by my role in the Faubus campaign and my election to the executive committee, I was keen to embark on my final political adventure of 1960—the effort to win the heavily Protestant state of Arkansas for John F. Kennedy.

With our six measly electoral votes, out of 535 at stake, we were not exactly high priority. The Solid South had voted Democratic for most of the century. Even Al Smith, the first Catholic presidential nominee, had carried Arkansas. Franklin Roosevelt's New Deal, generating programs that extended aid to the rural poor, deepened loyalties to the party during the Depression. But the Solid South was breaking up. Increasingly Democrats were perceived as the party of liberalism and East Coast licentiousness, and the support northern Democrats gave to civil rights measures made matters worse for the party in Arkansas. Brooks Hays's defeat in 1958 had been an early-warning signal for local Democrats.

Just as in the Faubus operation, I was given the title of youth director for the statewide JFK campaign, and once again I worked in something of a vacuum. Arkansans were not exactly rushing into the arms of Kennedy. Faubus had appointed his aide Dan Stephens as the state director, but Stephens was a figurehead at best and never came to the headquarters. Control was in the hands of Pat Mehaffy, the national Democratic committeeman from Arkansas and a leading lawyer in Little Rock. Despite widespread doubts about Kennedy, Mehaffy applied pressure to keep restive Democrats in rank.

Like Truman Baker, Mehaffy didn't need a title to exercise power. He was a member of the high-powered Little Rock law firm of Mehaffy, Smith & Williams. His partner Bill Smith maintained the Faubus line in the legislature while Mehaffy represented the Missouri Pacific Railroad, one of the great corporate powers in the state.

Mehaffy had been a prosecuting attorney back in the 1940s. A short man, he favored expensive suits, fine broadcloth shirts, and silk ties. His immaculate appearance won him respect, as did his political wiles. Mehaffy, who had Faubus's ear, was an intimate of our senior U.S. senator, John McClellan.

Mehaffy stayed behind the scenes. He never visited our forlorn campaign headquarters. If something needed to be discussed, the meetings were held in the hotel room of Fred Coleman, Mehaffy's associate. Coleman was the Missouri Pacific's lobbyist in Washington, but he spent a great deal of time in Little Rock at the sedate Grady Manning Hotel, a block east of the frantic Marion. In spite of my aversion to the railroad industry, I never really identified either man with the cold-hearted owners. Their strong Democratic credentials and personal generosity meant more to me than their affiliation with the Missouri Pacific.

A half block west of the Marion, the Kennedy campaign occupied a dingy suite in an office building. Unlike the spacious Faubus headquarters upstairs, the JFK campaign was relegated to storefront space on the first floor, one big room divided by a partition. We lived like underdogs.

Arkansas was seen as a forlorn hope by the Kennedy people, another southern state in the process of breaking its traditional ties to the Democratic Party. Our local races had already been decided in the primary. There was little enthusiasm for Kennedy in the general election. Instead of rushing aid to JFK's embattled faithful in Arkansas, the national Kennedy organization had given up on us and gave us nothing but boxes of campaign literature. Instead of receiving support, we sent money to them.

Fact is, we were persuaded to purchase our Kennedy buttons and bumper stickers from national headquarters on a budget of thirty-five thousand dollars that Mehaffy had raised locally. The JFK campaign in Arkansas was so threadbare that a pay phone served as our only means of communication. We could only receive incoming calls and were not even given credit cards. A WATS line, the device used in most campaigns to place unlimited calls, was never offered. When a Kennedy representative from the Washington office deigned to visit us one day, it became a memorable event. He had a telephone credit card and we were able to make a flurry of calls on the Kennedy account.

A few women volunteers occupied desks in the front of the office, but no salaried official managed the local campaign. By default, I ran the day-to-day operations and answered to Mehaffy.

Kennedy never made an appearance in the state, nor did his running mate, Lyndon B. Johnson, nor any of their high-powered surrogates. Actually, we thought we'd be better off handling the campaign ourselves. During the period after the Little Rock crisis, a Yankee visitor, especially a Roman Catholic, might have further alienated the Arkansas voters.

The only weapon we received from the national organization was a huge shipment of *Reader's Digest* reprints of the story of Kennedy's bravery in the Pacific during World War II. We showered the state with the reading material, hoping heroism would transcend Catholicism.

My partner was R. D. Randolph, a state employee delegated to help the campaign. R.D. worked for the State Apiary Board, an agency responsible for the honeybee business in Arkansas. Provided with a car and mileage expenses to drive around and talk to beekeepers, R.D. let me ride with him. For a while, there was an arrangement to put me on the payroll of the apiary agency.

Composed of a handful of honeybee owners, the apiary board met annually at the Marion Hotel and approved its budget over lunch. It was easy to sneak me onto the staff. The next year, when the legislature conducted a review of expenditures by the apiary board, one of the representatives spotted my name and asked, "What does Jim McDougal know about honeybees?"

R.D. and I trucked the *Reader's Digest* material all over the state, paying kids fifty cents a bundle to stick the reprints under every door and to distribute hundreds more at public gatherings. Our favorite forums were the livestock auctions. R.D. owned a few head of cattle and knew the schedule for all the sales, which served as weekly social and commercial events in each town. Amid the sweet smell of cow manure and the swirling dust, farmers would sit under the tin roof of the sale barn, listening to the auctioneer's spiel with one ear and gossip and bad jokes from their buddies with the other.

After handing out the stories of Kennedy's PT 109 exploits, I would usually be allowed to speak during a lull in the auction. I tried to be entertaining and to appeal to the farmers' instincts, which ran strongly in the direction of regional pride and military service.

"You know John Kennedy's a war hero!" I shouted. "He patrolled the Pacific waters, and when the enemy cut his boat in two, he didn't surrender! He swam for miles—severely wounded—to an island so he could continue to fight!" I paused. "He won more decorations than you can find on a Christmas tree!"

Most farmers were veterans, and I hoped they would respond to tales of bravery. But I was met at first with the sound of shuffling feet in the bleachers, and not much more.

So I moved to make Arkansas connections. "You know Senator Kennedy is a close friend of our Senator McClellan! He's worked closely with him on many issues affecting our state. His brother Bobby Kennedy has been Senator McClellan's chief counsel on the Senate Rackets Committee. They're working together to cleanse this country of organized crime!"

That led to a few murmurs of support.

"You know all of our senators and congressmen in Washington are Democrats! They work hard to bring government programs to Arkansas. They've worked tirelessly, in the face of an uncaring Republican administration, to help our state. Think what they could do with a Democrat in the White House." At this point, a few spectators stomped the planks with their boots and whooped approval.

My voice rose as I neared the climax. "Who do you want? Tricky Dick Nixon?" My rhetoric reflected the old-time religion—already out of date, but I pressed on, invoking that heartless Republican trio Martin, Barton, and Fish, the men who'd tried to obstruct Franklin Roosevelt in the 1930s, and suggesting that Nixon was one of their group. "No," I thundered, "you want a man like Senator John Kennedy, a Democrat from the mold of Roosevelt! A man who'll be the champion of the farmer, the small merchant, and the working folks everywhere!"

◆ ◆ ◆

Despite my activity on Kennedy's behalf, I feared he would lose Arkansas. The morning of his first televised debate with Nixon, Mehaffy sent me to represent JFK's Arkansas campaign at a southern governors convention at the Arlington Hotel in Hot Springs. Using my legislative bus pass—compliments of Joe Hamilton—I wound up riding with a reporter from Boston on his way to cover the convention. Drinking whiskey from a half-pint bottle, the visitor seemed sardonic and wise to the ways of the world, disinterested in the historic confrontation between the two presidential candidates and already jaded by the Kennedys of Boston. After we watched the debate together that night, he declared Nixon the victor. I disagreed, saying Kennedy looked cool and in control, while Nixon appeared fretful, even shifty as if he were guilty of some heinous crime.

The debates gave me a glimmer of hope, but the Arkansas political establishment remained unenthusiastic. Faubus withheld a formal endorsement. Even those powerful members of the Arkansas congressional delegation, those very men whom I'd claimed would gain strength with a Democrat in the White House, were reluctant to be identified publicly with a Catholic candidate perceived as a liberal.

Finally, Mehaffy coerced everyone into late endorsements to project a united front. On the last weekend before the election, he prevailed upon Faubus to issue a carefully worded, lukewarm statement, something to the effect of: "I'm going to vote for every Democrat I can find on the ticket." It was better than a denunciation.

The greatest resistance to the Democratic presidential campaign came from the fundamentalist denominations, the Baptist Church and the Church of Christ. Their leaders muttered that Kennedy's election was the first step in a plot involving the pope—shades of the Know-Nothing movement of the nineteenth century.

By the end of the campaign, most of the Democratic officials were grudgingly on board for Kennedy. Fortunately, many of them happened to be Baptist deacons. It occurred to our campaign—which is to say, Mehaffy and me—that these Democratic deacons could render political service through their positions in the church. We feared that the Baptist ministers would rally their followers with the tired chant "Rum, Romanism, and Rebellion," as they had when thrashing Al Smith some thirty years earlier. We feared a tirade would be unleashed against Kennedy on the final Sunday of the campaign. But we also knew that Baptist churches were autonomous; each congregation controls its minister and its policies, without answering to any denominational dictates. We called upon every Baptist deacon who was a Democratic committeeman and persuaded each of them to warn their local ministers: if the name of the Democratic presidential candidate was mentioned in church, prominent Democrats were prepared to walk out of the congregation and take their money with them.

To avoid such an unseemly scene, the ministers held their tongues. There were no diatribes against Kennedy from the pulpits that final Sunday. On Tuesday JFK carried the state with just over 50 percent of the vote.

5

couple of months after John F. Kennedy's inauguration, Pat Mehaffy telephoned me. "Look son," he said, "we can't make you ambassador to Kenya or anything like that. You're only twenty." Still, he told me people should be rewarded for their efforts in politics. As a result of our success in the Kennedy campaign, Mehaffy was in line to be nominated by the White House to the U.S. Circuit Court of Appeals, one of the highest judicial positions in the land, and he said I was being recognized for my contribution to the Democratic victories with a job in Washington working for Senator John L. McClellan.

The offer was both fortuitous and flattering. Joining McClellan's staff would be a godsend. McClellan was a venerable figure in Washington, and respected in Arkansas as a self-made man. At the age of seventeen he read the law—studied for the legal profession without attending law school—and won admission to the bar without a degree. Nothing had come easy. McClellan had experienced great personal tragedy in his life: one son had been killed in World War II and another in a car wreck. The senator had also been broke and had lost an election or two. He understood hard times.

Still, he radiated power and seniority. With his commanding voice and handsome wardrobe, McClellan cast an impressive profile. He was a key chairman on Capitol Hill. If America had been a theocracy, he would have been a high priest.

Both McClellan and Bill Fulbright, Arkansas's other senator, defied the cornpone image America had of Arkansas. Our two senators were intelligent, dignified men, not given to backslapping or demagoguery. They were held in such high esteem that constituents constantly sought their approval.

Intrigued by my opportunity, I went off to Washington, a city I had never visited, while Kennedy was still in his first one hundred days in office. I wish I could say I was thrilled to reach the threshold of the New Frontier after eight sleepy years of Eisenhower. But I knew I wasn't joining Camelot's court. I was going to work in Congress, which I considered a larger version of the Arkansas legislature. I had no illusions of grandeur. A good thing.

When I reported for work, I was given an assignment as a "research assistant" on the staff of the Rackets Committee, the investigative unit created in 1957 to resolve a dispute between a couple of Senate committees fighting for jurisdiction over racketeering. With Bobby Kennedy as counsel and McClellan as chairman, the committee had conducted a series of nationally televised hearings on Mafia operations and mob infiltration of labor unions. The hearings had sparked the bitter exchanges between Bobby Kennedy and Jimmy Hoffa, the Teamsters boss, that helped demonize Hoffa and drive the union toward the Republican Party. Bobby Kennedy, of course, had gone off to become his brother's attorney general, but McClellan still controlled the committee.

The research assistant had several duties, none of them significant. Performing as a glorified office boy, I fetched coffee and ran errands for the more vital staff members. I was expected to talk to all of the nuts who came to the office to report on gangsters destroying the brains of their foes with radioactive waves. When these characters arrived, the receptionist would direct them to "Mr.

McDougal, the chief counsel," and I would sit there, nodding sagely, listening to their tales of conspiracy and danger. On occasion my reverie was interrupted by colleagues plunking a dime on my desk and telling me, "One, with sugar."

McClellan was my boss, but Fred Coleman controlled my destiny. A big guy, Fred carried on wisecracking conversations, and for a fellow from Lafayette County in southwest Arkansas, he was debonair. Fred dressed in the white-on-white shirts and ties fashionable among the gambling set in Hot Springs. As lobbyist for Arkansas's most powerful railroad, Fred's duty was to keep Arkansas's preeminent man in Washington comfortable. "One God, one country, one client," Fred said. Since McClellan didn't like to drive, Fred picked him up in the morning and drove him home at night. Fred shopped for McClellan, choosing shirts and accessories for the senator at an expensive men's store in downtown Washington. They had an easy relationship. Once Fred remarked that he was going to Little Rock; McClellan pulled eight dollars out of his billfold and asked, "While you're down there, could you get me a pair of those alligator shoes?"

Fred pretended to be insulted. "Goddamn, Senator," he said. "They cost sixty-four dollars. And besides, that's the first time I ever saw you pull anything besides a handkerchief out of your pocket."

McClellan rarely paid for anything. It was a reflection of the Washington culture. Members of Congress made it a point to walk around without money. When a bill came for dinner or drinks, the politicians didn't even bother to fumble for their empty billfold; an obliging lobbyist was always there to pick up the check. It was reminiscent of the Marion Hotel, writ large. Not only were meals free; big corporations paid for plane tickets and hotel accommodations when the senators and representatives went out of town. They inundated congressional offices with gifts. No one was embarrassed by the system. It was standard operating procedure in Washington in the years before Common Cause and the ethics police.

Given the Missouri Pacific's relationship with McClellan, Fred had the senator's ear. Fred first landed me a $5,600-a-year job on the Rackets Committee; within a few months he saw that I was promoted to an $8,800 patronage position McClellan controlled in the secretary of the Senate's office. Fred even tried to get me a $17,000-a-year job as a full-time investigator on the Rackets Committee, but McClellan balked. "My God, Freddy," McClellan told him. "We can't appoint this boy to that." At the time, senators were making only something like $22,500 a year.

My new assignment in the Senate secretary's office seemed swell—good pay and great hours except when the Senate held sessions at night. As the junior member of the staff, I had to keep the office open until midnight or later when there was protracted debate, but my buddies would bring over a couple of six-packs and keep me company until the Senate recessed for the night. It was a dream job. I attended classes at George Washington University in the morning and came to work at noon. With floor privileges, I was able to come and go in the august chambers of what was known as America's most exclusive club.

Just a few steps off the floor, the Senate secretary's suite functioned as the clubhouse. I had a desk in a large, ornate room with high ceilings, fireplaces, and mirrors appropriate to the grandeur of the capitol building. My title was assistant bill clerk, and I shared the room with such functionaries as Bud Ast, the bill clerk, and Ted Mansur, the reading clerk. There were others whose duties were less clear: Bill Vaughan, who originally got his patronage slot from old Senator Alben Barkley of Kentucky before Barkley became Truman's vice president, and Mr. Ed Hickey, who kept the journals and had been there since about 1900. A couple of the official recorders of debate, those guys who prowled the Senate floor like violinists at a Viennese restaurant, writing down the speeches and colloquies on large pads for the *Congressional Record*, also had desks in the room.

The most essential staff members in the room were seven distinguished-looking black men: Mr. Taliaferro and six servants in livery.

I had never seen such formality outside a fancy restaurant. While Mr. Taliaferro's six helpers were listed as "messengers" on the payroll, they were actually bartenders.

The secretary's staff was deferential to the senators, but the older clerks were as imperious as Romans to anyone outside the Senate. We kept a ledger of all the legislation that had been introduced, tracking progress in committees. Legislative offices and government agencies would often call us to determine the standing of certain bills. The staff had a game they enjoyed playing with self-important folks in the administration. If an assistant for a cabinet member called and instructed one of our guys, "Please hold for Secretary Freeman," my associates would hang up immediately. They wouldn't hold for anybody from downtown, not even Orville Freeman, the secretary of agriculture. They saw themselves as grandees.

My colleagues were incredibly blasé. One afternoon, one of the elderly recorders of debate sneaked off for a matinee—a sexual ring-a-ding with a young lady. He suffered a heart attack and expired on the scene. Ted Mansur was reading the *Wall Street Journal* and smoking a cigar when someone told him the news. Mr. Mansur had worked with the newly deceased gentleman for about twenty-five years. He looked up from his paper for a moment and declared, "Well, I'll be goddamned." Then he resumed reading.

The private office of the Senate secretary, Felton "Skeeter" Johnston, a Mississippian who held the plum patronage appointment, operated like an exclusive lounge. I never saw Mr. Johnston do anything except entertain the senators. He had an unlittered desk. Instead of fooling with paperwork, he tended to his own well-stocked bar. On a pleasant evening, there might be as many as twenty senators gathered in Mr. Johnston's office, partaking of drink. He did big business when there was a filibuster boring the bejesus out of the senators.

This was long before television invaded the Senate chamber, a drastic change that forced members to appear sober at all times.

When I worked there, alcohol was an essential factor in senatorial comity. After leaving the floor, the senators were courtly to one another and set aside party differences. The secretary's suite was a bipartisan watering hole, and all of the great figures of the day mingled there. Russell Long of Louisiana, the son of my hero Huey, spent a lot of time around the bar, as did another favorite of my youth, Estes Kefauver. Warren Magnuson of Washington seemed to keep a drink in his hand perpetually. Prominent Republicans, such as the patrician Leverett Saltonstall of Massachusetts and Everett Dirksen of Illinois, also enjoyed a nip. I remember Dirksen, with shocks of his wiry hair shooting in all directions, coming off the floor after making a speech, getting about six ounces of Scotch, and drinking it down with the loud, gulping sounds of a horse at a water trough.

Richard Russell of Georgia was the towering figure in the Senate, and his presence awed me. The chairman of the Armed Services Committee, Russell was a stern and learned man, and his words were like commandments from God. It was said that the office host, "Skeeter" Johnston, regularly imbibed with the senators until the day he stepped on Senator Russell's foot. The Georgian grabbed the tipsy Johnston and warned him: "The next time you have a drink, you'll be out of a job." Mr. Johnston went on the wagon.

I saw more of McClellan at the secretary's office than when I'd worked on his committee staff. One of my tasks was to look for articles and editorials about his hearings in the newspapers kept in the Marble Room, a private lair of the Southern Democrats. All of the old lions, men like Russell and McClellan, Jim Eastland of Mississippi, and Herman Talmadge of Georgia, hung out there. It was an intimidating parlor. As I crept into the room and rustled through the papers, the senators looked at me scornfully. After they realized I was McClellan's aide they tolerated my intrusions.

I loved the Senate floor. If I knew that Dirksen, the most mellifluous orator of the day, intended to make a speech I'd grab a position on one of the couches in the rear of the chamber. If I was in the office and someone came off the floor to report that Jacob Javits, the liberal Republican from New York, and Willis Robertson, the conservative Democrat from Virginia, were "really going after each other," I'd rush to the floor to watch the debate. It was great, free theater.

Although I worked for McClellan, I visited Mr. Mills at his capitol office regularly, sitting with him in the late afternoon as he signed mail. A master politician, Mr. Mills not only controlled the Ways and Means Committee, he attended to petty issues affecting his district. He followed constituent problems personally and kept up on details, such as the county road systems, which were not his responsibility. If a group of country folks from White County came to Washington, he would ensure that they were given the full treatment, with tours and audiences with VIPs.

He had an owlish face with prominent glasses, a dumpy physique, and a voice that sounded as though it came from a gravel pit. Mr. Mills may not have looked impressive, but he controlled the legislative agenda and wielded enormous power.

Because of his friendship with my grandfather and my own involvement in Democratic politics in White County, we shared a bond, and I believe it was strengthened on a flight back to Arkansas the year after I arrived in Washington. Although several powerful Arkansans were aboard the plane, returning to Little Rock for a state Democratic convention, Mr. Mills asked me to sit with him. He worked crossword puzzles for relaxation, and usually he was so quick he could fill the blanks as fast as he could write. But one word stumped him, and he asked me: "What's German for goodbye?" My family had German relatives in Milwaukee, and I knew the answer: *auf wiedersehen*. Mr. Mills thought I was fantastic. He announced to the other Arkansans, "This boy's a genius."

To demonstrate what a genius I was, around this time, the Berlin

Wall had been built, the conflict in Vietnam was heating up, and I had done nothing to escape a military mobilization. I was ripe for the draft and summoned for a physical examination at a military hospital in Baltimore. My group of potential draftees included one other scrawny white guy and about thirty-five young blacks in porkpie hats. Every one of the black fellows, who appeared in strapping condition, was turned down by the Army doctors because of flat feet or some other kind of problem. My own body groaned from nightly dissolution, but I passed the physical. So did the other white guy, who couldn't have weighed more than 115 pounds. Suddenly, I worried for myself and the defense of my country. Riding the military bus back to Washington, all the guys were bitching. "I can't go home," one fellow said, "my daddy already spent money on my going away party." There were moans and numerous suggestions that the United States Army regularly had carnal relations with its mother. I whispered to the other white guy, "I think if they ask, we better say we failed, too."

As soon as I got back, I called to volunteer for the Air National Guard: there were 461 people on the waiting list, and it would be years before they got to my name.

I took my predicament to Mr. Mills. "I don't want to bother you, Mr. Mills," I said, "but I need to get into the Air National Guard because I'm about to be drafted." While I sat there, Mr. Mills placed a call to the White House. Within seconds, the president was on the line. They exchanged pleasantries, then Mr. Mills asked, "Mr. President, can we get something moving on Wimpy Wilson's appointment?" It was obviously a follow-up to Mr. Mills's recommendation that Wilson, an Arkansas man, be named adjutant general of the Air National Guard. As I eavesdropped, it sounded as though President Kennedy agreed to make the appointment. The conversation was over in less than a minute.

Mr. Mills looked at me, winked, and placed another call. "Wimpy," he said, "I think I got your appointment okayed. But there's one thing that worries the White House and worries me, and that's this boy Jim McDougal." The following Saturday I enlisted in the Air National Guard.

Though I had come to Washington with a certain naïveté, I always knew that our congressional delegation enjoyed extraordinary influence, far more than that of New York or California. During the three years I was there, I came to appreciate the way the Arkansans took charge in the nation's capital. While senators and congressmen from other states were busy fighting off challenges from rival parties in each election, Southern Democrats returned to Washington routinely from our one-party region. They took advantage of the seniority system, of course, but they also mastered the rules of the Senate and the House.

The southerners also seemed to have a natural advantage in an environment requiring give-and-take. They were principled, but not abrasive, preferring polite colloquy and cloakroom compromise to obstreperous debate. Courtly senators, such as Sam Ervin of North Carolina and John Stennis of Mississippi, symbols of Old South courtesy and gracious manners, were far more likely to charm adversaries and strike satisfactory deals. Northerners with sharp edges made headlines with their liberal stands, but they usually failed to manage a majority.

Control in Congress, like power in the Arkansas legislature, was actually held by a handful of men who were experienced, clever, and able to make accommodations with their colleagues. In Washington, most of them happened to be southerners.

Historians refer to the Kennedy era as a time of glamour and grace. In fact, Washington was an overgrown state capital, with no more than a half dozen fine restaurants, little legitimate theater, and few intellectual salons. Even the movie houses were rundown and dirty. President Kennedy wryly observed that the nation's capital operated with southern efficiency and northern charm. I'm not sure the city had even that. Rats roamed the streets, and Georgetown had not yet achieved high-society status. The center of downtown Washington lay at the intersection of Fourteenth and F Streets, where Garfinckel's department store anchored the northwest corner. Now lined with batteries of elegant restaurants, K Street was at that time barren, dotted with only a few nondescript office buildings.

The city marched to the beat of politics. And after government hours, we partied. There were events almost every night: receptions for congressional barons on Capitol Hill, Democratic fund-raising dinners downtown, cocktail soirees hosted by lobbyists, and black-tie banquets attended by the president and other dignitaries.

Because Mr. Mills and his wife rarely went out at night, he passed on many of his invitations to me. His prominence assured him tickets to most social events, and my evenings were often brightened by the company of a young woman from Little Rock named Carol Tucker. A recent graduate of Woods College, Carol represented Sunshine Mining, a client appreciative of her Arkansas connections to the chairman of the Ways and Means Committee. Carol's main duty was to lobby Mr. Mills. He liked her and approved of our using his tickets together.

Carol's personality bubbled. Vivacious and funny, she developed a coterie of friends in Washington. Though she dated one fellow fairly regularly on the weekends, and I went out with a lot of different girls, on weeknights we ran around together in the company of other congressional aides. Capitol Hill may have been run by the old bulls of Congress, but the congressional staffs turned out beautiful young women and ambitious young men like an assembly line.

The invitations to fancy dinners arrived so often that I bought a tuxedo. We were on the proverbial power trip. One night, as we walked past Senator Ervin, he turned his head and remarked that I was lucky to have such a "strikingly beautiful redhead" on my arm. I seemed blessed by good fortune. I didn't own an auto, but Carol had an MG sports car and I used it to tool around town. Through my Senate connections, we parked it overnight in front of the Capitol steps.

One summer, Carol's brother, Jim Guy Tucker, arrived from Harvard to stay in my apartment on New Jersey Avenue, a few blocks from the Capitol. From the very first day I met him, I thought Tucker was a young man bound for stardom. Though a student, Jim Guy had the looks and bearing of a movie actor. His face appeared to have been cut from stone, and his manner was more urbane and articulate than that of any other boy from Little Rock (or New York, for that matter). After she introduced us, Carol whispered to me, "Jim Guy's too serious. He's eighteen and he's already worried whether he'll be president by the time he's thirty-five."

Carol was usually buoyant company, but at one point she grew distressed over a stalemated piece of legislation, a measure Sunshine Mining was pushing. As I recall, the bill—designed to free the price of silver by removing the mineral as support for the dollar—was stuck in a House committee. The mining company expected Carol to shepherd the legislation along, but it seemed hopelessly mired. The next time I stopped by Mr. Mills's office, I confided to him, "Carol's in danger of losing her job." I explained the situation regarding the silver bill. He listened patiently, then simply said, "I'll take care of it in the morning." The bill was called out of committee, taken to the floor, and passed.

It was another example of Mr. Mills's awesome power. He exercised it quietly, in the privacy of his office or behind the closed doors of his committee meetings, yet everyone in Washington recognized that Mr. Mills held life-or-death authority over the agenda on Capitol Hill.

In the evenings, my social group was composed of congressional aides and lobbyists, flitting from house to house, party to party, bar to bar. I enjoyed a platonic relationship with Carol Tucker. Though she eventually began going steady with another fellow, we kept up our Arkansas friendship. I counted David Lambert, a young man from West Memphis, Arkansas, as one of my best friends. A product of the state's political pipeline, David had my old job at the Rackets Committee. He was extremely likable, never lost his temper, never caused any trouble.

One night, Mr. Mills's administrative assistant, Jack Files, and I went to an F Street nightclub. A pretty girl performing the "Dance of the Bashful Bride" diverted us from our cocktails. Jack recognized her as the sister of a woman working for "Took" Gathings, an Arkansas congressman. After we sent business cards backstage, identifying ourselves as Arkansas political aides, the dancer came out to chat between acts. Her name was Julie Gibson, and from the crisp, confident way she talked, I judged her well educated and well-to-do. She made hundreds of dollars a week. Though her dance number was considered risqué in those days, it pales in comparison to much of prime-time TV today. Julie and I became good friends.

The *Washington Daily News*, a tabloid now defunct, published a feature story on Julie and her "Dance of the Bashful Bride." Afterward, I went with her to look at a fancy, four-story house in Georgetown listed for sale. The broker panicked when he saw that his client was the infamous dancer and began criticizing things about the house to discourage her from moving into the neighborhood.

I worried that Senator McClellan might disapprove of my liaison with Julie. The senator was a serious man with a deep, brooding personality. His friends said he had become withdrawn after the loss of his sons. For a while, he drank in the morning in the privacy of his office, and there were whispers of an incident where police officers stopped McClellan while he was driving drunk and let him off with a warning. By the time I came to work for him, he had given up drinking as well as driving.

Though a staidness surrounded him, McClellan was no bluenose. His manners were gentle and tolerant, and he always called me Jimmy. I liked to think I reminded him of his boys. Following Christmas holidays at home, I drove Mrs. McClellan's car back from Arkansas. Before returning it, I used the auto to go to a New Year's Eve party, where I stayed up all night, swilling cheap champagne.

About ten that morning, the telephone by my bedside rang. A soft voice asked: "Are you awake?"

"Well, goddamnit, I am now," I shouted.

After another question, which I couldn't comprehend, I grew quite agitated. "Who in the hell is this?"

The voice said, "John McClellan."

I bolted from my bed and used my best Air National Guard training to stand at attention. I barked: "Yes sir, Senator!"

"I was wondering if you wanted to bring Mrs. McClellan's car over," he said, explaining, "I need to get a hat out of it." It was New Year's Day. Arkansas was playing Ole Miss on TV in the Sugar Bowl. He added, "Bring somebody with you and come watch the ball game with me."

A buddy—another survivor of the New Year's Eve party—and I drove to the McClellans. The senator could tell we were dying of hangovers. He teased us with a malicious smile, and let us suffer for a few minutes. Then he asked, "Would you boys like a little drink?" God, we were dying for a drink.

For all of his formality, Senator McClellan was a down-home politician who kept in touch with Arkansas. In the summer of 1962, I asked to take a leave of absence to go home and assist my good friend Sam Boyce, who was running for attorney general. I knew Sam from my work with the Young Democrats, and we both came from White County. Sam's opponent was Bruce Bennett, a former attorney general with a reputation as a segregationist and a witch-hunting anticommunist. When I asked McClellan about taking time off, he told me, "I loaned that damned Bruce Bennett a book once, and it took me four years to get it back. Go down there and beat the son of a bitch."

The campaign bristled with intrigue. Bennett had challenged Faubus in 1960, but agreed not to run for governor again in exchange for Faubus's backing in the attorney general's race. Faubus, meanwhile, was opposed by Dale Alford, the former congressman who had defeated Brooks Hays only to be gerrymandered out of his seat. The Faubus-Bennett coalition against Sam became the first fissure in my break with Faubus, and it pushed me into a path with Alford.

Using a gospel quartet to drum up crowds, Alford staged rallies around the state, and I trailed along with him. According to Arkansas political protocol, candidates who hosted events were expected to extend speaking privileges to candidates for other offices. I piggybacked on Alford at almost every stop to speak on Sam's behalf.

I also wrote speeches for Sam, and I claim authorship of the line Sam used to refer to Bennett: "the silver-haired sinner from south central Arkansas." In the midst of the campaign, Bennett accosted me on the steps of a country courthouse. "You're not supposed to be doing this," he said. "I'm going to call McClellan."

I told him, "Go ahead and call him. You'll find out he sent me down here to beat your ass."

Alas, it was our ass that got beat. When I telephoned Ralph Matthews, McClellan's top assistant, to see if I still had a job, he told me, "Hell, McClellan himself lost once or twice—come on back."

I returned to Washington, somewhat humbled. But before long, I was flying to Memphis, on the first leg of a trip to Helena, Arkansas, for the dedication of a new Mississippi River bridge. Senator McClellan had gone into considerable debt en route, playing gin rummy with Senator Fulbright and a couple of their aides.

The plane touched down in Memphis, where the cream of eastern Arkansas aristocracy waited on the runway to meet the delegation and accompany them on the drive downriver to Helena. A beating sun pushed the tarmac temperature past the 100-degree mark.

McClellan announced, "Nobody's getting off this goddamned airplane until I'm even." While the important constituents wilted in the sun, the gin rummy game continued for another half hour until McClellan won back his losses.

The various members of our delegation had odd ways of throwing their weight around. On the motorcade to Helena, I rode with the east Arkansas congressman "Took" Gathings. His full name was Ezekiel Chandler Gathings, a moniker typical of the planter Brahmins of his region. Pale and cool, he reminded me a bit of Fulbright. As we motored down the highway, Gathings turned to his driver, a fellow called Chester, and said archly: "Chester, turn off the air. I'm getting a little cold."

We drove along for a while, and the temperature reached about 120 degrees in the car. I rolled down my window, then made the mistake of coughing.

Gathings said, "Jim, I'm afraid you're catching a cold. Roll that window back up."

He was the most lifeless character I've ever seen. I have no idea where the name "Took" came from; perhaps from the pronouncement of the old Tammany Hall boss George Washington Plunkitt: "I seen my chances and I took 'em."

The nickname stumped Hubert Humphrey when he delivered a speech later in Little Rock. After Humphrey had plowed dutifully through the list of Arkansas Democrats, hailing the accomplishments of everyone from McClellan to Mills, he reached the most obscure member of our delegation. The vice president took a breath and, thinking of nothing else to say, shouted, "Toot! A great American!"

I drank deeply from the cup of Washington; I tasted the proximity to power and the ambrosia of good times. But as the days of 1963 fell away, I became increasingly anxious to make a move.

It was a conflicted time. That summer, I had gone to basic training for the Air National Guard in San Antonio and met Peter Edelman, a thoughtful young man serving as a law clerk for U.S. Supreme Court Justice Arthur Goldberg. In our conversations, I found Peter an idealist, far more liberal than the practical politicians with whom I had been associated. Peter had strong beliefs about racial equality, and he forced me to consider the question.

New views were being pushed on the South. Even as the Southern Democrats in Congress resisted civil rights initiatives, their home states were being turned into battlegrounds. Arkansas's crisis had passed in 1957, but conflict gripped other parts of the Deep South. Freedom riders had rolled into Alabama and Mississippi and been met with violence. Bodies were beaten and buses burned. Waves of black demonstrators were filling the streets and jails of southern cities, demanding an end to Jim Crow laws. In the spring of 1963 in Jackson, Mississippi, NAACP leader Medgar Evers was shot to death by a sniper, the same night President Kennedy addressed the nation on civil rights.

It was a period of dramatic change in the country, and a time of personal evolution for me and other Arkansans. When I passed through Bradford following summer duty, I happened to be watching TV in a cafe when Martin Luther King delivered his "I Have a Dream" speech. As a student of great orators, I appreciated the force of his language, but I also approved of his message. I found myself surprised by my own reaction.

Catharsis came on November 22. David Lambert, my friend from McClellan's committee, and I used our staff passes to go into one of the House dining rooms in search of a fine Friday lunch that might get our weekend off to a good start. The Speaker of the House, John McCormack of Massachusetts, was seated a few tables away. Someone approached him frantically and spoke in his ear. The Speaker bolted from the room. Suddenly, there was a silence, broken by the sibilance of whispers. Something had happened. David and I went directly to the Senate side of the Capitol, where a wire service teletype pounded out the news from Dallas.

Although the president had become increasingly unpopular in the South because of his civil rights position and his decision to send troops to the University of Mississippi to enforce a desegregation order there in 1962, my admiration of him had grown from the time I'd traveled the sale-barn circuit in his campaign. The word *charisma* seemed created for him. He projected movement; for the first time in my life, there was a sense of youthfulness in the federal government. Even though they were skittish over his views on race and religion, other members of the Arkansas delegation had warmed to Kennedy. They discovered that the Kennedys were Irish politicians with many of the same instincts as southern politicians—including an ability to talk through troubles with a twinkle in the eye. We call it southern charm; the Irish call it blarney.

The death of John F. Kennedy had a profound effect on everyone. Back home in Arkansas, framed dime-store photographs of JFK were tacked onto walls in tenant homes, alongside likenesses of Jesus Christ. The poor felt as though they had lost another hero. Washington's character soon changed from a city at play to a capital at war in Vietnam. The columnist Mary McGrory said it best: we would be able to smile again, but we would never be young again.

The national trauma coincided with my own sense that I was spiraling downward. After three years of the high life, consorting with political celebrities and pursuing a schedule of gaiety, I was besieged by depression. I attributed some of it to too much drinking, too little sleep. Troubled by my inability to control alcohol, I feared I was becoming a drunk. The party circuit in which I once reveled had become tiresome. Though only twenty-three, I worried that I had already seen it all, that my remaining years would be an anticlimax. My mood that winter was black.

It was time to go home. In March 1964, I returned to Arkansas. I thought home would be my panacea. I was leaving a trouble spot behind me, all right, but as I passed the Potomac, I was plunging into a deeper abyss.

6

hings in Bradford had changed little since I was a youngster. A sense of grinding poverty was gone. Industry in Newport had brought jobs to the area, and many people commuted to work there. However, our town was still a small, rural crossroads. After watching three years of big-league politics first hand, I was suddenly back where I started as a child, working in my family's business. Faubus was still governor; it seemed as though he had been forever. Depression gnawed at me.

My father faced surgery for cataracts and needed my assistance at the store. But I needed help myself. Alcohol was consuming my life. I had begun drinking as a teenager, and my thirst had intensified at the University of Arkansas. We couldn't drink in the Acacia fraternity house because of our Masonic affiliation, so we'd go to the Tea Table or the Rockwood Club in Fayetteville. Even though I was a teenager, I had no trouble buying drinks. And those wild days at the Marion Hotel, when the legislature was in session, were one long party. During the whirl in Washington, where nightly revels were followed by morning hangovers, I had begun to worry about myself. I had experienced blackouts from the time I was a teenager. I would be filled with remorse, yet I couldn't stop. Instead of taking charge of the situation after I gave up the high life in Washington, I ignored it and my problem deepened.

The time I burned up Truman Baker's car during the 1960 campaign had its amusing side, but there was nothing humorous about the scratches and dents that began to appear on my own car. Though I lived with my parents, in the same room where I'd spent my high school days, my innocent outings to the theater in Bald Knob had been replaced by excursions to a juke joint at Possum Grape, the nearest place where beer was sold legally, across the Jackson County line.

A real country honky-tonk, the place rocked with a juke box and live music on Friday and Saturday nights. The owner, G. B. Kennedy, didn't put up with any crap. If a customer caused problems, G.B. would wait until the troublemaker went into the men's room. Then he'd slip behind him at the urinal, slug the fellow, and throw him out the door. In the South, country physicians were revered, but when Dr. Bernard Smith jovially addressed the proprietor as a "son of a bitch," G.B. reached across the counter and coldcocked the doctor. Broke his nose. Once I made the mistake of remarking, "Hey, son of a bitch, give me a Bud." My blood froze when I realized what I had said. I stood there waiting for my nose to get busted, but G.B. was in a good mood and let it pass. On weekends, he had crowds of more than a hundred people, dancing and drinking, and G.B. kept the joint unusually orderly for a roadhouse.

The place was originally named G.B. and Helen's. After G.B. and Helen split up, G.B. married a woman named Loretta. He instructed his new wife to ask the Coca-Cola people to change the name on the sign the bottling company furnished. She had it changed, all right, to Loretta's. We didn't dare tease G.B. about it.

I spent some long nights in Possum Grape. I would drive the five miles home at ungodly hours, trying to get to bed quietly. Some mornings I'd wake in a motel, and couldn't remember how I got there. I would peek through the window to make sure my car was there. Then I would creep outside to look for blood on the front bumper. Quite often, there would be new dents where I must have sideswiped another car or a telephone pole.

During the day, I might see someone I'd been with the night before, and they'd say, "Did you make that phone call for me?" Or they'd ask about some promise I didn't remember, and I'd fake a reply.

Almost daily, I suffered the physical pain of hangovers: the throbbing headaches, the nausea and queasy stomach, the sweats soaking my shirts. And, always, the pangs of guilt and feelings of worthlessness.

Even though I knew it led to no good, I headed to Possum Grape or Newport or Little Rock almost every evening. After a while, I began drinking during the day, too.

Autumn brought a respite from the routine in Bradford. The Arkansas Democratic Party called me to Little Rock to act as youth director for President Lyndon B. Johnson's 1964 campaign in the state. I had never admired Johnson. After the stylish years with JFK, I felt Johnson was a comedown, a towering, boorish figure known for browbeating his colleagues when he was Senate majority. When I worked in the Capitol, I had once seen Johnson, as vice president, dismiss someone rudely as he entered an elevator. Still, he was a Democrat and committed to following Kennedy's policies.

I passed much of the fall campaign in an alcoholic haze, and I remember that our greatest problems in Little Rock involved Faubus rather than Johnson. While many lifelong Arkansas Democrats were deserting the party in favor of the conservative Barry Goldwater, we spent most of our time maintaining a balancing act between the liberal Democrats and the Faubus loyalists.

In pursuit of an unprecedented sixth term, Faubus had sailed to the Democratic gubernatorial nomination with little opposition. For the first time, a formidable Republican confronted him in the general election. Winthrop Rockefeller, a grandson of John D. Rockefeller and one of the heirs of the family fortune, had moved a few years earlier to a ranch he owned on Petit Jean Mountain in the Ozarks. Faubus had actually introduced Rockefeller to Arkansas politics by asking Rockefeller to use his business connections to bring commerce to the state as head of the Arkansas Industrial Development Commission. Rockefeller did such a good job, luring hundreds of industries to the state, that he decided to run for governor himself.

Even though Faubus seemed to have a stranglehold on the governor's office, Rockefeller saw opportunity in Arkansas's inchoate political structure. His brother Nelson was a prominent figure in the national Republican Party. As governor of New York, Nelson Rockefeller had just lost the GOP presidential nomination to Goldwater. Win Rockefeller thought he had a shot in Arkansas if he could succeed in pulling together a strange coalition of blacks, white liberals, and conservative Democrats disaffected with the policies of their national party.

Faubus, who'd had to be pressured to make an eleventh-hour endorsement of JFK in 1960, gave a pro forma nod to LBJ early in the campaign and turned his attention to Rockefeller. With a plutocrat for a rival, Faubus showed his talent for expediency. He became a populist again, excoriating the Standard Oil Co.—the keystone of the Rockefeller empire—for antitrust violations that crippled the independent oil operations in Arkansas and surrounding states.

In his biography *Faubus*, Roy Reed wrote that Faubus's performance was "like coming home to his father's house. He touched every nerve in the Arkansawyer's defensive psyche: the resentment of wealth, of aristocracy, of high society, of anything from the East. He alluded to Rockefeller's well-known drinking problem, not directly but by mentioning the huge collection of liquor at Petit Jean. He quietly exploited Rockefeller's messy divorce from Barbara

(Bobo) Sears Rockefeller. He made fun of him for flying to New York for haircuts."

Some of Faubus's sallies were harmless, drawn from the school of playful, populist demagoguery perfected by Jeff Davis sixty years earlier. But the governor injected an uglier note when he suggested that Rockefeller's nickname, Win, was an acronym for "Wants Integration Now." The governor noted that civil rights demonstrators had begun lying in the streets in some southern cities to block traffic. If they carried their campaign to Arkansas, he said, someone should run over them. "If no one else will do it, I'll get a truck and do it myself," he said.

Faubus's return to racial themes, after a period of relative calm in the state, riled up the liberal Democrats. After we printed a Democratic campaign letterhead featuring the names of the three candidates at the top of the ticket—Johnson–Humphrey–Faubus—the liberals howled in protest. Although progressives were outnumbered in the party, they still constituted an important component.

The fraying Democratic Party in Arkansas was symptomatic of a dynamic sweeping Dixie. Though passage of the Civil Rights Act of 1964 was hailed as a triumph for the Johnson administration in most parts of the country, it was seen by Southern Democrats as a betrayal. For years, southerners in Congress had successfully bottled up civil rights legislation in committees. Now a son of Texas was using the might of the White House to uncork those bills and win passage of progressive legislation. While conservative whites were beginning to desert the party, grateful blacks—on the verge of eliminating the last barriers to their right to vote—were rushing to enlist. As a result, the composition of the two major parties in the South would be turned on its head.

Working together at the LBJ headquarters on the fifth floor of the Marion Hotel, my old friends Sam Boyce and Jack Files and I held our forces together for one more time, for President Johnson as well as Faubus.

The Arkansas AFL-CIO, which had grown in number and strength since World War II in a state with a history of enmity toward organized labor, threw its wholehearted support to the Democratic ticket. The Arkansas Education Association, which represented the teachers' interest even though it did not carry the stigma of a union, also encouraged its membership to rally behind the Democratic ticket. Blacks, naturally inclined to vote for Johnson, were persuaded to pull the lever for Faubus, too. And most of the disgruntled liberals, weighing a hawkish Goldwater and a silk-stocking Rockefeller, stayed on board to vote a straight Democratic ticket.

Although the only electoral votes Goldwater won outside his home state of Arizona came from the Deep South, Arkansas stayed in the Democratic column in November. Johnson carried the state, and Faubus, winning sixty-five of the seventy-five counties, was re-elected.

We rejoiced in victory, but we recognized that the days of unchallenged Democratic supremacy in Arkansas were over.

Following the election, I returned to Bradford to resume my duties with the family businesses. Earlier in the year, while my father recovered from surgery, I'd expanded his variety store at 101 Main Street, a shop he opened after selling off his grocery stores and furniture business in a series of manic transactions. The store offered an assortment of dry goods: clothing, household items, and hand tools. Thinking the business had capacity for growth, I obtained a 3 percent Small Business Administration loan, bought the building he was renting, knocked out a wall, and doubled the size of the store. Sales and profits increased.

The McDougals have always had business acumen. Years later, when Senator Fulbright and I were real estate partners, he told me, "You know, Jim, you're just like my father. You're a generalist. My father would have a John Deere place, a wagon factory, a mill, and a furniture factory. All at the same time. He thought he could do anything, and you're the same way."

With the store expansion completed, I took an additional job, helping Bryan Nick prepare tax returns for the farmers in the region. Nick served as the town's all-purpose man. He delivered mail and coordinated veterans affairs. With no lawyer in town, Nick offered legal advice and handled tax returns, too. In the spring, when taxpayers swamped him, he asked me to help. I had a knack for numbers.

The tax-return business led to one of my most memorable ventures: organizing a cooperative for the men who combed the White River for mussel shells.

Freshwater mussel shells were used to form the nucleus for cultured pearls. The process involved inserting a piece of the mussel shell in the membrane of an oyster. By attempting to expel the intruding shell, the oyster actually secreted juices that formed a pearl. Demand for mussel shells was high in Japan after supplies from the Tennessee River had been depleted. The beds of our river systems in Arkansas were filled with mussels, and the Japanese were so pleased with our product that they called the White River shells "gloriously wonderful."

I was vaguely aware that White County farmers and river rats—men who scrounged a living by fishing for catfish and gar—supplemented their income by raking the bottoms for mussels, but I never understood the business. Earlier in the century, shells were taken from the river and used for buttons. Small factories, later abandoned, had been erected on the banks of the White River to stamp the shells into buttons. But a market remained for the shells.

Sometime in 1965, as I prepared a tax return for a mussel digger, he told me about the business. He was paid only eighty dollars a ton, and he felt screwed because so many middlemen were involved. He knew I had contacts in Washington and wondered if I could help.

The situation aroused my populist instincts, and I thought of forming a diggers' cooperative to deal directly with the Japanese buyers. Drawing on my political connections, I called Lee Williams, Fulbright's administrative assistant in Washington. As chairman of the Senate Foreign Relations Committee, Fulbright could give me entrée to the Japanese. Mr. Mills, whose committee dealt with trade issues, also helped the project.

In Washington, I met with the commercial attaché for the Japanese embassy, and sent samples of our "gloriously wonderful" shells to Japan. We agreed upon a contract, and soon the shell diggers of White County were quadrupling their money in the name of the White River Mussel Shell Association. To me, it was like a labor union for the diggers. Our operation antagonized J. R. Sink, a Newport man who bought shells in White County. For years the diggers had been selling to Sink, who shipped the shells to a Memphis buyer. The Memphis businessman sold the goods to a New Orleans buyer; in turn, the New Orleans agent sold the consignment to a Japanese buyer. I did away with three middlemen. Paid a twenty-dollar commission on every ton, I made more money than I had in my life, and I also raised the diggers' income from eighty dollars to nearly four hundred a ton.

I thought we were big-time exporters until the Japanese sent a $50,000 letter of credit and the banking establishment in northeast Arkansas had no clue what to do with it. Since I did little business with the bank in Bradford—they wouldn't give loans—I took the letter of credit to the Merchants & Planters Bank in Newport. They were baffled. Nobody had dealt with exports before. Percy Copeland, the president of the Newport bank, called and said, "I got all this money, aren't you going to come up and get it?" I had to explain that there were certain things we needed to do before we could claim the money. Finally, I opened an account at a Memphis bank with experience in exports.

Most of the members of the association wanted to be paid in cash; a lot of them were illiterate and had never endorsed a check. Some days, I would return from Memphis with $20,000 in five-dollar bills.

There were so many people on the river digging that the *Arkansas Gazette* dispatched a reporter to Bradford. His story described me as a "jack of all trades" who had organized hundreds of mussel diggers. "We're trying to show them that they can get out of the sharecropper class and become wage earners," I told him. The story noted that twenty-six people had bought licenses to take mussels in 1963, and in the first eight months of the current fiscal year, the state Game and Fish Commission had already issued more than one thousand licenses. The bubble burst when big business interests in Memphis sent a mechanical dredger to join the White River digging spree, a move that touched off trouble. Some of our members took potshots at the dredger. They were tough guys who employed their wives and children in a family operation, digging the mussels from the river, boiling them open in a backyard vat at home, and using the mussel meat as feed for hogs and chickens. But they were no match for Memphis.

To diversify my enterprises, I sought a charter to establish a new bank in Bradford. Sam Boyce, who practiced law in Newport, handled the legal work, and I tried to take care of the politics, dealing with people like Bill Smith, the high-powered Little Rock attorney. I raised the capital and had the money in escrow, ready to start.

The only banking institution in Bradford was a branch of the Citizens State Bank in Bald Knob, and Truman Baker, the governor's chief ally in White County, controlled an interest in it. Under Arkansas law at the time, branch banks were forced to close if a local bank was chartered in the same town. Despite our political experience, Sam and I were given another lesson in the interlocking interests of banking and politics in Arkansas. Inasmuch as our proposal posed a threat to Mr. Baker's Citizens State branch, we were denied a charter. During all the years Faubus served as governor, no new banks were chartered in Arkansas. He permitted no competition, giving the existing banks a monopoly.

The great champion of populism had become an apologist for the establishment. Not only had Faubus protected the banking interests, he'd presided over a series of rate increases and extended favorable treatment to the Arkansas Louisiana Gas Co., the increasingly powerful utility known as Arkla.

The company was purchased in 1954, the year Faubus was first elected, by Witt Stephens, a Little Rock financier and arguably the most powerful citizen in the state. Stephens saw Arkla as an instrument to broaden his control of the private sector in the state and to extend his influence to the political arena. The utility had potential as a moneymaking machine, but it could also be used by Stephens to eclipse the Arkansas Power & Light Co., a rival that had long dominated Arkansas politics.

Though he had not supported Faubus in 1954, at a time when the candidate from Greasy Creek was flaying the utilities, Stephens soon ingratiated himself with the new governor. Wealthy beyond the dreams of ordinary Arkansans, Stephens became one of Faubus's major benefactors.

For good measure, Stephens won election to the state legislature in 1960 and served a couple of terms. Eventually, Stephens and Faubus created a revolving-door arrangement. At Stephens's behest, the governor appointed Stephens's acolytes to key positions in state government, and when someone left Faubus's staff, Stephens usually found a place for them on his payroll.

After four terms, Faubus had shucked all traces of his native populism. Even before my unsuccessful attempts to obtain a bank charter, I had grown disillusioned over his handling of bond issues. Faubus lost a referendum in 1961 on a $60 million bond issue because folks suspected it would put money in the pockets of Witt Stephens and his brother Jack Stephens. But Faubus was undeterred. In 1965, he proposed a $150 million bond issue to build roads. Truman Baker called to ask my support in Bradford, but I had to turn down my old patron's pleas. It looked like a sweetheart deal to make the Stephens family an unreasonable amount of money.

Prior to the referendum, I teamed with Bryan Nick to oppose Faubus publicly. In addition to his various small businesses in Bradford, Nick was president of our local school board and a wounded World War II veteran. With a following among veterans groups, Nick enjoyed high popularity in the town. We denounced Faubus's proposal as a camouflaged gravy train for the big-business boys in Little Rock, and the township voted heavily against the bond issue. It lost statewide, by a two-to-one margin, a stinging rebuke to Faubus only a few years after his glory days.

Faubus was a cool strategist, but he had little personal magnetism. Unlike Congressman Mills or Senator Fulbright, whose natural reserve was offset by a warm personality when talking with their constituents, Faubus showed little emotion. When he smiled, I thought he looked like a catfish aspiring to be a barracuda. Despite the populist rhetoric he used against Win Rockefeller, it was apparent Faubus had become a captive of Arkla; it was as if Huey Long had gone to work for the Standard Oil Co.

The time had come, I believed, to bring Faubus down, and many of my friends in the state's Young Democrats organization felt the same way.

When the governor helped rejuvenate the YDs in the 1950s, he had hoped to set up a new political apparatus for himself. But as Saint Thérèse said, "More tears are shed over answered prayers than unanswered ones." The YDs were dutiful toward Faubus for a few years, but my faction of the organization was in full revolt by the time of our annual convention in Little Rock in May 1965. Faubus sought to control the group through his son, Farrell, and several influential accomplices, including one of the governor's aides, John Browning, who served as state YD president. The Faubus crowd had settled on one of Witt Stephens's employees at Arkla, a rising young politician named Sheffield Nelson, to succeed Browning.

Supported by a coalition of labor unions, liberals, and moderates, my faction backed Sam Boyce for president. I had first met Sam in

1961, when he represented Mr. Mills during a congressional redistricting fight in the legislature, and I had taken a leave to work with him in the attorney general's race in 1962. Now I was committed to his new effort to lead the YDs.

The convention turned into a public challenge of Faubus, and every daily newspaper in the state followed developments.

The YD rules committee was stacked with Faubusites, and they planned to seat a number of delegates chosen by county judges, all Faubus cronies, and to deny credentials to our popularly elected delegates. Knowing we would have the Faubus delegates outnumbered when the convention was called to order, we decided to strike before the question of our delegates' legitimacy could be raised.

As the delegates assembled in a ballroom of the Marion Hotel, our rivals, including Browning, the outgoing president; House Speaker J. H. Cottrell; and Claude Carpenter, another top Faubus strategist, huddled in a room on the fifth floor. We knew they usually arrived at conventions a bit late, to sweep onto the floor in a grand gesture of gubernatorial authority. We also knew one of the hotel's elevators was broken.

Joe Hamilton gave five dollars to the operator of the other elevator, a fellow who was something of a nitwit anyway, and instructed him not to stop on the fifth floor. We had a spy up there, another guy from Newport named Dean Ponder. When Dean saw the Faubus gang had tired of waiting for the regular elevator and decided to use the freight elevator, he dashed down the stairs, stopping at each floor to push the freight elevator button. Since the lumbering elevator inched at a slow pace, Dean's tactic delayed the Faubus team another minute or two.

In Browning's absence, Roy Lee Hight, who worked for Mr. Mills and served as first vice president of the Young Democrats, bounced up to convene the meeting. I was immediately elected chairman of the convention. Just as quickly, I took nominations for president. Jim Blair nominated Boyce, and Sam was on his way to election by the time Browning arrived and attempted to take over the podium.

Harry Pearson, a reporter for the *Pine Bluff Commercial,* described the scene in the next day's newspaper: "McDougal refused to budge. Browning tried to squeeze his way to the rostrum. McDougal, with perfect aplomb, elbowed him back."

In somber tones, I announced to the convention: "The appointed hour having arrived and the president being absent, the vice president assumed the chair." I turned to Browning and said, "An election has been held and a new president has been elected. You're no longer president. Mr. Browning, if you don't remove yourself from the podium I shall be forced to ask the sergeant at arms to remove you."

There was a ruckus from the Faubus people. I threatened to have them all evicted. A deputy sheriff from Independence County, Frog Henson, was acting as sergeant at arms. Frog was on our side, but so hungover he couldn't have evicted himself; he was sitting on the stage with his head in his hands. The Faubus people left, stomping off to another room to "elect" Sheffield Nelson as president. But when they appealed to the national Young Democrats convention, which Sam and I attended later in the year in New York, delegates from every state sided with us. In a move that reflected the shifts in the state Democratic Party, the AFL-CIO—long an ineffectual political organization—paid our expenses to take the fight against Faubus to New York.

Our success against the governor was another indication of his waning powers. After twelve years in office, he had exhausted the last of the goodwill he had built up as a man of the people. Smelling blood, challengers lined up to take a shot at Faubus. His era was about to end, as was the Democrats' long control of the governor's office.

After beating Faubus's proxy in the Young Democrats battle, Sam Boyce declared as a candidate against Faubus. Sam foresaw a David-versus-Goliath battle, a young prosecuting attorney against a mythic governor who had lost his strength. Faced with the prospect of defeat, Faubus chose at the last minute not to run for re-election and threw his support to a rising politician, Frank Holt. Since Sam and Frank had worked together in the attorney general's office, their friendship made the contest a bit awkward. I took another leave from the family business to join Sam's campaign, advising him to lay off Holt and bash, instead, the Faubusites and their patrons, the Stephens family. I wrote a speech for Sam suggesting that "commenting on Witt Stephens's honesty is like commenting on Judas Iscariot's loyalty." The line made the newspapers, antagonizing the Little Rock establishment. Although Faubus had gotten his start hammering the power structure, there had been no such impertinence in recent years.

The Democratic primary continued in the wilting summer heat. The Boyce campaign had a few cars at our disposal, but only one was air-conditioned—the candidate's. Sam claimed I rolled up the windows of my car so it appeared my car was air-conditioned, too. I accused him of rolling down the windows of his car to keep from looking too prosperous.

With the Democratic Party in flux, neither Sam nor Holt managed to electrify voters. The angry white masses turned to Jim Johnson, the segregationist warhorse who had run against Faubus in 1956 and was returning to politics after serving as a judge. Johnson roused his troops with warnings of a racial Armageddon. His campaign rallies became theaters for bigotry; he dismissed civil rights leaders as so many blackbirds, and his followers responded with rebel yells. Johnson prided himself on his principle of refusing to shake hands with black voters, and he whipped the Citizens Council crowd into their first good lather since the Central High controversy. In the end, Johnson claimed the Democratic nomination, but his intemperate behavior frightened many people in the party.

Confronted with Winthrop Rockefeller as his opponent in the fall, Johnson took his tactics to a new low. Affecting a lisp, he called the Republican candidate "a limp-wristed, wet-lipped New

York cowboy." Rockefeller was a bit more substantive. Reminding voters of the six hundred industrial plants that had been located in the state during his tenure as head of the Arkansas Industrial Development Commission, Rockefeller ran as a progressive. Warming to the prospect of a new face for Arkansas, hundreds of college students volunteered for Rockefeller. Liberal and moderate Democrats also sided with the Republican candidate. My parents and I were appalled by Jim Johnson, but unwilling to support a Republican. We were, after all, still Yellow Dog Democrats. We voted for neither candidate in the fall, but the shifting forces across the state produced an upheaval. Rockefeller won 54 percent of the general election vote and became the first Republican governor of Arkansas since Reconstruction.

The 1966 election also saw the demise of Paul Van Dalsem, the cranky old legislative powerhouse who'd dominated debates by creating chaos. First elected in 1944, he was considered unbeatable in his Perry County stronghold on the edge of the Ouachita forests. But one-man, one-vote reapportionment had been ordered by the Supreme Court, and to comply legislative mapmakers had merged Perry County with part of Pulaski County, the home of Little Rock.

Van Dalsem suddenly found himself in a more metropolitan district, and he sought to reach out to his new constituency in a speech to the Little Rock Optimists Club. In the course of his remarks, Van Dalsem offered a commentary on the feminist movement. "We don't have any of those university women in Perry County," he said. "But I'll tell you what we do up there when one of our women starts poking around in something she doesn't know anything about. We get her an extra milk cow. And if that doesn't work, we give her a little garden to tend. And if that's not enough, we get her pregnant and keep her barefoot."

Van Dalsem intended for his remarks to be treated humorously, but the "pregnant and barefoot" line created an uproar, becoming part of the state's political lore. It also led to his political demise. Within months, he was beaten by a city slicker from Pulaski County.

Dispirited by the turns in Arkansas politics, I returned to my shell operation, but its days were numbered. The goose had destroyed the golden egg. Within a year, the White River's mussel beds were wiped out. The diggers had been unable to drive away the dredger from Memphis. The device harvested a ton of mussels an hour and destroyed the river bottom where the mussels grew. Although we petitioned the state to stop the dredging, no one did anything during the transition from Faubus to Rockefeller, and by 1967 the riverbed was ruined.

The mussels ran out, and I had run out, too. Drinking day and night, totally in the grip of alcohol, I turned to liquor for medication instead of sociability. I used vodka to get started in the morning, driving to Jackson County to buy a half-pint, thinking that would be all I needed. By the time I'd driven back to Bradford, the vodka would be gone, so I'd return to buy another half-pint. Empty bottles piled up in my office as rapidly as the shells in the warehouse. Once, when I was trying to clean my place, I filled an old feed sack with dozens of bottles.

Life was hell at home, too. Disapproving of drink, my parents grew distressed, and a darkness settled over our meals. My mother and father didn't nag, but they picked at their food and exchanged worried glances.

One morning, after I had been unable to go to work, my father approached me. "Son," he said, "we just have to do something. I've been talking to this place out in Arizona. They can help people with problems like yours. It costs eight hundred dollars a month, but I'll pay for it, and you can pay me back when you get better."

"I'll think about it," I mumbled.

Instead, I kept up a steady schedule of benders. I wound up in Little Rock, out of control. Sam Boyce drove down and brought me back to the hospital in Newport, where a doctor admitted me with a diagnosis of "upper respiratory problems." I checked myself into the hospital several times, in Bradford, in Newport, a couple of times in Little Rock. The doctors always wrote down some phony illness. I'd spend a few days getting the alcohol out of my system, taking pills to ease the pain of withdrawal. Then I'd begin drinking immediately after each time I was released.

In the summer of 1967, as the mussel business played out, I sat in my office in the warehouse, brooding. I was feeling especially useless when a stranger walked in and introduced himself as Paul Carroll, the minister of a small Baptist church out in the country. A big, friendly fellow, he carried none of the sanctimonious bearing you see in some preachers. He looked well acquainted with misfortune.

After we talked for a couple of minutes, Paul spotted my Xerox copying machine and said, "I've been praying for one of those."

I told him: "If you're praying for a machine, you've got this one, and you can use it." Then I added a confession. "You might say a prayer for me, too, because I'm an alcoholic and I can't stop drinking."

"You know, I'm an alcoholic, too," he told me, relating how he stayed sober through his ministry.

In that moment I experienced an epiphany. My visitor inspired me to try to bring order to my life, and I resolved that day to arrest my drinking. Later, I realized that Paul's visit was not accidental. He had been sent by Howard Masters, a friend of mine who was troubled by my drinking. And after a decade of dissipation, from the Washington nightclubs to the Jackson County juke joints, I, too, turned to the church.

Even while I was drinking heavily, I had continued to attend the Bradford Missionary Baptist Church with my family. After my conversation with Paul, I talked with the minister and deacons of my church and obtained a license to preach.

My faith, at the time, was a bit wobbly. I suppose I was agnostic. When invited to preach at several churches in the area, I felt most comfortable with the story of the prodigal son and the gospels of redemption and repentance. Avoiding hellfire and brimstone themes, I dwelt on the New Testament God, loving and forgiving. I told the congregations how practical it was to live goodly lives. "It will help you here," I told them, "as well as in the hereafter."

I thought I had found my calling. That autumn I enrolled at the Southern Baptist Seminary in Little Rock, the school Paul Carroll had attended. He was the only person I knew who had found a solution to alcoholism, so I followed in his footsteps.

My parents were pleased. I overheard my mother tell my father, "This will take care of it. Jim's been fighting the Lord, and he's finally given in. If you resist the Lord's call, it causes you a lot of trouble."

At the seminary, for the first time in years, I found peace. Although the classroom buildings were nothing fancy, and the dormitories resembled army barracks, there was a spirit to the place. At first, I did fine. I was elected as a class representative to the student body senate, and I plunged into Bible studies. Snobs laugh at Baptists as red-tie illiterates, but there were some deeply knowledgeable teachers at the seminary. They had studied in Hebrew and Greek, and they knew their theology. Enrolled in their masters program, I found it intellectually challenging. In many ways, seminary study addressed my skepticism and gave me a stronger basis for belief in God.

I had been sober from July into October. Then, for no reason at all, I got drunk. I simply walked into a package store, bought a bottle of vodka, and drove around Little Rock, drinking. On Saturday morning, October 21, 1967—the date is clear in my mind—I woke at a hotel. My hands were shaking so badly I couldn't shave. I looked and felt horrible. I came downstairs and discovered it was a crisp fall day, a football day in Little Rock. I saw waves of pretty college girls and their handsome dates getting into cars, dressed for the game, and I thought that I'd never have a girl on my arm again, never enjoy anything wholesome again. I felt finished.

Sunk in a spiritual slough, I was ready to commit myself to the state mental hospital, to spend the rest of my days in confinement. Knowing I needed connections for admission to the state hospital, I called Jack Files. He had worked for Mr. Mills when I was in Washington and now ran Senator Fulbright's office in Little Rock. A generous man, Jack was the kind of guy who couldn't resist giving a home to stray dogs. Over the years, he and his wife, Jo Anne, had let me sleep at their house in North Little Rock when I was sobering up.

"Jack," I said, "I think I've gone crazy. I can't stop drinking. I want to stop, but I can't. I want you to get me into the state hospital, and I don't care if I ever get out."

He told me to come to his office Monday. Somehow, I managed to get through the weekend without another drink, though I remember being convulsed with pain in the hotel room.

When I arrived at the Federal Building on Monday, Jack said: "I don't think you're crazy. I think it's all alcohol, and I think I know what you need to do." Jack said he had already discussed my case with Pat Mehaffy, now a federal judge with an office upstairs in the same building. Jack told me Mehaffy was waiting to see me.

Mehaffy had been a heavy drinker when he was a young man, but after joining Alcoholics Anonymous he had been sober for thirty years. After his secretary admitted me into his office, there was no small talk between the judge and me, no happy recollections of our 1960 JFK campaign, no swapping of political rumors. He took me into a conference room, an austere place with a long, polished wood table and shelves filled with law books. He told me sternly that he had asked a couple of his friends to come over. "You just wait for them," he commanded, and left.

I waited by myself. In less than an hour, two men arrived and introduced themselves as Doyle Rowe and Buddy Keeley. They were Mehaffy's contemporaries, years older than I, and just as tough-minded as the judge. I didn't know it at the time, but all three were pioneers in the AA movement in Arkansas. They had been drunks, and now they had been sober for three decades. Doyle had pulled himself up from poverty to become a successful auto dealer. Buddy had done a little bit of everything, and was now working for a state alcoholic rehabilitation program.

Quite abrupt in their approach, Doyle and Buddy gave me no psychological sweet talk about what a good fellow I was, or what great potential I might have if I didn't abuse myself.

Doyle was short and bald but well dressed, with the confident, no-nonsense attitude of a self-made man. He took one look at me and said in a harsh voice: "You know, McDougal, we figure you're a liar, a thief, and a con artist."

I had this tremendous sense of elation. These guys were going to be able to help me.

Buddy had a gruff voice, too. A big bear of a fellow, he said, "McDougal, put it all behind you. You're going to come with us, and you're going to do exactly what we say for the rest of your life."

Although Bill Fulbright grew up in Fayetteville, in Ozark country, he was the antithesis of a hillbilly. He had the manners of an Oxford don and often practiced the politics of a British Tory. His voice had the archness of the British ruling class, and even the formal name he used—J. William Fulbright—carried the ring of authority. He was thirty-five years older than I and completing his seventeenth year in the Senate when I went to work there in 1961. I was not intimidated by the other members of the Arkansas congressional delegation; even staid old Senator McClellan had a warm and human side. Yet Fulbright appeared aloof from the issues affecting Arkansas and preoccupied with the greater international questions of the day.

During the years I was in Washington, the only time I saw Fulbright relaxed was the night Jimmy Driftwood, a hillbilly singer from Arkansas, performed on Capitol Hill. Driftwood had written "The Battle of New Orleans," a popular ballad, and he brought several fiddlers with him. A crowd of Arkansans came to Fulbright's party, and the music was rousing. When Fulbright shouted, "Goddamn! That's good!" he surprised me. When I looked closely, I saw that the elastic in his socks was worn out, causing them to droop inelegantly. Maybe the man wasn't a complete elitist, after all.

Fulbright entrusted most of his constituent work to his administrative assistant, Lee Williams, a native of West Fork, an Ozark town near Fayetteville. While Fulbright was reserved, Lee was gregarious. I never knew anyone who didn't like him, and after I had followed Arkansas politics for a while, I realized that anyone needing a favor from Fulbright's office called Lee. He was Fulbright's alter ego, and it was said that he could sign Fulbright's name better than the senator could.

I'd gotten to know Lee on the trip the Arkansas congressional delegation took to dedicate the Helena bridge. There was nothing self-important about him, yet he understood the levers of power. He was the one I'd called when I was looking for help in setting up the mussel shell business with Japan. And in the winter of 1967, Lee came to my assistance again when I desperately needed it.

After my meeting with Doyle Rowe and Buddy Keeley, I had been sober for a couple of months. On a strict regimen, I was installed in an upstairs room of a house the AA rented for meetings in Little Rock. I was given a bed and a chest of drawers. That was my furniture. They loaned me two dollars a day for food and other expenses. I was so broke I rolled my own cigarettes. I was instructed to write a personal history of everything regrettable I had done. Mine was a long, long list. I had run up bad debts, insulted associates, created embarrassing situations, let down friends. That was painful enough. Now I was expected to visit the people I had offended.

I particularly dreaded my return to the Southern Baptist Seminary, where I'd washed out so ingloriously. The president of the school was typing a translation from Greek scriptures when I went to see him. "I'm writing this out for you," he said. "You know, the apostle Paul was a drunk, but he was one of God's favorites. He'd go out and preach a bit, then he'd stay on the road and get drunk and pass out in a ditch. He was the first person to use the word *crackpot.* Paul would pray to God and say: I've got to stop this or people are going to think I'm a cracked pot." His minisermon, I thought, conveyed the Christian principle of forgiveness better than anything I had ever heard. Salvation was possible, even for the hopeless drunk.

As the Christmas season approached I struggled to get back on my feet. My friends on Fulbright's staff, Jack Files and Lee Williams, were aware of my problem and monitored my rehabilitation. To build my confidence, they gave me a key to Fulbright's Little Rock office and let me handle minor projects for them. When that temporary arrangement worked out, Lee agreed to give me a full-time job.

Just as I thought I had stabilized my life, my unit of the Air National Guard was called to active duty because of a flare-up in Korea. But I knew things could have been much worse. We were stationed a few miles from home, at the Little Rock Air Force Base. In Vietnam, American servicemen were dying by the hundreds every week, and the conflict was tearing our country to pieces.

Protest had taken to the nation's streets again. Antiwar demonstrators stormed the Pentagon and boiled through the narrow canyons along Wall Street. Yet in Arkansas and across the South, support for the war remained strong. Southerners take pride in patriotism and military tradition, and an inordinately high percentage of American servicemen have always come from the South, drawn into the military ranks either by family custom or the need for a regular paycheck and daily meals. The wars of my childhood, World War II and the conflict in Korea, were considered worthy commitments, and now few questions were being raised publicly in Arkansas about the American involvement in Vietnam. Sentiment to escalate the war burned brightly in the local halls of the American Legion and Veterans of Foreign Wars, and no local politician dared challenge the old saying, My country, right or wrong. Yet in Washington, one of the leading congressional opponents of the war was Bill Fulbright.

Shortly after I completed my Air National Guard duty in the spring of 1968, Lee asked me to write Fulbright's introduction for a book by my friend Jim Guy Tucker on Jim Guy's experiences as a journalist stringing for Arkansas newspapers in Vietnam. The assignment was something of a tryout. Knowing that Fulbright liked his material tightly written, I made the introduction short and succinct. Lee told me Fulbright called it "so concise it's almost terse."

I was given a raise after a trip with the senator to inspect tornado damage in the Jonesboro area. Fulbright had become a creature of the nation's capital; he no longer knew a lot of people in our state. "All my friends are either dead or in nursing homes," he told me. On the other hand, I knew all the legislators and state Democratic leaders we encountered on the trip. I whispered their names to Fulbright. He was positively amazed when we stopped at Newport and I knew everyone in town. He didn't know I had grown up just down the road.

My awe of him vanished as my admiration grew. Behind that patrician bearing was a tough old man from the mountains who enjoyed a challenge.

He had been one of the youngest presidents of the University of Arkansas, fired when he was only thirty-six by a conservative board of trustees controlled by Governor Homer Adkins. Within the year, Bill Fulbright defeated one of Adkins's candidates in a race for a northwest Arkansas congressional seat. Two years later, he beat Adkins for a U.S. Senate seat.

Fulbright took delight in running against the grain. The only senator to oppose funding for Senator Joe McCarthy's communist witch-hunt, Fulbright also angered a Democratic president early in his career. As a young congressman, he feared Harry Truman was leading the party toward an electoral disaster. Fulbright proposed that Truman appoint Arthur Vandenberg, a Republican senator from Michigan, as secretary of state and then resign as president. Under Fulbright's plan, the line of succession would make Vandenberg—without a vice president—president. Truman, who had a flair for a pithy phrase himself, called Fulbright an "overeducated Oxford S.O.B.," as well as "Senator Halfbright."

To survive in Arkansas politics, Fulbright knew he had to appeal to the right in his positions on some issues. He embraced any number of initiatives by religious groups and cultivated church interests in Arkansas.

He seemed comfortable walking this tightrope between liberalism and conservatism. Even though the liberals of Arkansas held Fulbright in esteem, approving of his courageous stands against McCarthyism and the Vietnam War, he was notoriously tightfisted and clung to southern shibboleths on race. Coming from a region where there were few blacks, Fulbright seemed to have little understanding of black aspirations. I never heard him utter a word in support of civil rights. He signed the Southern Manifesto, which asserted states' rights over the Supreme Court school desegregation decision, and he opposed the Civil Rights Act of 1964 as well as the Voting Rights Act the following year. To have done otherwise would have cost him his seat.

Ultimately, however, he risked his career by alienating the Johnson administration and the voters of Arkansas with his dogged opposition to the Vietnam War. As chairman of the Foreign Relations Committee, Fulbright felt he had been deceived by President Johnson into introducing the Tonkin Gulf Resolution in 1964, a measure that legitimized the U.S. military operation in Vietnam. When it became obvious to him that the war's premise was faulty—at a cost of thousands of lives and billions of dollars—Fulbright broke with Johnson and said he would never again trust government statements. His 1966 book, *The Arrogance of Power*, was a blistering attack on U.S. policy, and his Senate hearings galvanized the movement against the war.

Fulbright's stand won him worldwide renown, but cost him political capital at home. He was assailed as a communist sympathizer giving aid and comfort to the enemy. By the time I joined his Arkansas staff, he was fighting polls indicating that 70 percent of the Arkansas voters supported the war. Confronted with the candidacy of cantankerous old Jim Johnson in the Democratic primary, Fulbright never flinched.

At the start of the campaign in the summer of 1968, I was driving him around the state, escorting him to speaking engagements on courthouse steps and in private homes. The reception was not always warm. At one event at the Poor Boy Duck Club in Lonoke County, the grounds were swarming with Jim Johnson supporters, conservative farmers and hunters. They hated the Viet Cong as much as they depised the civil rights workers who had been spreading leftist beliefs around the South. There were about four hundred men there, most of them drunk and spoiling for a clash with the senator. Fulbright had taken a couple of drinks himself, and I feared we might have to fight our way out.

The senator climbed up on the porch of the hunting club and proceeded to take on the crowd standing in the yard. "I'll tell you what," he shouted. "I'm gettin' a little tired of hearing this communist business. I may be a goddamned communist, but I'm your communist." His sarcasm got their attention.

"Let me tell you something else," he continued. "You all are the guys who raise soybeans and rice. You're the experts on this, and you tell me what to do on soybean and rice issues. I do it immediately. I do it without arguing. Now, here's my position on the war: I'm against it. I'm the expert on that, and you should listen to me. If you don't like my position, then don't return me. But if you do send me back, I'll do exactly what's best for you for the next six years."

He just buffaloed the bastards. They respected him because he was always in everybody's face.

Although Fulbright was steadfast in his opposition to the war, he agonized over it. By June 1968 the war and the protests against it had escalated. After running for the Democratic presidential nomination as a peace candidate, Bobby Kennedy was assassinated on the night of his triumph in the California primary. Fulbright showed the strain. We spent the night at Jack Files's house in North Little Rock. As I tried to sleep in a bedroom on the floor below him, I could hear Fulbright pacing the floor upstairs long after midnight.

With Jim Johnson, backed by the Citizens Council, spewing his venom, the Senate campaign grew vitriolic. In *Faubus*, Roy Reed wrote that "Johnson and his people resembled one of those ragged bands of outlaws that roamed the South after the Civil War. They continued to assert their grievance, tired and increasingly frustrated but stubbornly refusing to surrender."

By the time he challenged Fulbright, Johnson had been elected to the state supreme court and used the moniker Justice Jim. Johnson encouraged the notion that Fulbright was a closet communist, a turncoat betraying American interests, an Anglophile out of step with Arkansas ways.

Fulbright, one of the most sardonic men I ever met, held Johnson in utter contempt. One night, after making a circuit of Fourth of July picnics in northeast Arkansas, we wound up at a motel in Marked Tree. R. D. Randolph, my comrade from the Kennedy campaign in 1960, was a staunch Fulbright supporter, and he met us there. R.D. and Fulbright had a couple of drinks before dinner. Fulbright could get more out of two drinks than any man I ever saw. With two drinks, he could charm birds out of the trees. For him, alcohol served its purpose as a relaxing potion. But this night, he got a little loose.

We went to the dining room, and Jim Johnson's wife, Virginia, came in with a couple of Johnson's minions. She was running for governor, in tandem with her husband's pursuit of a Senate seat. The Johnsons had a built-in base of support; either one of them was assured of getting at least a third of the state's vote any time they ran. The Johnson bloc was never big enough for election, but it represented a major force in the state. After Virginia Johnson sat down, about twelve feet from us, Fulbright took one look at her and announced, in an insulting, high-pitched voice, "She looks like a goddamned Harpy."

I thought we might have to fight our way out of there, too, but nobody wanted to fool with Fulbright. He was not a big man, but he was wiry, and despite his reputation as an elitist, he had a hot temper.

Although he was sixty-three at the time, Fulbright's physical attributes were intimidating. Justice Jim would send hecklers to harass the senator at his public appearances, thinking they could cow him. They didn't understand his true character; he never shrank from the threat of a fistfight.

Fairly early in the campaign, Lee pulled me off Fulbright's traveling detail to work at our headquarters at the Marion Hotel. I began spending days and nights on the phone, calling upon my Democratic contacts to line them up as local Fulbright chairmen.

One day at headquarters, Lee interrupted my calls to introduce Fulbright's new driver, a young fellow from Hot Springs who had been working for the senator in Washington while attending Georgetown University. His name was Bill Clinton, and he seemed like a nice twenty-one-year-old kid. Affable and obviously smart, Clinton had won a Rhodes Scholarship and planned to go to England in the fall. His southern manners were spiced with just a bit of eastern brashness. Bill was quick to voice opposition to the war in Vietnam, but he seemed just as happy to talk about Arkansas folkways and personalities. His steady eye contact and ability to discuss various subjects demonstrated a natural flair for politics. Though the lines of his face were still rounded by baby fat, Clinton looked promising.

Clinton's assignment as driver didn't last long. Fulbright expected the deference normally paid to senators. Convinced of his own brilliance, Clinton expressed opinions at variance with Fulbright's views. Neither yielded. They rode around jabbering at each other, and it drove Fulbright crazy.

On their first day on the road, Fulbright called to report that the car's floorboard was filling with water. After talking with them, I figured out that Clinton had opened the external vents while running the air conditioner wide open—two goddamned Rhodes scholars in one car and they couldn't figure out that they were making it rain.

Fulbright and his young driver made it to Hot Springs, where the senator booked a room at the Arlington Hotel, the fine old resort spa. Fulbright looked forward to the medicinal waters. As soon as he checked in, he undressed, donned a robe, and headed to the baths. Before he opened his room door, the phone rang.

Afterward, Fulbright told me the story, in great detail:

The desk clerk was calling. "Senator Fulbright, I'm sorry, but your car is blocking the driveway."

"Well, why in the hell don't you get my driver to move it?"

"We don't know where he is, sir. But we do know your car needs to be moved."

Cursing under his breath, Fulbright put on his clothes and went downstairs. He found his car, parked in the middle of the driveway. He located his driver. Only a few feet away, Bill Clinton was embroiled in a loud debate with Alex Washburn, the editor of the *Hope Star*. They were arguing over Vietnam. Clinton had just informed Alex that his newspaper's editorial position was stupid. Fulbright had always been talented in schmoozing these small-town editors. After a conversation with the senator, editors usually wound up writing columns that called Fulbright wrongheaded on the war, but a valuable asset to Arkansas nonetheless. After all his efforts to mollify the newspapers in the state, Fulbright couldn't believe that Clinton had the gall to alienate a local editor.

Fulbright chewed Clinton out. When they returned to Little Rock, Fulbright insisted that I resume my job as his driver. Lee Williams told the senator I couldn't be spared from my organizational work. Fulbright said he would never take another trip with Clinton.

Disgusted with his staff, Fulbright vowed to wage the campaign by himself and set out alone in his car to take a five-day trip around the state. We received ominous reports from the field, and it was apparent that Fulbright's foul mood affected his campaign style. He stopped at a Forrest City barbershop, where some of the patrons began arguing with him over the war. One guy barred the barbershop door and told Fulbright: "You're not leaving here until you answer some questions."

"Fuck you," Fulbright said. "I'm leaving." And he threw the guy aside. He lost Forrest City by an overwhelming margin in the primary. Hell, he lost every county he visited on that trek. Fulbright wandered aimlessly. He left Little Rock without any luggage and had to borrow clothes from supporters along the way—living off the land, so to speak.

He was a peculiar character. Although he came from great wealth, Fulbright never spent a nickel without a sigh. The Fulbrights owned a newspaper, a bank, and a furniture factory in Fayetteville. They controlled a railroad that operated between Fayetteville and their lumber mill in neighboring Madison County. When Fulbright's father died, young Bill became, at nineteen, president of the family conglomerate. As an executive, he paid notoriously poor wages. After he became president of the University of Arkansas, some of the janitors called upon Fulbright for a raise and he refused. "My God," he was said to have told them, "I'm already paying you more than we're paying the help at our furniture factory."

His penny-pinching was legendary. While I drove him, he bummed so many cigarettes I was forced to complain. He bought a pack himself and offered me one with a sheepish grin. Another time he refused to share a package of mints with me. "I've only got four left," he explained.

"Jesus, Senator," I said, "I only want one. When we get to the next town I'll buy you a case of Life Savers."

He reluctantly handed over one mint.

He was what the hill folks call "careful." He wore one pair of shoes for forty years and refused to give up an old raincoat from his Oxford days, a garment that hung to his ankles and made him look like a member of the Russian general staff at the time of Nicholas II.

Jim Johnson sneered at Fulbright's English affectations. He called him "British Bill." To counter this criticism, we took Fulbright to a department store and bought him four gingham shirts to wear at campaign appearances. We promoted the idea that he was "just plain Bill."

The campaign grew nastier. Besides Johnson, we had another opponent, named Bobby K. Hays, who really twisted the Vietnam issue. Hays sponsored a television commercial with a voice-over saying something like: "You can hear the crack of AK-47s. Another American boy dies, thanks to Bill Fulbright." A third adversary was Foster Johnson, one of those perennial candidates for public office.

Through all the Arkansas Sturm und Drang, Fulbright survived the primary, which ensured his re-election in the fall. With Justice Jim repudiated again at the polls, it appeared Johnson's brand of demagoguery would always energize the kooky right but never win him an election. Our other opponents faded into oblivion. Foster Johnson managed to get only about six thousand votes. After the primary, the simpleton came to our headquarters and asked for a job. "Foster," I said to him, "I guess I better explain some basic facts of life to you. We give jobs to people who helped us. You not only ran against us, you said every vicious thing you could think of. So why don't you just go to hell."

I spent the next six years on Fulbright's Arkansas staff. For all his eccentricities, it was obvious that he had a high-minded belief in every man doing the best he could for our country. As a student, I had read Jefferson, Jackson, and Woodrow Wilson, all good Democrats and visionaries. An internationalist, Wilson had a certain idealism about doing good in the world, the same sort of trusting, naive idealism I embraced. Fulbright's similarity to Wilson was one of the reasons I admired him.

Never playing to the passions of the crowd, Fulbright took his role as senator very seriously. He believed that demagogues such as Jim Johnson and Faubus were the lowest form of political life. Although Fulbright could never be accused of being an integrationist, he finally spoke out against Faubus's tactics of racial division. He deplored yahoos.

Bill Clinton remained a Fulbright admirer, and as we got to know each other better during the summer of 1968, we often talked of the old man's knowledge and courage. More often, however, we talked about girls. Bill always made observations about pretty girls on our staff. "Gosh, she's something," he might say of a buxom secretary, and I would agree. Neither of us was married. In fact, neither of us had a steady girlfriend, but we appreciated young women.

During that summer, I came to think of Bill as an improvident younger brother, good-hearted but prone to cause problems. Because he was bright as hell and wanted everyone to know it, he rubbed some people the wrong way. As David Maraniss wrote in *First in His Class:* "Fulbright exasperated Clinton because he could never win an argument with the old man. Clinton exasperated Fulbright because the young buck would never shut up."

At my campaign post, I served as the lightning rod for every irritation and resentment Fulbright developed on the road. He would call to gripe about events that went awry. Whenever he thought about the incident at the Arlington Hotel, it set Fulbright off and he would begin bitching about Clinton. I defended Bill as a loyal follower, even while I acknowledged to the senator that "the boy" was a bit of a pain in the ass.

The next year, when I was running Fulbright's office in Little Rock, I traveled to Washington to discuss an effort to build the Democratic Party in Arkansas. Under the leadership of Governor Rockefeller, the Republican Party had begun to organize in the state, and those of us who still identified ourselves as Democrats thought it prudent to convert the old feudal machine into a functioning operation. When I saw Fulbright at his office in the morning, he seemed in a good mood, and as he studied my long sideburns and checkered vest, he told me I resembled Edward VII. That assessment would change at lunch.

Clinton was heading back for his second year at Oxford and happened to be in Washington at the same time, so we met Fulbright at the Senate dining room. Bill was dressed casually, with his hair coiled around his head like a weed. As soon as we sat down,

Fulbright snapped at Bill, calling him "a goddamned hippie." He decided he didn't like my looks either. Fulbright's face grew white with fury. He upbraided us so loudly that Senator Russell glanced toward our table.

I was holding a letter from our new state party chairman, Charles Matthews, which noted that "Jim McDougal will use the full resources of Senator Fulbright's office" in a drive to build the party organization. I made the mistake of putting the letter in front of Fulbright when I was trying to show him an organizational chart. He glared at the letter. "Well, goddamn," he snarled, "I can see Matthews is a pretty good lawyer, getting you to commit us on all this stuff."

Instead of calming down when the meal was put on the table, Fulbright grew hotter with Bill and me, raising hell about our hair, our woebegone political sense, and anything else he could think of. We both left the lunch chastened.

I thought I was going to be fired. When I returned to Little Rock, I got a call from Lee Williams. He said he was amazed. It was rare for Fulbright to give a raise, but the senator had told Lee to add two thousand dollars to my salary, raising it overnight from eight thousand dollars a year to ten. Lee reported one other instruction. Fulbright had said, "Tell him to get a haircut."

Over the years, Clinton and I forged a lasting friendship with Fulbright. After Clinton achieved high office, he recalled that "people dumped on our state and said we were all a bunch of back-country hayseeds" even though Arkansas had a senator "who doubled the I.Q. of any room he entered. It made us feel pretty good, like we might amount to something."

Fulbright survived his challenge in 1968, but McClellan faced strong competition when he next ran for re-election. David Pryor, an attractive young Democratic congressman from McClellan's own hometown, Camden, represented the new wave of politicians in Arkansas. A graduate of the University of Arkansas and its law school, Pryor was only thirty-two, but he had already been an editor and an attorney by the time he'd won election to Congress. Six years later, after making a name for himself in a crusade against disreputable nursing homes, Pryor thought he was ready for the Senate.

McClellan failed to win a majority in the first primary and was thrown into a runoff with Pryor. Quite often in Arkansas, if an incumbent could not manage a strong first primary majority in a field of multiple candidates, it gave the opposing forces an opportunity to coalesce against the incumbent in the runoff. McClellan and Pryor ran neck-and-neck in the first primary, drawing more than 40 percent each in a contest that eliminated a liberal candidate, whose vote was expected to go to Pryor in the runoff.

Witt Stephens decided that one of his "put sessions" was in order. As I heard the story, Stephens summoned about a dozen of Arkansas's wealthiest planters and bankers to a boardroom at a Little Rock bank controlled by the Stephens family. McClellan sat glumly at the table.

In somber tones, Stephens announced, "Boys, I'm glad you came, because this is a serious matter." He turned to McClellan.

"It looks like it's over for me," the old senator said. "They're going to gang up on me in the runoff. Maybe this is the time for you all to get right with David."

"Not so fast," said Stephens. Appealing to his guests, Stephens reminded them of McClellan's conservative leadership through the years. "You don't know what will happen when David gets in there with all his labor buddies and leftist friends," Stephens said. "I want to go around the table and see how much you all are willing to put up."

The meeting was held just before election reforms put limitations on campaign contributions. A Delta planter offered $50,000. A Jonesboro banker put up $25,000. Truman Baker pledged a large sum. The contributions came to nearly $300,000—enough to buy advertising and provide "street money" on election day, when organizers are paid to produce voters at the polling places.

Stephens assessed the commitments from the group with satisfaction. "Okay, boys," he said. "I'll put up the rest that's needed." A suspicion lingered that Stephens never gave a nickel; regardless, his "put session" enabled McClellan to hang on to win re-election even though the old order was crumbling.

My own finances were not so rarefied, and I had not been invited to the meeting. I gave $250 to McClellan. As a Fulbright aide, I probably shouldn't have taken sides in a contest between two Democrats, but I hoped my small contribution would help my old friend.

After going to work with Fulbright, I moved into a house Jim Guy Tucker and I bought together in Little Rock. It was an old two-story frame structure, nothing fancy, but it had more room than the apartment where I'd been staying. By pooling our interests, Jim Guy and I lowered our monthly payments on housing. Creating a classic bachelors' pad, we each had a floor to ourselves. There was a constant flow of young women, as well as Jim Guy's buddies from his Vietnam days, sitting around the house drinking and smoking pot. Jim Guy had a liver problem and didn't drink much, but he smoked a lot of pot. Downstairs was wreathed in smoke, but I didn't mind. I was a three-pack-a-day smoker myself. Jim Guy and I got along fine, joking with each other and talking politics. I thought he was my friend for life.

Other than the dope smoking, there was nothing bohemian about our household. We were just a couple of conventional guys. I had my job with a United States senator and Jim Guy worked for a big law firm and intended to run for prosecuting attorney in Pulaski County. Already hustling for public office, he was very conscious of his image. He kept his hair groomed neatly and dressed fashionably.

Away from the house, Jim Guy and I pursued our different interests, but we were linked politically by our involvement in the progressive wing of the Democratic Party. We might have been a far cry from the New Left, the campus-oriented movement touting free speech, free love, and participatory democracy, but by Arkansas standards, we were liberals.

While working in Little Rock's Federal Building, I met Delores Winston Lieberman, an attractive woman who ran Mr. Mills's district office in the same complex. Though a couple of years older than I, Delores appeared to be about eighteen. She was petite, with blond hair and shining eyes, and dressed as neatly as a model in a women's magazine. Occasionally we shared problems relating to the Arkansas congressional delegation, and her professional manner impressed me. Delores measured her words carefully and had her thoughts in order before she spoke. Our work led me to invite her to dinner.

Delores was divorced. She had married at a young age; her three sons lived with their father in Atlanta. There was no man in her life at the moment. I found excuses to drop by Mr. Mills's Little Rock office, to talk with Delores about our casework and other things. We had mutual interests, talking with the same bureaucrats and sometimes the same constituents. We laughed about the drones and dummies we dealt with in the federal government, and we marveled at some of the ridiculous requests Arkansans brought to our offices. We had plenty to talk about, and in the evenings, I enjoyed taking Delores to dinners and movies.

In 1970, we were married in a little Baptist church in Rosebud, the White County village I often visited. Delores's mother was dead and her father quite old, but she had a favorite aunt in Rosebud who helped arrange the wedding. Lee Williams served as my best man, and Fulbright flew in from Washington to attend the ceremony.

Delores and I moved to a house just outside Little Rock and dwelled happily together, at least for a couple of years. Then David, one of her sons, sustained severe brain damage in an accident, and Delores rushed to Atlanta to be with him. She stayed for weeks, tending to her son, refusing to accept a diagnosis that he would never get better. I flew to Atlanta every weekend to be with her, and the stressful situation grew into an emotional and financial strain. We brought the boy back to Little Rock to live with us for a while. He was a sweet child, but the damage had reduced his ability to care for himself. He spent his days in a school for the blind and returned to us in the evening, but he showed no sign of progress.

David's helplessness consumed Delores. Mr. Mills gave her an indefinite paid leave of absence; he was good about that. And Delores poured all her physical resources into caring for her child. Finally, she snapped under the strain. David was returned to his father in Atlanta, and Delores had to be hospitalized herself. She was found to be manic-depressive.

Although I had lived with a father and grandfather with the same affliction, and had suffered my own emotional ups and downs, I knew little about the illness.

Delores stayed in the hospital for weeks; I despaired of our future. Throughout her ordeal, she never lashed out at me. She was sweet, and one day she presented me with a piece of stained glass she'd made in the hospital crafts room, accompanied by a note: "To Jim McDougal, a good man." Yet she seemed distant, and I could sense her slipping away.

When she was discharged from the hospital, Delores moved to California to live with her sister. After she left, one of her friends in Mr. Mills's office told me of Delores's previous manic behavior. I learned that Delores had had a pattern of binge shopping. Once she'd rushed out and bought hundreds of dollars' worth of towels and washcloths that she'd neither needed nor could afford. I had been oblivious to her problem, and now she was gone.

In 1974, Delores asked for and obtained an uncontested divorce. It was as though I had married a will-o'-the-wisp. I never heard from her again.

While my personal life was in tatters, my relationship with Fulbright grew stronger. Even though he never spent money, he loved to make money, and he appreciated my talents as an investor. Shortly after my friends in Alcoholics Anonymous drummed me into shape for the job with Fulbright, Doyle Rowe, the successful AA business-man who'd helped break my drinking cycle, suggested that I buy a piece of property near Little Rock. To meet the $20,000 price, I put $500 down on a credit card and arranged a loan with payments of $100 a month. Within six months, I sold the land for $40,000. The transaction launched my career as a developer. I dabbled in other real estate deals and mentioned one venture to the senator, but he didn't appear interested. When I told him later of the quick profit I had turned on the investment, Fulbright was indignant. "I thought we were going to get that together," he complained.

I let the issue chill for about a year, then asked Fulbright if he wanted to invest in a partnership to purchase two hundred acres in Saline County, just southwest of Little Rock. Together, we bought the land for $60,000 and named our company Rolling Manor. The incorporation papers listed Fulbright as the chairman of the board, and me as the president. After he signed the papers for the loan, Fulbright had nothing more to do with the property. He never even made the effort to look at it.

During the 1974 campaign, when Fulbright's seat was up for elec-tion again and things weren't going well, the senator and I stopped to buy some fruit at a Safeway store. Fulbright believed fresh fruit cured all ills. I thought it was a good time to tell him some news.

"You know that piece of property we bought down in Saline County?"

Fulbright grunted.

"Well, it might cheer you up to know that we've already paid for the thing and made a hundred thousand dollars."

Fulbright's eyes lit up and he had a happy exclamation: "God-damn!"

He always worried that inflation was going to eat up his riches. When Fulbright told audiences of his fears that he might end his days eating beans, they chuckled because they knew of the Ful-bright family's wealth. But he was possessed by these fears. He told me of a recurring dream: "My father died, and somebody moved into our house and started to go through all our papers. My mother and I were under tremendous pressure to save our business, and we failed. I dreamed, over and over, that my mother and I were in a car, and somebody was driving us to the poorhouse."

Fulbright was never able to rid himself of the nightmare. "I'll think I need a new suit," he told me, "and then I'll think: Oh, hell, I don't need a new suit. I can't afford to spend that money."

Once, when I accompanied him to a family meeting in Fayetteville to discuss the Fulbright business interests, he blew his top at one of his nephews because the poor guy had spent five hundred dollars to renovate an office. From Fulbright's reaction, you would have thought the fellow had murdered his grandmother.

By 1974, Fulbright had been worn down by his battles, by endless clashes with the far right on his home front in Arkansas, and by his epic struggles against the Vietnam policies in Washington. The long war was over, but Fulbright felt little satisfaction. Fifty thousand American lives had been lost, and the nation no longer enjoyed a worldwide reputation as a moral force. Fulbright was sixty-nine; he had seen the United States rise as a superpower, a liberating force in World War II, and he had lived to see the country castigated overseas as a vicious bully.

With changes sweeping Arkansas, Fulbright appeared increasingly out of touch with his home state. A new generation had gained power in state and local offices, and Fulbright barely knew its members. He had been preoccupied by the war, and I felt his political problems were compounded by his Foreign Relations Committee staff. The committee aides were internationalists, close to Fulbright intellectually, but with no grasp of Arkansas politics.

I quarreled with the Washington staff. They were horrified by the way I handled his correspondence. When writing letters for the senator, I made a point of addressing recipients by their first name, and I signed the mail "Bill." The committee staff thought the use of "Bill" uncouth. Once they had Fulbright refer to Arkansas as "the buckle on the Bible Belt" in one of his speeches, and that infuriated a lot of Arkansans.

When I campaigned with him in northwest Arkansas, he tried to rely on his old magic. He strolled the sidewalks, shaking hands and introducing himself to young voters as "Bill Fulbright from Fayetteville." They seemed surprised to learn he was from Fayetteville. He was no longer a local personality. They saw him on the network news, and thought he was a national figure.

Fulbright's opponent in the Democratic primary that year was Governor Dale Bumpers, a progressive leader who had sprung from small-town law practice in Charleston, in western Arkansas. I first heard of Bumpers in 1969 from my friend R. D. Randolph, who grew up in Bumpers's home county. R.D. had said, "We've got this guy up here named Bumpers and I think we can get him elected governor." I had a fit of laughter and told R.D. nobody with the name of Bumpers could get elected anything. But the next time I traveled in that part of Arkansas, I stopped to talk with Bumpers, and his intelligence and easy manner impressed me.

In 1970, Orval Faubus had attempted a comeback. Willing to do anything to block Faubus, Fulbright supported Bumpers in the fight, even though it was unusual for a Democratic officeholder to take sides in a primary. Faubus spoke darkly of a "Fulbright machine" arrayed against him. At the state Democratic convention that year, Fulbright wisecracked to reporters, "I had to unleash my machine—all three of them." He was referring to his three-man Arkansas staff. Fulbright had no machine, but he commanded respect. Our efforts with Charles Matthews, the state chairman, to organize the Democratic Party helped Fulbright's reputation among county leaders. I'm convinced his endorsement was instrumental in Bumpers's victory over Faubus in the primary as well as in Bumpers's defeat of Rockefeller in the general election.

But just as Faubus had created a monster when he'd revitalized the Young Democrats a decade earlier, Fulbright had sown the seeds of his own political destruction.

Bumpers was a skillful, popular governor who built a formidable organization. He used patronage wisely, winning the loyalty of prominent businessmen by appointing their wives to state commissions. He filled the state payroll with workers who reciprocated with political support. No Arkansas politician, other than Faubus, had succeeded in assembling a real machine in my lifetime, but Bumpers understood the mechanics of building a strong, statewide organization.

He was telegenic at a time when television was replacing the newspaper as the source of information. When Bumpers spoke on TV, he had a gift of reaching out to the Arkansas voter; he exuded common sense. When Fulbright appeared on *Meet the Press* or another of those Sunday shows from Washington, he sounded far removed from Arkansas. And Fulbright's criticism of the administration of President Richard M. Nixon—who in 1972 became the first Republican to win Arkansas's electoral votes in the twentieth century—grated on the folks back home.

In a departure from his conservative position on domestic issues, Fulbright had voted against G. Harrold Carswell, Nixon's nominee to the Supreme Court, during a bitter battle that Nixon lost. Martha Mitchell, an eccentric Arkansan married to John Mitchell, Nixon's attorney general, targeted Fulbright in one of her quirky late-night telephone calls. After reaching the news desk of the *Arkansas Gazette*, she told an editor, "I want you to crucify Fulbright."

Fulbright could smile and brush off the barb from Martha Mitchell, but he couldn't dismiss Bumpers so easily. In 1974, Bumpers challenged Fulbright for his Senate seat, and the polls showed we never had a chance. Even though voters might have preferred to keep Fulbright in the Senate and Bumpers as governor, Bumpers held a big advantage in a one-on-one race. Like any good politician, Bumpers saw his chance to move to the national scene and seized it, even if it displaced an ally who had held the seat for thirty years.

In 1968, we'd probably spent no more than $100,000 in an old-fashioned re-election campaign that depended on local talent. In 1974, a troubled Fulbright brought in highly paid specialists from Washington. Before he became a TV commentator, Mark Shields worked as a Washington consultant. He had labored for Edmund S. Muskie's presidential campaign in 1972, and though unsuccessful, Shields had won praise as a smart inside operator. Fulbright brought Shields to Little Rock. When we were introduced, the senator sarcastically informed Shields that I was "the intellectual in this office."

We sat down to hear our visitor. The consultant had a presentation featuring a flip chart with illustrations. Shields turned to a page with a picture of a cherry tree. "If you want to pick cherries, you've got to go where the cherries are," he instructed us.

Fulbright and I exchanged looks. After Shields left the room, Fulbright said, "That fellow has a genius for overstating the obvious."

Things were falling apart. Our campaign manager was Jim Blair, the political operative from northwest Arkansas whom I had first met at the University of Arkansas in 1957. I thought of Blair as a big, blundering Saint Bernard who wanted to be helpful but didn't understand Arkansas politics. Blair's role as campaign manager reflected Lee Williams's wishes; Lee always liked to have weak managers so he could manage the campaign himself.

Blair seemed aware of his own inadequacy. One day he came into Fulbright's office at the Federal Building to discuss the failing campaign. I normally sat at Fulbright's desk, but when the senator came to town I moved across the room to a conference table. I sat there as Blair talked with Fulbright. In the middle of the conversation, Blair began sobbing. Then he slapped himself back and forth across the face several times and said: "I needed that." (Around this time, there was a TV commercial for an aftershave lotion showing a fellow who slapped himself in the face and said, "Thanks, I needed that!")

My thought was similar to that of Alice in Wonderland: Things are getting curiouser and curiouser.

On the night of the primary, Fulbright's staff gathered with his family and close friends at a Little Rock hotel to await the results. The senator was expecting a long night with late returns. He went downstairs to have dinner with several family members shortly after the polls closed. Before he had been gone long, one of the local television stations called the suite and told us they intended, within ten minutes, to announce that Bumpers had won.

Seth Tillman, a Fulbright aide on the Foreign Relations Committee staff, said to me, "You need to go and tell him."

I said, "Seth, why don't you go tell him, you're the one who got him beat." I felt Seth and others on the Washington staff had been insensitive to Fulbright's need to stroke his Arkansas constituency. I thought they had watched his fight for political survival from an ivory tower.

Seth was unwilling to carry the bad news to Fulbright. "You're just a lot closer to the senator than I am—you tell him," he said.

I went downstairs to find Fulbright enjoying a spirited conversation at the dinner table. I said simply, "Sir, you need to come up to the room." We went upstairs, into an empty room in the Fulbright suite, which had become deathly quiet.

"Well, sir," I said, "it looks like they got us." Fulbright poured a straight shot of vodka—I'd never seen him do that before—and drank it down. Then he prepared for his concession speech and the interviews that would follow. He took his loss, just as he took everything, like a gentleman.

Later in the same year, after Washington police stopped Mr. Mills late one night for driving his car erratically, a sequence of bewildering incidents unfolded. Mr. Mills's passenger, Fanne Fox—a stripteaser known as the Argentine Firecracker—leaped from the auto and into the shallow waters of the Tidal Basin near the Jefferson Memorial. Mr. Mills lurched about incoherently with his eyeglasses broken and scratches on his face, according to the police report. While the nation's capital was still clucking over the story, Mr. Mills appeared on stage at a seedy nightclub in Boston, leering drunkenly while the Argentine Firecracker went through her routine. A news photographer was on hand to freeze the moment.

When I heard the news, I flashed back to my flight from Washington with Mr. Mills in 1962 to the state Democratic convention, the day he'd pronounced me a "genius." After we'd checked into the Marion Hotel that afternoon, I'd gone to Mr. Mills's suite and noticed an opened fifth of vodka on his sideboard. Returning later in the evening, I saw that Mr. Mills had consumed the whole bottle. He muttered that he wanted to go eat dinner, but he was staggering and could have caused a terrible scene in public, in front of many constituents who had no idea Mr. Mills drank. Jack Files, his top aide at the time, and I eventually put Mr. Mills to bed. I hoped it was an aberration, but other events convinced me that Mr. Mills was a heavy drinker.

In 1968, when I was working in Fulbright's campaign against Jim Johnson, I called Mr. Mills at his Capitol Hill office. Though it was midweek, his receptionist suggested that I call him at home. Mr. Mills answered the phone, and immediately I sensed that something was wrong. He began boasting. "Well, I guess I'm just going to have to come down there and bail Bill out," he told me. "You remember forty-eight, don't you? When I had to come down and bail Truman out?"

Mr. Mills's decision to run for the Democratic presidential nomination in 1972 appeared to be the product of a drunkard's grandiose dreams. A few big wheels in Arkansas, men like David Parr of the Milk Producers Association and Charles Ward, a major school bus manufacturer, pushed Mr. Mills to run. The effort, which petered out shortly after a dismal showing in the New Hampshire primary, mortified many of Mr. Mills's friends. Even Mr. Mills was embarrassed.

Fulbright told me of a strange telephone conversation he once had with Mr. Mills, who'd spent an hour rambling about a trip to Aruba. After Fulbright bumped into him at the Democratic national convention in Miami Beach in 1972, he confided to me, "I just saw Wilbur. He was red in the face and acting crazy." His conduct fit the convention. The sessions lasted until all hours of the night. Senator George McGovern of South Dakota, running on a peace platform, had locked up the presidential nomination, but the Mills people kept floating ridiculous rumors, insisting that Ted Kennedy was off-shore in a family yacht and lobbying to put Mr. Mills on the ticket.

There had been intimations of Mr. Mills's problems earlier. When Delores had worked for him, she'd told me how she'd had to keep a large supply of towels at the Little Rock office when Mr. Mills was in town. He constantly washed his face and patted his cheeks with cologne in a transparent effort to disguise his condition.

It was obvious that Mr. Mills had been a closet alcoholic. He and his wife, who had a secret drinking problem herself, led a reclusive lifestyle in Washington. Mrs. Mills seemed a fragile character, like Blanche DuBois in *A Streetcar Named Desire*. The Millses never went out socially. That's why he'd passed on his invitations to Washington functions to Carol Tucker and me.

The incident with Fanne Fox destroyed his career. Even though the voters of our district sent Mr. Mills back to Washington, his colleagues moved to strip him of control of the Ways and Means Committee. Reduced from a satrap to a shadow, he served out his last two-year term and returned to Kensett, a broken man, to live out his days in his modest frame house there.

The world of Arkansas politics in which I had been reared had quickly disintegrated. The men who'd served as my mentors and father figures were leaving the scene. Faubus and Fulbright were gone and Mr. Mills discredited. Senator McClellan was contemplating retirement. Republicans had already breached the Democratic wall with Rockefeller's victory, and fresh faces were taking over Democratic affairs.

Philosophical over the transition, Fulbright resigned from the

Senate early to give Bumpers a head start in seniority over the other new senators elected in 1974. Although Fulbright was hailed for making a generous gesture, I understand he gave up his office because of a loophole in the Senate pension law. By quitting when he did, Fulbright actually increased the amount of his pension. In the end, it was just a matter of dollars and cents.

Bumpers and David Pryor, who had just been elected governor, were the new powers in the state. And waiting in the wings were two other rising stars in the Arkansas firmament, my friends Bill Clinton and Jim Guy Tucker.

S

I f Bill Clinton seemed like an improvident younger brother during this period of my life, Bob Riley was a benevolent older brother, a lovable legend in Arkansas politics. The first time I saw him, I was in the midst of nominating Lowell Whittington, my friend from the legislature, for the presidency of the Young Democrats at a convention in Camden. As I built toward my rhetorical climax, Bob burst into the room and the YD delegates erupted, far more interested in greeting him than listening to me.

In order to enlist in the Marine Corps the day after Pearl Harbor, when he was only seventeen, he'd had to persuade his father to forge his mother's signature to the parental consent form. By 1944, he was part of the American force fighting across the South Pacific. During the Marines' initial assault on Guam, his unit was pinned down by fire from a Japanese pillbox. Bob ran ahead to try to take out the enemy position. As he fired, a land mine detonated under him, striking him with hundreds of pieces of shrapnel. His unit fell back and the Japanese thought him dead, but he crawled to safety.

He came home, severely wounded. Like my Uncle Bert, Bob was blinded, left with only a tiny bit of light perception in his right eye. He wore a black patch over his left eye, and it gave him the swashbuckling appearance of the John Wayne character, Rooster Cogburn, in *True Grit.*

Perhaps it was because he reminded me of Uncle Bert, but I felt a kinship with Bob as I worked in the various Democratic campaigns. A veteran of Arkansas politics, he had a treasury of funny stories, and his self-effacing humor endeared him to Democrats across the state. When I joined Fulbright's staff, Bob was chairman of the political science department at Ouachita Baptist University in Arkadelphia, and he supplied me with student interns for our Arkansas office. Our friendship deepened, and I began traveling back and forth between Little Rock and Arkadelphia to visit Bob and his wife, Claudia.

The Rileys made me a member of their family after Bob persuaded me to come to Ouachita to teach a night course in national government a couple of times a week. I had no college degree, myself, but Bob didn't care. He felt my background qualified me, and I suspect he believed my connection with the Baptist school would help keep me on the straight and narrow path of sobriety.

After my exposure to Jim Johnson's appeal to the worst instincts of Arkansas voters, and to Faubus's embrace of the big-business interests he had once denounced, I felt my idealism recharged by Bob Riley. He had political rivals, but no enemies. Bob was an ordained Baptist minister, and Christianity influenced his service in government. Bob would raise anyone's idealism quotient. He believed in the equality of races, in a fair shake for everyone. Bob enjoyed telling the story of how he met Claudia, a pretty ballet student who drove a new Oldsmobile. He thought dance and a fancy car an attractive combination, he said, until they married and he had to assume the payments on the Olds. Claudia was the perfect mate for Bob. When Bob campaigned, she walked with him every step of the way, telling him the names of approaching people so he could greet them effusively. I told Bob that while handicapped people sometimes won a sympathy vote, his act was so deft that should he stumble, voters would think he was drunk instead of blind.

Bob had been a member of the Arkansas House of Representatives, served as Senate parliamentarian, and been twice elected as lieutenant governor, a part-time job that enabled him to keep his position at the university. But in 1974, as he sought the Democratic gubernatorial nomination, he was swept away by the new generation. Beaten by Pryor, he intended to give up politics in order to devote all his energies to the school in Arkadelphia.

Before he left Little Rock, Bob had a final moment in the sun. When Fulbright yielded his Senate seat early and Bumpers resigned as governor, Bob became acting governor of Arkansas for a couple of weeks. He asked me to join him as his executive secretary, the top staff position in the office. For a brief period we were caretakers of the state.

Bob attempted no major initiatives. He didn't even try to sell a pardon, a lucrative technique that some southern governors have practiced on the eve of their departure from office. Bob named Francis McBeth, a well-known music instructor from Ouachita Baptist University, as the state's composer laureate. Beyond that, we simply occupied the office, experiencing only one flap. After one of Bob's aides authorized the printing of stationery bearing Bob's name as governor, we were criticized. To offset the cost of the stationery, Bob and I offered to serve without salary. When a bureaucrat warned that the gesture would foul up the state's accounting system, we donated our paychecks to Ouachita Baptist University.

At the beginning of 1975, Bob delivered the traditional farewell address by the departing governor to the legislature. He and I prepared the speech, and after Bob made a few impromptu remarks he stood by my side at the podium while I read the formal message for him. He knew everyone, and the folks in the legislature loved him. His speech described the joys of Arkansas politics, and as he walked out of the chamber many of the members reached out to

hug him. Even the gruffest character in the place, Max Howell—
who had beaten Bob for a Senate seat years before and had held it
ever since—had tears in his eyes.

When Bob went home to Arkadelphia, he took me with him. I had
made money in several real estate deals and my bank account was
in no danger of being overdrawn. But I was divorced, a recovering
alcoholic, and feeling somewhat rootless. I leapt at the invitation to
move into his home and begin a career as a college professor. Bob
put me in charge of courses in international relations, constitutional
law, and state and local government.

Ouachita was a small, cloistered Southern Baptist college with a
student body of about fifteen hundred, drawn primarily from Arkansas and east Texas. I stood out there like a libertine at a religious
revival. I smoked in class and drove an imported automobile alien to
the area, a Mercedes I had given myself following Fulbright's defeat.
Eventually, I moved into my bachelor's quarters, a mobile home the
Rileys had converted into a cottage on the grounds of their home.

Because my own academic record was spotty, I didn't care for
tests. In my constitutional law classes I'd call on students to give
legal opinions, and I graded them accordingly. At the end of the
semester, I gave the students a choice between accepting the oral
grade and taking a final exam. No one opted for an exam, and I
never had to flunk a single student.

I enjoyed the campus life, my colleagues on the faculty as well as
my students. One of my favorites in the political science department was Jim Ranchino. Jim had been one of the first to try his
hand at polling in Arkansas. I'd met him during the 1970 campaign
for governor when he'd used the WATS line in Fulbright's Little
Rock office to cut the cost of his telephone polls. Since Fulbright
was backing Bumpers, I'd doctored Ranchino's survey results to
exaggerate a trend toward Bumpers, the dark horse, and leaked the
misinformation to newspaper reporters. The tactic built up a per-

ception of momentum for Bumpers, which was helpful. The polls turned into a self-fulfilling prophecy. When Bumpers narrowly won the election, Ranchino looked like a seer.

In the summer of 1975, Ranchino unwittingly returned the favor. He introduced me to his student intern, Susan Henley. I was attracted to her from the moment we met. She had an upbeat personality, and her quick-witted repartee hinted at high intelligence. I asked her out for lunch that day, but she said she had other plans.

A couple of days later, I was delighted when she showed up at my office. Ranchino had gone to Little Rock, and Susan had lost his keys. Could I help? I could certainly try. Acting out a Ouachita version of the knight-in-shining-armor routine, I accompanied her to Ranchino's office. Inspecting the door with burglarlike efficiency, I saw it was held by an old-fashioned lock that could be opened by almost any door key. With one quick movement, I kicked the lock plate off the door jamb. The door swung open. Susan might have been a bit shocked, maybe even a little frightened, but I got her attention.

I asked her to join me for some waterskiing at a nearby lake where the Rileys had a houseboat. When Susan demurred, I told her, "I've never asked a woman a second time." She changed her mind.

A picture lingers in my mind of Susan in her black bathing suit on our first date at DeGray Lake. She was twenty and I asked her where she had gotten those curves. "They just showed up," she said. Susan had been very skinny as a kid, she said. But no more. Our hosts, the Rileys, liked her, and I was smitten. After my sad experience with Delores, I was not shopping for a new mate, but Susan seemed something special. She was spunky and she made me laugh.

Despite my reputation as a loner, I found I craved her company. We started dating regularly, and took off one weekend for Little Rock. While we were there, I introduced Susan to the world of real estate. We drove to Saltillo Heights, a twelve-hundred-acre tract between Little Rock and Conway that Fulbright and I had bought for a hundred dollars an acre. We'd gotten it cheap because there were no roads into the land. My initial inspection of the property consisted of a quick look from a hilltop to see if the timber had been cleared. When I called Fulbright about the deal, he asked, "Have you been over the land?" I responded, "Every inch of it, sir." We had owned the property for only a few months when I took Susan out there, but we had built four miles of roads and already sold some of the lots. I felt the project was moving nicely, and I took pride in explaining to Susan the business of turning an unappreciated piece of property into a profitable development.

On the way home, my Mercedes began coughing. I had filled the tank with fuel that must have been watered down. As the level of gas lowered, the water content grew proportionately higher. Since the Mercedes was designed to block water from its fuel system, the car simply stopped. Repeatedly. We were forced to sit on the roadside until the water evaporated, then start up again. Sometimes I pumped water manually from the filter. I had been trying to impress this young woman, and it took me four hours to drive sixty-five miles.

Despite that inauspicious start, our relationship grew more serious. Susan enrolled in a couple of my classes, and for the first time in years, I felt really good about myself. During my drinking days, I had been dogged by depression and remorse, and I still wrestled with mood swings. Susan brought me out of my funk.

That winter, I took a group of my students to Washington. We visited the Arkansas congressional offices, I showed them my old work space at the secretary of the Senate's office, and I took the group to meet Fulbright at his law office. Later, Susan and I had lunch with Fulbright. He told me privately he approved of her. So did I; we had been dating for about six months.

Before leaving Washington, Susan and I had breakfast at an Irish restaurant next to our hotel. I asked her to marry me. She hesitated, but accepted my proposal before we left the table. Delighted, I called my friend David Lambert, who had moved from his job with McClellan to work as a Washington lobbyist for the New York Stock Exchange. I told him I was in Washington with my fiancée—the first time I'd ever used the term—and invited him to join us for lunch. Afterward, we went to a jewelry store to choose Susan's wedding ring.

I looked forward to an opportunity to start married life over again. Where Delores had been restrained, Susan was effervescent. We talked, with enthusiasm, of all the great fun we would have.

After we returned to Arkansas, Susan took me to meet her family in Camden, an hour's ride from Arkadelphia. I was surprised to see that the Henleys lived in an old, ramshackle house. Her father, J. B. Henley, was a retired Army man. He ran a service station, and it soon became apparent he knew little about business. J.B. struck me as the kind of guy who gets preyed upon by con artists selling house siding or vacuum cleaners. Susan's mother, Lauretta, was a Belgian whom J.B. met while stationed overseas. Susan had been born in Heidelberg, West Germany. She had four brothers and two sisters. Three of the siblings still lived at home, and it seemed the others were always around with their own children, each determined to outshout the other. To an only child who had grown up in a quiet household, the Henleys' noise level was unbelievable.

Her parents were a bit troubled over the age difference between Susan and me—she was fourteen years younger than I—yet they treated me cordially. Susan later told me that her father warned her, "You know, you're marrying this old man and you're going to wake up every morning to the sound of a hacking cough." Both J.B. and I were heavy smokers.

Before we were married, Susan began to spend nights with me at the cottage on the Rileys' property. It was a neighborhood where the university president, Daniel Grant, and other faculty members lived. I had bought Susan a yellow Audi that was conspicuous when parked outside my place. A devout Baptist, Dr. Grant summoned me to his office one day.

"People are talking because they see Susan's car there over-night," he told me. "I know you're engaged and have honorable intentions, but this looks bad."

His sanctimonious attitude annoyed me, and I drew my response from the King James Version of the Bible. "Dr. Grant," I said, "the wicked flee where no man pursueth: but the righteous are bold as a lion." Then I added, from the gospel according to Jim McDougal, "Frankly, I don't give a flip how it looks."

Dr. Grant was so flustered he didn't press me on the issue. He even sent me a new contract for the next semester, but I was planning to leave the school, get married, and move into the real estate business.

This was the halcyon time of our lives. Susan and I were young, in love, flushed with the prospect of success, and surrounded by family and friends. Susan enjoyed meeting my political associates—she had few close friends herself in spite of her bubbly personality— and we ran around with a group that included the two promising young Democrats Clinton and Tucker.

While I had known Jim Guy for years, my friendship with Bill blossomed during the period I worked for Fulbright. Bill and I were both absorbed in politics. When he came back from Oxford, he often popped into our Little Rock office, flirting with secretaries on his way to my desk to hear the latest statehouse gossip. After he finished his scholarship, Bill moved into the big leagues quickly, managing the McGovern campaign in Texas. In our postmortems following the 1972 election, we both concluded that the McGovern campaign had been a hopeless cause, and it was apparent that twenty-six-year-old Bill thought he, himself, could have done better. After he moved to Fayetteville in 1973, I saw more of him when Fulbright and I visited the Ozarks. Clinton would show up at my motel room to talk about Arkansas personalities and exchange political intelligence. One night, instead of paying for a motel, I stayed at a house Bill rented in the countryside. It was a modernistic stone structure with slashing lines, and Bill proudly pointed out that it had been designed by Fay Jones, a prominent architect in Fayetteville. Perhaps it was a thing of beauty, I told him, but the place looked like a cave to me.

I met Bill's girlfriend, Hillary Rodham, during the 1974 state Democratic convention in Hot Springs. I represented Fulbright, who had had no interest in attending. Charged with delivering Fulbright's endorsement of Bumpers, I tried to be as diplomatic as possible, visiting all the Democratic officeholders and office-seekers. As the Democratic nominee for the Third Congressional District seat, Bill had set up a hospitality suite in the Arlington Hotel, the same place where he had abandoned Fulbright's car in 1968.

The old hotel was still garishly decorated to please its mob-linked clientele from Chicago, and Clinton held forth in a suite filled with delegates. I had heard of Hillary, but we had not met. After Bill introduced me, I sat and talked with her for a while. She was a northern girl, trying very hard to get along in a strange southern setting. Unversed in Arkansas issues, she sought a common denominator in the subjects we discussed: Fulbright's defeat and Bill's chances. We had a good chat, and when I was leaving, Hillary remarked to Bill, "I like your Mr. McDougal!"

My first impressions of Hillary were favorable. She was not one of the strikingly beautiful women who often caught Bill's eye. Still, she seemed smart, sophisticated, and devoted to him. Though Bill and Hillary were children of the 1960s, a period symbolized by sex and drugs and rock 'n' roll, Hillary had stable credentials that would appeal to the Arkansas electorate: a well-to-do family from the suburbs of Chicago, and degrees from Wellesley and Yale Law School. She looked like the kind of person who could clean up after Bill, and God knows he always needed that. To put it bluntly, Bill was a mess, never on time and chronically rushing from one event to another.

Though Clinton lost his 1974 race, he made a name for himself as a tireless campaigner with a bright smile and a mellow voice that often grew hoarse from overuse, and it was impossible to dislike him.

Susan and I socialized with Bill and Hillary. We attended their engagement party in 1975. Though Clinton is not much of a drinker, I brought him an expensive bottle of brandy someone had given me.

He responded with a handwritten thank-you note. Bill was preparing to run for attorney general in 1976, and he wanted to set up a time when we could have dinner to discuss his next race, but he couldn't resist adding, "I hope you will bring that long, lanky girl—I liked her."

Susan and I also spent time with Jim Guy and his wife, Betty. Elected attorney general in 1974, Jim Guy had his own plans. He intended to run next for Congress. Betty had already been brushed by Arkansas fame. She had formerly been married to Lance Alworth, a star for the Razorbacks who had gone on to an outstanding career as a wide receiver in pro football. After she married Jim Guy, Betty went to law school. A smart, attractive woman with an appealing personality, Betty never lived in either husband's shadow.

When I shared a house with Jim Guy, I'd heard him deliver rambling monologues on the merits of the various girls he dated. It was almost as if he were prospecting for the proper political wife. In any event, I thought he found the right mate in Betty.

When Susan and I were married on May 25, 1976, a simple ceremony was conducted in front of a little house I owned a few miles west of Little Rock. Bob Riley officiated. Susan was the portrait of a bride in her white veil and scalloped white wedding dress. She carried a white Bible and one long-stemmed red rose. I wore a pastel-colored summer suit. We stood under a flowered arch Susan had set up in the front yard.

With summer approaching, there was no breeze to beat back the afternoon heat. Our guests sat on folding chairs, stirring the air with hand fans. My mother and father, Aunt Ola and some cousins, and most of the Henleys were there, too, as well as Bill and Hillary, and Jim Guy and Betty.

I took Susan to Europe for our honeymoon. On the way, we stayed at the Algonquin Hotel in New York. I wanted Susan exposed to its literary tradition. Susan was interested in books, and I showed her the lobby where the *New Yorker* crowd used to gather to deliver their urbane commentaries over cocktails. I thought of our trip as the latest phase in the education of Susan McDougal. In Europe, we visited many of the cities that we knew only through postcards. A couple of Arkansas pilgrims, we toured museums filled with priceless art and strolled through ancient neighborhoods, soaking up a culture foreign to our home. In a suburb of Liège, we stopped to see Susan's aunt. I found that her Belgian relatives spoke English fluently and lived in an impressive home. They seemed far more sophisticated than Susan's parents.

By the time we returned, the election year was well under way. I was too busy with my real estate ventures to become deeply involved, but I gave money to the Clinton and Tucker campaigns. When Clinton wrote to thank me for my fifteen-hundred-dollar contribution, he added a postscript about our old boss, Bill Fulbright: "British Bill didn't think much of my idea to have him endorse Carter. I was mildly surprised but at least amused to have him giving me hell again."

That fall, Jim Guy was elected to Wilbur Mills's old seat in Congress. Bill was elected attorney general. Jimmy Carter, a fellow southerner, became the first Democrat to win the presidency since LBJ in 1964; he appointed my old friend Carol Tucker, Jim Guy's sister, assistant secretary of agriculture.

Looking back on this political high point years later, I was reminded of Mary Tyrone's line at the end of Eugene O'Neill's tragedy *Long Day's Journey into Night*. Life had once been good and I "was so happy for a time."

My partner in marriage became my closest business associate. Although Susan had no background in real estate, she was extremely well organized and almost Prussian in her efficiency. She took over a project near Friendship, Arkansas, where Bob Riley and I had bought sixty-four acres. Between my teaching chores and handling the property I owned with Fulbright, the development we called Riley Farms had been neglected. I showed Susan the site and gave her a list of things that needed to be done: cutting the timber, bush-hogging the brush, clearing a roadway. I told her the object was to make enough money to help the Rileys financially and to buy me a new Mercedes.

The next time I went to Riley Farms with Bob and Claudia, it looked as if Susan were orchestrating the Normandy invasion. Workers were all over the place. The property sold quickly, and we enjoyed a nice return on our investment.

Susan and I settled into the house where we were married. It was a shotgun-style dwelling I had bought, along with a couple of sur-rounding acres, for eight thousand dollars a few years before. I had the place air-conditioned, built a porch, and made a few other im-provements, but it was quite ordinary. I fancied fine cars but had never really cared about owning mansions. Instead of using our profits to buy expensive furnishings, Oriental rugs, and artwork, we reinvested in our real estate operation.

Life with Susan was good. If I attended an AA meeting in the evening, I hurried to get home. Our business grew so rapidly we rented an office on University Avenue, a main artery in Little Rock. Weary of commuting over a twisting, twenty-minute drive to our little house in the country, we moved into the city. Only six months after we were married, Susan and I bought a house at 2 Shadow Lane in the Heights, a popular neighborhood in Little Rock. We paid $74,000 for a two-story brick house with four bedrooms and two and a half baths. The building had been neglected over the years and needed work. Using her gift for decoration, Susan had the house renovated. I didn't realize it at the time, but this home would be the finest place I ever lived.

Even though we enjoyed our home life, the great chefs of Amer-ica had nothing to fear from our competition. I could barely boil water, and Susan burned the first chicken dish she tried to prepare after we married. We ate all our meals out.

The Clintons lived in the Lower Heights, in a tasteful Swiss cot-tage. We saw them often. Occasionally, I visited with Bill at the attorney general's office. He had a receptionist whom we both admired. Beyond talk of women, Bill discussed his ambition to run for higher office, and wondered whether he should run for governor or senator in 1978.

Jim Guy Tucker, serving his first term as a congressman in Washington, was also restless, looking for another political office himself. Bill knew that Jim Guy wanted to run for either governor or senator, and a rivalry soon developed between these two progressive, eastern-educated men. I wanted to maintain my neutrality, but it was becoming more difficult. Their egos made it impossible for one to accept the other.

Although Arkansas had nurtured several powerful politicians at the same time, suddenly it seemed as though the state was not big enough to hold both Bill and Jim Guy. In their bids for high office, they turned their followers into factions inside the Democratic Party. With little subtlety, Bill strived to cut off Jim Guy's re-entry from Washington, and Jim Guy tried to use the prestige of Congress to eclipse Bill.

One Saturday morning in 1977, Clinton was at our house, lolling on the floor and dominating the conversation—making himself completely at home, as was his habit. Jim Guy had returned to Little Rock for the weekend, and he dropped by, unannounced. Although we had been together in groups, it was the first time I had been with the two of them privately, and it was a thoroughly miserable experience. The atmosphere grew charged. When Jim Guy walked through the door, Clinton reminded me of a house cat acting indignant when a new cat shows up. He and Jim Guy engaged in a painfully forced conversation, with hollow laughter and brittle bonhomie.

Publicly, Bill and Jim Guy projected the appearance of Democratic allies, but they could not stand each other. After Jim Guy's election to Congress, I had made an arrangement with him to hire Susan's sister Paula for a job in his district office in Little Rock. I knew he was tightfisted with his expenses and told Jim Guy that if he paid Paula three hundred dollars a month I would provide the balance of her salary. When I later mentioned the deal, in passing, to Clinton, he seized on it. "Tucker's not paying minimum wage," he said. As attorney general, Clinton said he wanted to conduct an investigation. It took some persuasion, but I talked him out of it.

It became a burden to talk to them. When I saw one or the other, I would be subjected to their soliloquies, talking of each other's perfidy and their own political dreams. Susan and I tried to make the best of the awkward situation when we were thrown together with the other two couples.

My own life was shaken when I discovered a document while cleaning out a drawer at home. It showed that Susan had been admitted to a Little Rock hospital at a time when she had told me she had gone to Camden to visit her mother. The piece of paper made me curious, but I was also troubled by what it might mean. I wanted nothing to jeopardize my marriage, but I had to ask Susan about it.

She flushed when I showed her the hospital document, but she didn't try to lie. Susan was never good at lying. I think she knew that when she tried to shade the truth, her words were unconvincing. She took a breath, then told me she'd had an abortion as an outpatient. Embarrassed, she explained that her mother had encouraged her. Lauretta had warned Susan that she was too young to be tied to a baby, and that she had not been married long enough to start bearing my children.

She attempted to pass it off as inconsequential, as if we could plan more carefully for a baby, as if there would be a next time. I felt a numbness spreading through my body. Childless and approaching middle age, I felt I should have had a part in her decision.

The more I thought of Susan's explanation of her mother's role, the more infuriated I became. I felt Lauretta was the matriarch of one of the most dysfunctional families I had ever seen—presiding over a house full of screaming kids—and I told Susan her mother had no grounds to judge our marriage or to dictate Susan's decisions in the matter of our children.

I was mad, but even more so, I was hurt. As an only child, I had wanted children. I yearned for a larger family, a wider range of friends. My desire for closer associates had drawn me to my business partners, and to my friends from the political world, people like the Hamilton twins, the Rileys, the Clintons, and the Tuckers. I held Victorian beliefs about abortion. Although I supported a woman's right to choose, as a political position, I deplored the concept. In this case, it involved my own offspring, whom I desperately wanted. And Susan hadn't even mentioned that she was pregnant. I couldn't help conjuring up images of blood and gore.

By nature, I am an impulsive character, quick to draw conclusions and make decisions. On that day, my desire for Susan perished. We would continue to live and work together, to share good times and bad. But in many ways, our marriage ended the day I found the hospital admission slip.

A talk that had started with a question had turned into an ugly argument. When it was finished, I went into another room. It's over, I thought. Whether it's a building project or a personal relationship, when I decide I've finished something, I put it out of mind. But on this occasion, I felt terribly sad. As I sat alone, I remembered an old expression: "All moonbeams turn to worms and crawl away into the night."*

Tension between Clinton and Tucker continued to build. When it appeared both might run for the Senate seat, opened by McClellan's death in November 1977, I tried to avert a collision. I joked to them separately that if they ran against each other, I would join the race as their competitor and tell the public everything I knew about both of them. Finally I encouraged Clinton to run for governor. I told

---

* A close friend of the McDougals doubts Susan had an abortion and says that it was Jim, fearful of passing down his family's tendency toward manic-depressive behavior, who was doubtful about parenting. It appears indisputable—whatever the reason—that Susan and Jim ceased living as man and wife early in their marriage.

Tucker, three years older than Clinton, that he should seek the Senate seat. In the end, those were the races they chose and a confrontation was averted—for a few years.

The 1978 campaigns drew me back into a supporting role for my two friends. During the Democratic primary, I drove Jim Guy around the Ozark country in north Arkansas. Since the hill people thought of him as a city boy from Little Rock, I acted as Jim Guy's ambassador, introducing him to my friends in the region who might be helpful to his candidacy. Jim Guy didn't fit in. He looked, indeed, as though he had gone to Harvard, and he failed to relate to these people. When we met country women on the street, Jim Guy would blurt, "I consider this the most critical Senate race in fifty years," instead of making connections ("Well, you must be Bob Brown's cousin") or telling homespun anecdotes or discussing the weather. Jim Guy couldn't "shoot a line of talk," as the balladeer Jimmie Rodgers once said.

I made calls on his behalf and offered a generous campaign contribution. But Jim Guy finished a poor third in a race won by David Pryor. I figured Jim Guy's political career was finished.

On the other hand, Clinton sailed to election. He faced no serious opposition for the Democratic nomination, and encountered little resistance from the Republicans in the general election.

I was delighted by the prospect of having an ally in the governor's mansion again. Pryor, who had held the office for four years, had never been close. I didn't dislike Pryor; we simply kept winding up in different camps. He had made the run against McClellan in 1972 and had beat Bob Riley for governor two years later. To help ensure Clinton's advantage in the 1978 race, I used my pocketbook as well as my manpower. Although there was a fifteen-hundred-dollar limit on individual contributions, a loophole in the law enabled Susan and me to funnel nine thousand dollars to Bill's campaign through a series of six fifteen-hundred-dollar contributions from our various business entities. Bill was always grateful. At the bottom of one form letter thanking contributors, he wrote me a facetious yet prophetic message: "You are a great American who will live long in the hearts of your countrymen, your words carved in stone by devoted followers and members of the prison work gang."

I had helped Clinton's personal finances in 1977 when I'd suggested that he buy a tract of land in the Saltillo Heights project Fulbright and I had developed. We had bought the land for $100 an acre; now we were selling it for $350 an acre. I stood to make a profit on the sale to Clinton, but I was convinced he would do well himself.

"You'll make some money," I told him. He knew Fulbright was involved, and that was reassuring. Even though Clinton didn't have much money, he took me up on the deal. As I recall, he put about $500 down in cash and paid $100 a month on a note. We gave him one of the most attractive sites, and his lots sold within a year or so. Clinton received about $5,000 for a $2,800 investment.

Though Clinton was pleased with the return, he never cared much about money. He was a consummate political animal, preferring to build friendships and collect personal IOUs to advance his career. Business interests were secondary to him. Most investors would have gone to look at their property; Clinton never visited the land. To Clinton, it was like owning a share of stock. If the investment made a profit, it would make his personal finances more comfortable. But it never got him excited.

In early 1978, Susan and I decided to spend a weekend in Eureka Springs, deep in Ozark country, but a heavy snowfall buried the region while we were there and ruined our plans to trek around the hillsides. Confined to our motel with only the morning newspaper for entertainment, I found my eyes drawn to an advertisement offering twelve hundred acres of land for sale for $100 an acre in Marion County. I called the broker, but he was unable to tell me precisely where the property was located. It was made up of scattered parcels in a rural area near the Missouri state line, he said, and he gave me general directions. When the roads were cleared, Susan and I drove to Marion County to take a look. It was a beautiful wilderness, with soaring forests and small, unspoiled lakes. The price struck me as a fantastic bargain.

"Do you see anything here that's not worth a hundred dollars an acre?" I asked Susan.

She shook her head, as enthusiastic about the land as I.

At the end of the weekend, we drove back to Little Rock, and on Monday we bought the property.

After the transfer was formalized, Susan and I made the three-hour trip back to Marion County. Because of the distance from Little Rock, we needed to find an agent to resell the land for us. We visited several local brokers before stopping at Ozarks Realty in the town of Flippin.

We were greeted by a pleasant, moonfaced man who introduced himself as Chris Wade. He was suffering from an allergy attack. Between sneezes, he offered his background. He was a native of the region, and Ozarks Realty was a local, mom-and-pop operation run by Chris and his wife. Because of my own history of poor health, I immediately identified with his allergy problems, and as we talked it became apparent he was exactly what we needed.

Some country realtors take a relaxed attitude toward business. Not Chris. Within a week, he moved several parcels for us. The entire project sold out within six months, creating a profit of more than $100,000 for Susan and me, and a handsome commission for Chris. We were high on Marion County and high on our local real estate agent.

Knowing of our elation, Chris called to tell us about another piece of land in Marion County, 230 acres of Ozark forests fed by the coursing waters of the White River. The owners wanted a little less than $900 an acre—a total of $203,000. Susan and I returned to north Arkansas to inspect the land. One dirt road, running off a state highway, enabled us to look at part of the property by Jeep. Chris had a small airplane, and he flew us over the inaccessible stretches. We inspected the land closely, giving it more study than any other vast tract of land we had bought.

The land was bordered by the White River, an excellent trout stream and a picturesque waterway for canoes. I was attracted by the river because I had been successful on every project that had water frontage. To improve my earlier developments that lacked natural water resources, I'd dammed gulleys to create man-made lakes. This property looked far more splendid than the twelve hundred acres we had recently bought and sold so easily in Marion County.

High bluffs overlooked the river. I thought these tracts would attract buyers who wanted a water view but didn't want to live beside the water. Nearly all the property was covered with hardwood timber, oak and maple trees that burned with color in the fall, and a few ponds had been there since the last Ice Age. The air was pure—there was no industry within miles—and the setting pristine. Susan and I were convinced that this was premium property. We discussed how the land could be promoted. Susan was already imagining the advertising copy: "Nestled beside a beautiful, raging river . . ." We laughed.

We had been back in Little Rock less than a week when we went out to dinner at the Black Eyed Pea, a family restaurant near our house. As we stepped inside, we ran into Bill and Hillary, and the four of us took a table. The Black Eyed Pea specialized in chicken-fried steak, turnip greens, and peas. As we sat with the Clintons, the waitress brought us iced tea in large glasses. In this down-home setting, the seeds of a national scandal were planted.

As we waited for dinner to arrive, we talked of Bill's success. He was a solid favorite to win the governor's race. Susan and I told the Clintons of our own good fortune, the Marion County property we had just inspected, and our dreams for a profitable development on the banks of the White River. We felt it would appeal to buyers who visited the Ozarks regularly, especially vacationers from places as far away as Illinois and Minnesota.

The Clintons were interested in our idea, and without a moment's hesitation, we invited Bill and Hillary to join us in the venture. We were fond of them, and as governor and first lady of

Arkansas they would give the project cachet. The conversation about the property lasted no more than five minutes, and it was so casual that even now, in the eye of controversy, I can't recall all of the details. I remember that the Clintons accepted the offer instantly. Bill had nearly doubled his money in his other investment with me. But a businessman's blood did not run in his veins. He simply smiled and said, "Okay," as though agreeing to buy a potted plant.

Hillary was more enthusiastic. She clutched Bill's arm, remarking that the investment sounded like a terrific idea. Her eyes brightened with excitement over the prospect of getting a piece of the action in the development.

Susan was happy, too. She told the Clintons she already had a name for the project. It would be called Whitewater.

9

L ike the goddess Athena, sprung full-grown from the forehead of Zeus, Bill Clinton was born ready for political battle. He had a God-given gift for recalling names, making associations, and establishing empathy with people. His ability to speak extemporaneously was not learned at the feet of Arkansas politicians possessing quick wit and tongue; Bill's rhetorical skills came naturally. Though he had an easygoing manner characteristic of the region, Bill's style was not innately southern. His travels during the years he attended school on the East Coast and England made him far more cosmopolitan than the average educated Arkansan.

I always believed Bill could just as easily have been elected governor of Connecticut, where he went to law school, as Arkansas. In his student days, Bill had taken positions on two burning issues—civil rights and the Vietnam War—that would have been almost suicidal for a politician in Arkansas. Even as Jim Johnson continued to light fires with his segregationist speeches in the late 1960s, Bill was beginning to speak out for equal rights. As a Georgetown student, he ferried relief to beleaguered black neighborhoods in Washington during the riots after Martin Luther King's assassination in 1968. Not only had Bill campaigned for Fulbright, he had led demonstrations against the war in London while a Rhodes scholar. By the time he was in his mid-twenties, Bill had built up an enviable network of increasingly influential friends across the country. He probably could have staked out a political future anywhere. But Arkansas was his home, and the state's politics were in transition. As our automobile license plates once suggested, Arkansas was indeed a "land of opportunity" for bright young politicians, and Clinton chose familiar ground to make his start.

Within five years, he elevated himself from an untenured teaching position at the law school to the governor's office. Though unsuccessful in his first congressional race, he parlayed his intelligence and appealing personality to win election as attorney general the year he turned thirty. Two years later, Clinton became the youngest governor the country had seen in decades.

Bill looked even more boyish than his years, with his choir-boy cheeks and ready grin. At the time, Clinton's youth and progressive background so enamoured the national Democrats that they showcased him at the party's midterm convention in Memphis in December 1978, before he even took office. At the same conference, Senator Ted Kennedy issued his call for the party to "sail against the wind" on the issue of national health insurance, firing his first public shot at Jimmy Carter, the sitting president.

Nobody, neither the Democrats nor Clinton, had a premonition of the bloodletting that lay ahead over the next two years. But there had been an omen of doom in Arkansas. Jim Ranchino, my friend and Clinton's pollster, had collapsed and died of a heart attack on election night in Little Rock. Despite the loss of Ranchino, the situation seemed fresh and promising as Clinton assembled a team to help him run the state.

Following his election, I called Clinton and asked, "You got anything you want me to do?" He seemed enthusiastic about having me in his administration and asked one of his top aides, Steve Smith, to fit me into a position. Steve was even younger than Bill. From Huntsville, in the northwestern corner of the state, Steve had run Bill's congressional campaign in 1974. After Bill was elected attorney general, Steve had come to Little Rock as his aide at the Justice Department, even though he had no law degree. One day, when I dropped by Clinton's office for one of my periodic chats with Bill, I wound up having a long talk with Steve, in which two populists cussed the tycoons and lamented the closed banking situation in the state. Despite our age difference, we discovered we were kindred spirits.

With Clinton preparing to take over the governor's office, Steve was in charge of finding people to serve as liaisons to the various departments in state government. I agreed to handle the Bank Department, but Steve loaded me up with other jobs. He made me liaison with the Highway Department, the Securities Department, and the Arkansas Industrial Development Commission, the state's major economic agency. On top of that, Clinton assigned me responsibility for dealing with the state Senate.

At the ripe old age of thirty-eight, I found myself the éminence grise of the governor's staff. My salary was $28,000, not nearly as much as I was making in real estate, but I thought the experience would be worth it. Clinton brought several other friends into the office, bright and breezy guys who were full of ideas hatched in the groves of academe: Rudy Moore, a Fayetteville connection, and John Danner, one of Bill's college buddies. Danner's wife, Nancy Pietrafesa, became the only woman to hold a substantive job in the governor's office. Nancy kept her maiden name, as did Hillary.

At times, it seemed the first Clinton administration specialized in offending Arkansas values. In those days, about the only place you could find a beard in Arkansas was on a can of Prince Albert Tobacco. But Steve, Rudy, and John all wore beards. Rudy also had a white man's version of an Afro haircut even though he was going bald. Susan thought Rudy's hair was cute and naturally curly, but I told her, "Baby, let me tell you, since I'm getting to be an expert on baldness, myself: that Afro is just another subterfuge."

If those three guys had tried, they could not have designed hair styles to rankle the legislators more. Folks around the capitol began to refer to them, collectively and derisively, as "the Beards."

The key members of Clinton's staff were all men, and the place began to take on the trappings of a fraternity house. Guys wandered in and out of Bill's office willy-nilly. It was all very collegial and pleasant, but no way to run the state's executive suite.

Clinton failed to appoint anyone to direct the flow of traffic, yet he needed order in the worst way. Like most politicians, Bill was undisciplined about time and space, and much more disorganized than the garden-variety officeholder. I can't remember Bill arriving on time for any appointment. When out campaigning, he was reluctant to move to the next event in a timely fashion. If his audience liked him at one stop, maybe he thought that the next stop would be a disappointment. Lord knows, he needed to have everyone love him. In the governor's office, his daily schedule unraveled before noon. Unfortunately, he didn't function well in the mornings. After conducting bull sessions at the governor's mansion into the wee hours of the morning, he would arrive at work looking sleepy and out of sorts.

David Maraniss's biography of Clinton offers a couple of stories that demonstrated the office problems. One involved a Clinton aide who saw an advertisement in the Little Rock newspaper: "Will you commit larceny today? You could be stealing from someone important to you. If you steal time, someone else suffers." The assistant tore it out and gave it to Clinton, who laughed but kept stealing time.

The situation was so exasperating that when the governor's receptionist sent Rudy Moore a note warning, "Security downstairs is holding a guy who said he was sent here to kill the governor," Rudy quickly passed the note to the assistant handling Clinton's schedule with a request: "See if you can work him in."

Clinton's loose style of governing extended to the evenings. He used the governor's mansion to hold meetings, and he'd invite his aides, friends, and hangers-on to come for dinner and stay awhile. Hillary was not much of a presence at the capitol, but she would often sit in on the talks at the mansion. The meetings might start with a formal agenda, but the governor and his guests would soon slide into discussions of current books and films and recollections of whatever interested them.

Since neither the Clintons nor their friends consumed much alcohol, they must have been energized by ideas during these long nights of conversation. It was too much for me. Before I took my job, I reached an understanding with Clinton. I told him, "Bill, I just can't stay up all night. You know I'm an alcoholic and I have to have a regular amount of sleep. There are certain things I can't do."

Clinton was known to have a terrible temper that he would occasionally vent on his assistants. He often shouted and tossed papers around in anger, but the tantrum always passed quickly, like a summer thunderstorm. Perhaps it was because I was six years older, but he never talked to me like I was his employee. We never had a cross word.

Bill brought his attractive receptionist from the attorney general's office to the capitol, but at Hillary's insistence, she was banished to the basement, out of sight and, it was hoped, out of Bill's mind. That didn't prevent Bill and the boys from ogling female visitors. The governor knew better than to emit a wolf whistle, but he would surreptitiously raise his eyebrows to acknowledge a particularly handsome lady passing by.

One night at the governor's mansion, when Hillary was not at home, Bill hosted a party following a movie. It was a scene straight from my teenage years in Bradford, with girls flirting with guys, and vice versa. I remember a pretty young woman named Dolly Kyle, a classmate of Bill's in Hot Springs, playing a pinball machine in the basement. Other of Bill's old flames showed up from time to time.

He told Susan he marveled at one perquisite of the governor's office: after his high school years as a slightly plump, unathletic member of the band, he now could attract the interests of pretty women. I thought it curious that one attractive young woman worked as a volunteer in the governor's office even though her husband was fighting with Clinton over a waste-disposal site. It did seem that women were drawn to him.

Susan, who had begun managing our real estate business, came to the governor's office suite almost every day. I hated the Dictaphone machine and preferred to let her handle my business letters. She enjoyed the atmosphere at the capitol, and sometimes she created a stir herself. She didn't wear short shorts or miniskirts, but her clothes left little to the imagination. She had a good figure, and in the summer she flaunted it with low-cut dresses. If I knew Clinton was grumpy, I'd tell Susan, "Go in and see Bill. It will make him feel better."

I could usually disarm him with humor. When I found him fretting one day over a small problem, I began quoting Churchill's words from D-day: "Never in the field of human conflict was so much owed by so many to so few." Bill thought my imitations were funny as hell. He'd often call in another aide and insist that I repeat my performance. I always felt comfortable pointing out to Bill the absurdity of certain situations he took seriously.

Hillary recognized the chemistry between Bill and me; she appreciated my ability to make him laugh. She once told Susan, "I really like it when Jim goes in to see Bill because it makes him feel good." He and I had been political allies for a decade. We had come of age during the Faubus era, seen the repudiation of racial politics with the defeats of Jim Johnson, and witnessed the rise of the Republican Party in the state. We both realized we were players in a transitional period in Arkansas history.

One of the first issues Clinton tackled involved a multimillion-dollar program to improve the state highway system. Because of a scandal thirty years earlier in the McMath administration, when Truman

Baker and Faubus served on the highway commission, the department had been made independent of the governor's office. During Clinton's first administration, Henry Gray was in charge of the Highway Department, and I found him a tough and impressive figure in negotiations. Gray shared our interest in improving the highways, but the projects demanded money the state did not have.

The trucking industry—centered in Springdale, the home of the giant poultry producer Tyson Foods—was clamoring for a higher weight limit. Their trucks could pull eighty thousand pounds in neighboring states but were restricted to seventy-three thousand pounds in Arkansas. The higher loads would, of course, pound the highways into even poorer conditions, and Gray resisted a weight increase.

To find new sources of revenue for the rebuilding program, we constantly reviewed several options. One plan called for increased fees for the eighteen-wheelers in exchange for raising the weight limit. Another recommended a raise in the cost of car license plates, an annual fee that was already an irritant to every car owner. The plates cost only fifteen dollars, but car owners were forced to visit the state revenue office in their home county to obtain a renewal each year. At one meeting to discuss the issue at the governor's mansion, I suggested to Gray, "Look, I've got a Mercedes. You should charge me fifty bucks, and let me and everyone else renew by mail. Let's start charging on the value of the cars." I thought it was a simple and progressive solution, but other forces were at work.

The trucking industry, which had a powerful lobby in Little Rock, applied intense pressure to avoid paying their full share for the highway improvements. As it turned out, the automobile owners had nobody watching out for their interests, and failed to realize until too late that they would be asked to foot much of the highway bill.

In a decision that would characterize his style of leadership forever, Clinton came down on both sides. He signed off on a plan that would raise the truckers' fees slightly but give them the higher weight limit. At the same time, the price of the license plates went up.

I have come to realize through the years that Clinton's worst decisions have occurred when he has tried to be all things to all people, instead of taking a principled stand. Given his craving for approval, he has always sought some sort of compromise to ensure everyone's happiness. The process has rarely placated anyone.

Under the new car-licensing arrangement, assessments were based on weight, not value, and folks stuck with older, heavier models wound up having to pay higher fees than those owning lighter, newer cars. There was hell to pay the next year after car owners went to the revenue office and found they had to shell out more money for the same car—one year older and less valuable—than the year before. When they complained, the revenue officers told them, "Don't blame us, blame the governor."

The state workers were happy to direct anger at Clinton. They disliked him because he had tried to impose austerity on the system by cutting their expense accounts and reducing their number of days off to streamline state government.

Clinton's first year in office, 1979, was a time of belt-tightening across America. President Carter symbolically lowered thermostats and turned off the lights at monuments around Washington. A bona fide energy crisis gripped the land, and long lines of motorists clogged service stations. While Carter set the tone, concerns over the consumption of energy trickled down to the state and local levels.

One of the Arkansas legislative committees took a hard look at the mileage expenses run up by Russ Perrymore, a Clinton aide. Since I had prevailed upon Bill, when he was attorney general, to hire Russ in the first place, I was asked to check on the situation. It turned out that Bill and Hillary had been sending Russ around the state on personal errands, running up his expenses.

When I talked to him about the matter, I asked, "What am I supposed to tell the legislators, Russ?"

"Hell, tell them I'm prepared to take a lie-detector test," he said. "I'll say exactly how many thousands of miles I drove around for Bill and Hillary, going up to Fayetteville to pick up a suit, stuff like that."

The governor's office decided to quash the investigation. Russ was taken off the driving detail and appointed to the state athletic commission, a position that gave him a free pass to the wrestling matches. Russ loved the weekly spectacles at Robinson Auditorium, where Arkansans drove in from the boondocks to whoop at the vicious tactics of the villains and to cheer for the golden boys in the wrestling ring.

Clinton became more circumspect about dispatching aides on personal missions, and his top staff members grew obsessed over the conservation of energy. The issue triggered my only disagreements with Steve Smith. When Steve proposed to stop mowing the right-of-way along the highways in order to save fuel, I told him that was pretty dumb; the highways looked ragged if the right-of-way wasn't mowed. But Steve and other members of Clinton's staff had become environmental zealots.

They began overhauling the fleet of state-owned vehicles from full-size to compact in an effort to cut fuel consumption. Henry Gray, the highway chief, argued it was foolish to try to stuff a road crew, carrying all their gear, into a small pickup. He wanted Travel-Alls, a six-seat model similar to today's sports vehicles, for his department. Steve insisted that everyone use economy vehicles.

To resolve the conflict I said to Henry, "Look, we can't go through this whole administration with you and the governor's office at sword's point. I know some of these guys have idiosyncrasies, but I think Steve Smith's enough of a politician to understand a quid pro quo." I suggested that Henry undertake a road project in Madison County, which was Steve's home. Then I went to see Steve. "Show me a section of road in the state highway system in Madison County that needs paving and I'll get it paved," I said. Steve looked at the map and picked out a seven-mile stretch. It was not heavily traveled, and had no priority to be paved. But it was Steve's choice. Henry got his Travel-Alls.

It was typical of Clinton's first term that the governor lost out on the deal. One day he was riding around Madison County on the freshly paved highway, a lonely stretch that probably saw no more than ten cars a day. Bill spied a hillbilly woman sitting on her porch with several of her children and asked his driver to stop. "This woman's going to love me," the governor predicted. He walked to the porch to introduce himself, expecting praise for the paving work. Instead, the woman moaned, "This road plumb took over my yard."

Early in the administration, I did my bit to cut costs after I discovered that the Arkansas Industrial Development Commission had hired an outfit called Tropical Galleries of Little Rock to provide decorative plants for the department offices. The AIDC was paying $450 a month to rent plants—to rent plants, for God's sake; they were not even buying them.

I instructed the Department of Finance and Administration to withhold state payments to the florist and to take the cost from the salary of the office director, Jim Dyke.

Ordinarily, I got along with Dyke, even though he was a modern version of the silk-stocking crowd in Little Rock that Jeff Davis, our populist governor, upbraided at the turn of the century. Dyke was a real patrician, one of these guys who handled his fork in the European way—eating with the left hand, and holding the fork upside down with his index finger clutching the spine.

Clinton introduced me to Dyke at a postelection reception, telling me he thought Dyke would be good at attracting economic development to the state. With his high-brow tastes, he could move easily with the captains of industry, Bill said. But rented plants were foolish. Not only did I stop payment on the Tropical Galleries voucher, I saw that the item made its way to the hands of John R.

Starr, a conservative columnist for the *Arkansas Democrat* who had been kicking the crap out of the Clinton administration.

It won a bouquet for both Clinton and me.

"McDougal is a country boy from Bradford who spent a lot of his youth with grass poking between his bare toes," Starr wrote. "A city boy might not have been as responsive to the ridiculousness of spending $450 a month for greenery. The proposed expenditure, McDougal said, flies in the face of Gov. Bill Clinton's desire to hold state spending to the essentials."

When the legislature convened, I found myself back in my old element, though for some reason I had been asked to bird-dog the Senate instead of the House, where I had good relations with a number of the senior members whose service dated from my stint there twenty years earlier.

The session was not as exciting as the old days, and often we had trouble getting our message across. Clinton wanted to ensure passage of a special bill giving one of his buddies permission to open a liquor store in a tiny community. We bungled the assignment so badly that the legislature wound up authorizing three liquor stores in the same town and Clinton's pal got two unwanted competitors.

On another occasion, I was handling a bill to set up a state small-business investment corporation, working with Nick Wilson, an eccentric wheeling-and-dealing senator. When Wilson was called upon to defend the legislation, he spotted me and announced, "This is all complicated. There's Mr. McDougal, he'll explain it." It was like a pop test in college, and I struggled with the questions. The legislators were upset because the bill represented competition for the bankers; the legislature historically supported anything bankers wanted. I was trying to handle a volley of questions and couldn't hear everything in the uproar. A black senator, Jerry Jewell, got mad as hell when I didn't respond to his question. "You're hearing the white guys, okay," he snapped.

As Senate liaison, I was also stuck with the task of handing out passes to the racetrack in Hot Springs. It became just as big a pain in the butt as I remembered from years past, with members and their constituents pleading for passes.

But the job had its rewarding moments. Clinton asked Maurice Smith, his chief fund-raiser, to work with me in the Senate. I was fond of Maurice. He commanded enormous respect because of his wealth, background, and manners. His family owned about thirty thousand acres of valuable Delta land in Cross County, so that automatically gave him certain credentials among legislators from the poorer counties. About twenty years older than I, Maurice had attended the University of Arkansas when Fulbright was president of the school. Since Maurice was known as Clinton's money man, senators listened in the rare instances when he talked. He was the only man I ever met who was more taciturn than my father. His voice had a deep croak that you had to strain to hear.

Maurice had one affectation—he wore an old Stetson hat that must have been a quarter century old. The Stetson had been rolled up, creased, and beaten down over the years. I wore a homburg around the capitol, myself. Clinton said that when he looked at us, he became more interested in our headgear than the issues of the day.

While his staff had clumsy moments, the governor was skillful at working the legislature. He wandered the corridors of the capitol, with a cup of coffee in hand, buttonholing the state reps and senators to push certain items. He was always ready to give an informal hearing to their own measures, projecting the air of a big, friendly dog, anxious to please. He excelled at one-on-one negotiations.

The only time I saw his vindictive side involved a measure to help a bank in Hot Springs, the town where he grew up. Bill got a big kick out of blocking it. "I really enjoyed sticking it to those bastards," he told me. "One time when we were really desperate, my mother went in there and they wouldn't give her a loan."

Generally, the legislators liked doing business with Clinton because he operated on their level. Although the members of the legislature were more urbane than the crowd I knew in 1959, many of the state reps still came from the country. Clinton's eggheads, who were assigned as liaison to the House, couldn't understand them. While the legislators wanted to talk deals, the highly educated assistants to the governor preferred to discuss the nuances of public policy.

Guys in the House came to me, complaining they couldn't communicate with Clinton's liaisons. They begged me to intervene. One representative, Jerry King, pleaded: "You're the only one I can talk to." I had to tell him I was locked into the bureaucracy and could only work with senators. "The Beards" felt that by compartmentalizing our legislative chores it would bring order to the administration. Clinton's own success at informal give-and-take should have proved otherwise. Some of Clinton's aides were downright obnoxious, brushing off the country fellows in the House.

Vada Sheid, a tireless senator I had known since my Fulbright days, tried to break protocol. Pushing an education bill, she refused to discuss it with Clinton's liaison on education issues. She stopped Bill at his office door one day and told him, "Governor, I'd rather discuss this with Mr. McDougal. I like the sound of his voice."

"Lady, you're going to get me fired," I said. Bill laughed, in the loud, braying manner of a backslapping legislator.

Although Hillary made an effort to blend into Arkansas, taking on traces of a southern accent, she never quite fit into a culture heavily dependent on homespun humor and storytelling. At dinner one night at the governor's mansion, Steve Smith regaled us with a string of funny Arkansas tales and anecdotes about local politicians. With everyone else convulsed with laughter, Hillary sat there, tight-lipped.

She did not care for Steve. On the rare occasions when she visited the governor's office, she carped at him. Hillary had been critical since he'd worked for Bill at the attorney general's office. Steve appealed to the good ol' boy nature in Bill, a side that made Hillary uncomfortable. She preferred the company of the more sophisticated people on the staff, Rudy Moore and John Danner and his wife, Nancy.

Steve told me Hillary felt he was not a conceptual thinker, like his other bearded colleagues. Hillary's attitude hurt Steve; he had been having a hard time, working his way through a divorce and enduring public criticism because of some of his ideas.

While on Clinton's staff, I, too, had an unpleasant brush with Hillary. Knowing of my background in preparing income tax returns, Bill took me aside one day. "Hillary and Jim Blair made a bunch of money on the stock market," he confided. He didn't give any details, and I assumed Hillary had bought some shares in a venture company that produced a nice return. Maybe a few thousand dollars, like the profit Bill realized from his land deal with me. Bill seemed concerned about the tax implications of Hillary's investment, and mentioned the possibility of finding a tax shelter. This seemed a bit odd, considering the Clintons' finances. Even with two salaries, they could not have been making $100,000 a year at the time. I wondered why they would need a tax shelter.

I agreed to help Hillary find a write-off. She and I met at the capitol and drove downtown to see Charles Owen, a tax lawyer I had known since our days in the Young Democrats. As the meeting began, Hillary explained that commodities were the source of her windfall, but she didn't say how much money she had made. I asked Charles about putting the Clintons into one of the popular tax write-offs of the day, investing in a limited partnership in a gold mine. He said my scheme wouldn't work.

We failed to reach a resolution during the brief meeting, and as Hillary and I drove back, I casually asked how much money was at stake. When she said, softly, that she had cleared $100,000 on a small investment, I was astounded.

Driving up the hill to the capitol, I grew agitated as she laid out the mechanics of her deal. Hillary had made a $1,000 investment with Blair in October 1978, two months after she and Bill became partners with Susan and me in the Whitewater development. The money was applied to cattle contracts, and she cashed those out in less than two weeks, netting a profit of $8,000. Through Blair, she reinvested in more contracts and reaped even greater profits. By the time Hillary closed her account in July 1979, she had cleared $100,000—a 100-to-1 return on her investment in less than a year.

Several things troubled me. I knew fortunes were made and lost overnight in commodity trading, but the magnitude of her return and the tidy, round number—$100,000—defied belief. I had been taught by my family that commodities were not only dangerous, but a device by big-money interests to screw the farmers. Furthermore, I harbored suspicions about Blair, her adviser in the commodity market.

Although Blair and I had worked together in political battles, from the Young Democrats to the campaigns for Fulbright and Clinton, I felt increasingly estranged by his moves in the business world. He seemed to have forsaken his roots as a poor boy in northwest Arkansas, where he had been raised by his grandparents. After making his way, as a big man on campus, through the University of Arkansas, Blair had polished his rough edges and taken the title of general counsel of Tyson Foods. These days, he hung out at the country club instead of the country store.

I had coined a nickname for Blair. When I talked about him with Susan, I called Blair the "Main Chancer," a fellow on the make. He had become good friends with Bill and Hillary in Fayetteville, serving as a key fund-raiser for Clinton's first political campaign. Later, Blair married Diane Kincaid, a political science professor at the university, one of Hillary's best friends.

As Hillary described Blair's record of success in the commodities market, I smoldered. I had heard Blair was in league with a broker named "Red" Bone, a high-stakes gambler with a questionable reputation around Fayetteville. Both Bone and Blair had been privy to the ebb and flow of Tyson's massive chicken and egg shipments;

accordingly, they were in position to take advantage of this information on the commodities market, where there are few prohibitions against insider trading. Bone, who traded for Tyson as well as himself, could anticipate when the egg market would be glutted and invested accordingly. When the commodities regulators had handed Bone a year's suspension for manipulating egg futures, Blair had represented him.

After the egg reprimand, Bone and Blair turned to the cattle market, where they were again privy to inside information from Bone's new employer, Ray E. Friedman & Co., a commodities brokerage house. "There was a great fortune to be made in cattle," Blair later testified, and he enticed Hillary to invest in what was literally a bull market.

While Bone was advising Blair—and, by extension, Hillary—on the investments in the cattle market, I later learned that Blair gave Bone a tip. He told his buddy the Clintons had invested in some land in Marion County. Bone proceeded to buy a piece of property next to our Whitewater project.

I thought the whole business with Blair unsavory. Before we reached the capitol, I turned to Hillary and said, "Don't you understand it's gambling? That you shouldn't be able to make that much profit?"

Hillary was sheepish. "It really wasn't a risk, was it?" she asked.

I said Blair had probably used her contracts at the expense of some other poor sucker.

She blinked, as though she were an innocent, unable to understand the complexities of the commodities market. She spoke of "they" as if "they" were a just god overseeing the marketplace. She said, "If they made money, it would be properly recorded. And if there were losses, they would have to be handled."

"No, goddamnit," I responded. "They'd charge the loss to some sucker's discretionary account. That's the way they would do it."

The more we talked, the madder I became. It was the first time I'd exploded in front of Hillary.

"Goddamnit," I told her. "This is against everything I believe in. You're getting in with the 'Main Chancer,' and he and his buddies are cooking the books and screwing the farmers."

After we returned to the governor's office, Hillary must have told Bill of my anger because both of them treated me gingerly over the next few weeks.

I was annoyed with Hillary and weary of my job with Bill. I felt I had done all that I could do for him. My work had had an adverse impact on Susan. Our real estate operation had become static, and I had been inattentive to her interests. We had bought no new properties and there was not much movement with our old ones. It had been an especially unproductive year with the Whitewater project.

Susan was increasingly unhappy. She had few friends of her own, and I was away a lot. I suggested a change in routine to recapture the good times we had enjoyed in the years immediately after our marriage. Besides, I was ready to start making real money again.

Though I was fond of Clinton, his office seemed to have little of the magic of Fulbright's operation. I missed the wisdom of older men like Lee Williams and Jack Files. Clinton surrounded himself with young men with impressive educations but little common sense. Some of Bill's aides were so consumed with Ivy League public policy theories that they lost touch with the people of Arkansas.

As I neared my fortieth birthday, I felt it was time to move on. Susan and I made plans for new business pursuits outside Little Rock. I left on good terms with Clinton, but I soon realized that his future was endangered as I watched developments from a distance during the Democratic primary in May 1980. Clinton was opposed by a seventy-seven-year-old turkey farmer, Monroe Schwarzlose. In any other time, Schwarzlose would have been a joke. Even his name inspired mirth.

Yet Schwarzlose owned a country slyness. He knew how to needle Clinton, to get under his skin. Schwarzlose poked fun at one of

Steve Smith's environmental projects. The state had spent about $60,000 to buy chain saws to cut firewood. We had so many environmental enthusiasts in the governor's office that they probably hired ten guys who specialized in the purchase of environmentally pure chain saws. Touted as a bold effort to be energy efficient in Arkansas, the program made the news. But there was a problem. After all the publicity, only a couple of cords of firewood got cut. Schwarzlose divided sixty thousand by two and came up with an outrageous price for a stack of wood, suggesting that the state had spent $30,000 for a cord of wood that could be purchased for fifty bucks.

The press loved Schwarzlose and broadcast his contempt for Clinton across the state. A protest was growing, and when the old turkey farmer got 31 percent of the Democratic vote, I knew my friend Bill was in trouble.

10

Kismet brought me to Kingston. During the weekend Susan and I had spent in Eureka Springs in early 1978, the trip that led to our first purchase of land in Marion County, we had driven through Kingston, a quaint northwestern Arkansas village populated by no more than a couple of hundred people. I liked its looks, especially the unique architectural style of the Bank of Kingston. The building was covered with pressed tin inside and out, the exterior designed to look like cut stone. In an era when banks were being built to resemble automobile agencies, the Bank of Kingston was an antique artifact dating from 1911.

I thought no more about the place until a year later, when Jim Vaughn, a prominent Democrat from Madison County and a member of the Arkansas Industrial Development Commission, joined Steve Smith and me in a discussion of banks. After Vaughn mentioned that the bank in Kingston was for sale, I felt as if I had stumbled upon a secret. The little country institution I admired was available. It could serve as the outlet for my lifelong fantasies about banking.

Some boys want to grow up to be firemen or professional ball players. For years I wanted to be a banker, a people's banker. If I was unable, in the words of my childhood hero Huey P. Long, to let everyone "share the wealth," at least I could make money available to the working class in a small corner of Arkansas. I could extend loans to those who might be rejected elsewhere, treating every depositor, however humble, with courtesy. No one would be asked to beg for loans at my bank.

With a bank in my hands, I could carry on my father's tradition of offering credit to small farmers and realize the dream that Faubus had thwarted when his administration refused to give me a bank charter in Bradford.

The Kingston bank seemed the perfect solution to my search for a fresh start after life in Clinton's office. Steve Smith was interested as well. He had grown up a few miles from Kingston and wanted to go into business there.

The bank's price was a little more than $700,000. I talked not only with Steve, but with Jim Guy Tucker and Senator Fulbright about joining in the venture. Steve and his father came into the operation as equal partners with Susan and me. The Smiths put up about $300,000. In order to match that figure, we sold our home in Little Rock and obtained a loan for the balance. The Smiths and the McDougals each owned 43 percent of the bank. Tucker, who had been struggling as a lawyer since losing his bid for the Senate seat in 1978, and Fulbright put up the rest.

Susan did most of the paperwork to win approval of our purchase. She made the formal presentation before the Federal Deposit Insurance Corporation officials in Memphis, and we had no trouble on that level. Since I had been responsible for the appointment of the commissioner of the state Bank Department, I anticipated no problems in Little Rock.

After being stiffed by Faubus, it was good to have the right connections in state government.

Beverly Lambert, the father of my good friend David Lambert in Washington, had wanted the commissioner's job from the day Clinton took office. He visited me almost daily at the capitol. Lambert had a banking background and proper Democratic Party credentials. I thought he deserved the appointment, but Clinton kept hemming and hawing. The governor was being pulled in two directions—by my advice and by the big-time Arkansas bankers promoting their own candidate, a man likely to be more sympathetic to their interests. Finally, I went into Clinton's office and said, "Okay, Bill, I can't stand any more of Mr. Lambert coming around here with those big, pleading eyes. You either appoint him today, or I quit." Clinton laughed and said, "Get him down here."

Obviously, Mr. Lambert gave me no trouble on the acquisition of the Bank of Kingston. I took some papers over to his home and explained my interest in expediting our application. He said, "Oh, yeah, yeah. That'll be no problem." It was as simple as borrowing a cup of sugar.

In the fall of 1980, a time when I could tell that Clinton's re-election campaign was going down, the bank became ours. With our interests no longer tied to Clinton's political survival, Steve and I became absorbed with a new career, convinced that the bank had great potential.

In a related move, Steve, Jim Guy, and I had already acquired twenty-four hundred acres of scattered parcels of land from International Paper Co. in northern Arkansas. We bought it, sight unseen, for about ninety dollars an acre at a public auction. The property was spread across eight or ten counties, but Madison County was the geographic center of our land.

Shortly after we bought the property, Susan and I moved to Kingston to set up a sales office in another of the charming storefronts in town. It was an old barbershop, owned by the Bunch family, founders of the bank. I proposed to rent the building for ten dollars per month; they wanted twenty. That was the level of high finance in Kingston.

Despite the small-bore nature of the town, we had grand plans. The bank building had been neglected for years, so our first task was to restore it. Miraculously, we located the company that had supplied the original pressed tin and found that they could furnish matching squares to replace the damaged ones. We painted the building and knocked out the back wall to add office space.

We encouraged renovation in the town, gave loans for restoration work, and went so far as to paint some of the buildings on the town square that were owned by absentee landlords.

Steve and I developed the surrounding countryside, as well. We bought a beautiful piece of farmland that had been in cultivation for 150 years, with a pasture of green grass and clover that rolled down a hillside to meet the Kings River, a cold mountain stream. A sturdy barn, looking more permanent than the ramshackle facilities found on most southern farms, dominated the view from the highway, and we gave it a new coat of red paint to brighten the landscape.

For living quarters, Steve and I erected a couple of prefabricated buildings on the land. Susan had hated to leave our home on Shadow Lane in Little Rock, but she warmed to the little place in Kingston. Soon a double-wide trailer with two bedrooms became a comfortable home because of her deft touch.

Although Kingston was a hamlet, it served as a bustling trade center for the region. On weekdays, the street activity made Kingston seem like the home of several thousand people. A few stores did a thriving business, and the town was scenic enough to attract sketching classes from the University of Arkansas.

I became the chairman of the board of the institution we renamed Madison Bank & Trust Co. Steve was the president. Not bad for a couple of Arkansas populists. Subjected to ridicule for his environmental ideas, Steve had been increasingly unhappy at the governor's office. He had been divorced, and now he was back in his home county with a new wife, Julie Baldridge. Julie had been Clinton's press secretary, and she, too, had grown tired of the daily routine of defending the governor.

Steve and I loved sitting in our offices in the back of the bank building, exchanging shoptalk and savoring the idea of having our own financial institution. We no longer had to worry about the administration of the state of Arkansas. Informality was the word at the bank. I usually wore short-sleeve shirts without a coat or tie.

Since we were novice bankers, we hired an experienced chief operating officer, Gary Bunch, a big, jovial fellow who wore a cowboy hat and blue jeans all the time. The Bunches had not only founded the bank, they had been leaders in Kingston for generations. One of Gary's ancestors, Larkin Bunch, led a Confederate company during the Civil War. Folks around Kingston looked up to the Bunch family.

Our typical customers were farmers whose families had lived in the area for generations. They still held suspicions about city ways, but we did our best to allay their fears. If we erred, and a customer had to come to the bank to correct the problem, we gave him or her twenty dollars. Unsophisticated about money, most clung to the Depression-era mentality of rural Arkansas. Trying to save every penny they made, they kept cash squirreled away in safe-deposit boxes or pillowcases at home. They didn't trust the bank's solvency, and they didn't want to establish records that might reveal their true income to the Internal Revenue Service.

In our first year at the bank, interest rates soared well into the double digits. Certificates of deposit were paying 14 to 15 percent, and suddenly the people who had salted away their money in a box for years decided to take a risk. They began buying CDs to take advantage of the interest rates. Banks need a constant source of money to cash personal and payroll checks on a daily basis, so the rush of deposits made us feel like we were growing money. Another major source of deposits, we later learned, came from the hippie communes in the Ozark countryside. The hippies may have worn the ragged clothes of their counterculture, but they practiced the capitalism of Delta planters by raising huge cash crops of marijuana. Our assets doubled, from $1.5 million to $3.6 million within a few months.

◆ ◆ ◆

Though the skyrocketing interest rates attracted deposits, the economic situation discouraged real estate sales. With lending institutions charging more than 20 percent for loans, the market was frozen.

The Whitewater development, which we had bought with the Clintons in August 1978, failed to meet sales expectations. After we incorporated the project as Whitewater Development Company, Inc., Susan designed an impressive brochure, touting the rugged Ozark scenery. But sales were slow. The first problems occurred during the year I worked in the governor's office, far from the scene. We needed a survey before we could subdivide the land, but the work I commissioned turned out to be worthless. An entire year was lost.

Finally, the property was divided into forty-four lots, and we succeeded in selling one scenic lot along the river in September 1979. Over the next six months, we sold five more lots, but the income was not enough to cover the payments on the loans we had taken to buy the property.

The success of Whitewater depended on a steady cash flow. Under the system I used, my company provided financing for our customers. We held the buyer's promissory note and drew income from the principal and interest. But the lots were not moving, and by 1980, the Whitewater development was trapped by tough Arkansas usery laws, which limited the interest rates we could charge to 10 percent. Meanwhile, the interest rates the banks could charge the Whitewater company on our commercial loan rose above 20 percent. We were running a 10 percent negative interest spread.

The situation led to misunderstandings, and a renewal of my disputes with Hillary that had started when I'd criticized her commodities transactions.

Our principal loan to purchase the property had come from the Citizens Bank and Trust Co. of Flippin, where Chris Wade, our realtor, was a director and founder. Because we were required to put up at least 10 percent of the $203,000 purchase price, the Clintons, Susan, and I had obtained a smaller loan from the Union National Bank of Little Rock to make the down payment. During the first year, both families had shared the debt service. Saddled with an adjustable mortgage, subject to fluctuation, we watched helplessly as rising interest rates cost the Whitewater partnership thousands of dollars.

The two surveys and the construction costs of building roads into the property drove up our expenses. By the time Susan and I moved to Kingston, the project was already $80,000 in the red. Although I tried to cover most of the costs, I had asked the Clintons to make a payment to help maintain the loan during the first year. The continuing negative cash flow embarrassed me. I felt a responsibility for bringing the Clintons into an unprofitable deal and I decided to make the payments myself rather than ask Bill and Hillary for more money.

While Whitewater languished, Clinton's political woes mounted. In the two years since he had been elected as a symbol of youth and Democratic promise, Clinton had bounced from one controversy to another. His cadre of brash aides, out of sync with Arkansas, led him into conflict involving the auto-license tax and charges of environmental extremism. Meanwhile, the White House had its problems. Carter was unable to hold the Democratic Party together, and in his last year in office the president unwittingly helped bring Clinton down.

Carter was a compassionate man, but he seemed to have a talent for maladroit moves. In our case, he managed to draw landlocked Arkansas into the conflict between the U.S. and Cuba. Fidel Castro had raised the stakes in his long struggle with a succession of American administrations by expelling thousands of undesirable citizens during the infamous 1980 Mariel boat lift that brought masses of Cubans to the shores of Florida. The newcomers were hardly prepared for assimilation; and the U.S. wasn't ready to accept the wave of Cubans. Carter decided to house eighteen thousand of the refugees at Fort Chaffee, a military base outside Fort Smith, Arkansas.

Alarmed by rumors that many of the Cubans were thieves, prostitutes, homosexuals, and mental patients, the people of Fort Smith complained that their county had been turned into a dumping ground. The situation was not alleviated when hundreds of Cubans, restless over a delay in resettlement, broke out of the camp and attempted to storm the countryside. Brandishing bottles and staves and chanting, "Libertad!" the Cubans ran into barricades manned by state troopers outside the town of Barling. A brief, pitched battle broke out, and when it was over, dozens of Cubans and a few troopers were bloodied. Order was eventually restored, but Clinton's reputation was not. A few weeks after the confrontation, the governor of Arkansas watched helplessly as the president of the United States transferred even more Cubans to Fort Chaffee from resettlement camps in Wisconsin and Pennsylvania. Fort Chaffee was picked, Carter said, because of its warm weather and commodious facilities.

The incident at Fort Chaffee put the final block in place for Clinton's defeat. He had managed to overcome the campaign of Monroe Schwarzlose in the Democratic primary, but the rallying cry of Clinton's opposition became "Cubans and car tags." He lost the general election to Frank White. When reporters later asked Clinton his future plans, he answered that he might travel to Washington with a few refugees for Carter to sponsor.

Clinton became just one of many Democratic victims on election night. Not only would there be a Republican governor of Arkansas, there would be a new Republican president and, for the first time in decades, a Republican Congress.

Early on the morning after the votes were counted, Hillary called our house in Kingston. She sounded as though there had been a death in the family and said she needed money. She wanted to sell their stock in the Whitewater Development Company.

"That might not be easy," I told her. "It's not listed on the New York Stock Exchange." I tried to be comforting, but Hillary was distraught.

"I have to support everyone now," she said. "Bill's out of a job and I have a daughter to support." Chelsea had been born that year. "I have all these responsibilities. I've got to find means of support."

She was no longer talking as a proud political wife, but about herself. It seemed that every sentence began with "I."

There was little I could say to bolster her. No one wanted to buy into Whitewater at this point. The development had become a heavy burden, and Susan and I were already carrying the brunt of the financial load.

When I hung up, after explaining to Hillary that she should not expect a sudden influx of money from Whitewater, I turned to Susan and said, "She's in a panic."

When the Clintons first joined us in Whitewater, their original investment of about ten thousand dollars would have been a princely sum to them. Neither Bill nor Hillary had accumulated much money before he became governor. But I knew Hillary had since made ten times their Whitewater commitment in the commodities market, so they were not starving.

It was typical of Hillary to expect me to take care of her and Bill—the same way Jim Blair had brought in the big payday on cattle futures. Hell, other than putting up some money for the down payment on the property, the Clintons had shown no interest in our project. They had never even bothered to drive up to Marion County to look at it. Hillary may have been expecting money to gush from Whitewater like a geyser, thanks to Jim McDougal, but that's not the way it was working out.

My bleak assessment of Whitewater was not my first discouraging word on the subject to Hillary. We'd had earlier disagreements when she'd insisted on claiming deductions on the Clintons' personal income tax return for payments I made through the Whitewater company. Although the Clintons made an investment equal to ours in the early stages of the project, I assumed all obligations as the development continued. To spare Bill a potential election-year problem, I even relieved the Clintons of liability for the down payment by taking a loan from Maurice Smith's bank to pay off our note at Union National. I also took care of shortfalls, handling payments with new loans in my name or by writing personal checks.

The first year Hillary claimed tax deductions, I told her, "You can't do that. It's the corporation that's making the payments." She took the deduction anyway. The next year, she asked again and I repeated my advice. She did it anyway. In 1981, the third year of Whitewater's existence, Hillary told me she planned to claim further deductions. I lost my temper. "Goddamnit, Hillary," I said, "with that high-priced eastern education, don't you know you can't write it off unless you pay it? I paid it for you, goddamnit, so you can't take it out on your tax return."

Her face took on a startled expression, the kind of look stubborn or obtuse people use to show they don't want to understand.

I had my own frustrations as a bank executive. I wanted to expand the role of the Kingston institution, but we faced the limitations placed on a conventional bank. We were not allowed to invest directly in real estate, and we were forbidden from establishing branches in other counties. At one point, the Smiths, Jim Guy, Susan, and I bought some property in Huntsville, the county seat of Madison County, in hopes of putting an extension of Madison Bank & Trust there. My connections in the Arkansas government had been cut off by the election of Governor Frank White, and we were unable to get approval.

As an alternative, I turned to the idea of obtaining a savings and loan association. Once restricted to home mortgages, the institution had recently had its mandate expanded. Under new rules, the savings and loans were able to create their own financial subsidiaries and to invest in anything from junk bonds to condominiums. The expanded role seemed designed to help Republican investors, but I saw no reason why a Democrat couldn't profit, too.

Harvey Bell, an attorney who served as Clinton's securities commissioner, had gone into the business of brokering sales of savings and loan associations. I told him of my interest. Near the end of 1981, he called to report that the Woodruff County Savings and Loan in Augusta, a little town a few miles east of Bradford, was for sale. Located in familiar territory, the Augusta association was especially appealing because I felt certain I could establish a branch in Bradford.

Susan and I borrowed more than $200,000 from the Worthen Bank in Little Rock and bought a controlling interest in the Augusta operation. In the beginning, we had various stockholders, including Steve Smith and Julie, and a friend of mine from high school days, Dr. C. E. Ransom from Searcy. But within a year, Susan and I bought out their interests.

To obtain symmetry with Madison Bank & Trust in Kingston, we renamed the Woodruff association the Madison Guaranty Savings and Loan. From the outset, we conducted a campaign to increase capital, offering higher interest rates on deposits and buying accounts from other institutions. Before we knew it, our assets tripled.

As business accelerated in Kingston and Augusta, Whitewater slipped to the back of my mind. With the bank and the savings and loan producing money, the debts associated with the struggling land development were manageable. Our flight from Little Rock to northern Arkansas seemed to be paying off.

Just as my satisfaction with the political scene had been upset by the events of 1980, my pleasure over the banking successes was interrupted by an unexpected development in my personal life.

One day, while working at the bank in Kingston, I called home to talk with Susan. A new telephone system was being installed in the town, and I suspect that's what fouled up communications. Instead of hearing a ring, I found myself plugged into a conversation taking place on our home line. Susan and Bill Clinton were talking, an intimate conversation filled with giggles and sexual innuendo. Dispirited, I quietly hung up. I was left with no doubt that Susan and Bill were carrying on an affair.

From our friendship and many talks over the years, I knew how Bill felt about women, especially those he found sexy. His reputation as a ladies' man was well known, and rumors swirled constantly about Bill and other women: the women who worked for him, the women who seemed to show up by his side, as if they were hopelessly attracted. At times, Bill appeared surrounded by women, whether well-wishers at political events or acquaintances at parties. He basked in their attention. It occurred to me that they offered him escape from the stern dictates of Hillary at home.

At the same time, I recognized Susan's discontent with her life with me. Much of the fire had gone out of our marriage, after our quarrel over her abortion. We never had sex. Our friendship had evolved from high romance to co-existence as business partners and helpmates. In pursuit of a banking career, I had transplanted Susan from the house she adored in Little Rock to a mobile home in the country. Never one to make friends easily, Susan felt she had been catapulted into a town full of strangers. Her role in our real estate ventures became secondary to my own drive to build the bank. I spent more time at the office than with her, and sometimes, when I came home, I carried cranky moods with me.

In the minutes after I put down the phone, I reflected on my long relationships with Susan and Bill. Naturally I was hurt by Susan's unfaithfulness. I felt no rush of anger, just disappointment. But I was exasperated with Bill, as if the improvident younger brother had once again raised the level of misbehavior another notch. Jealousy never plagued me. I believed I could deal rationally with Susan's infidelity and Bill's betrayal. I recognized that my marriage was in trouble, but I had no interest in ending it. And I had no intention of mentioning the matter to Bill. What would have been the point?

As soon as I reached our house, I confronted Susan with the conversation I had overheard. Rather than lying clumsily, Susan acknowledged her relationship with Bill, in the same straightforward manner with which she had confirmed the abortion a few years before. Without histrionics, we talked this latest crisis through. Instead of making any precipitous decisions, we concluded that some sort of temporary separation was necessary to give us time to sort out our future. We decided that Susan should take over the management of the savings and loan in Augusta; she could stay with my parents, nearby in Bradford. No one would know there had been a problem.*

Later in 1982, I tried to do something that Bill Clinton had failed to accomplish—to take John Paul Hammerschmidt's congressional seat.

Hammerschmidt was one of the first Republicans to win a major office in Arkansas. Elected in 1966, the same year that Winthrop Rockefeller captured the governor's office, Hammerschmidt had faced only one strong challenge. That was in 1974, when Clinton had held him to 52 percent of the vote. Hammerschmidt had been unopposed in 1980. Now, as a close ally of President Reagan and Vice President George Bush, he had the White House fully behind him. Hammerschmidt had the pasty face of a small-town elder and the bland personality of a politician who marched in lockstep to Republican doctrine, I thought, but I knew he would be tough to beat. Using his party connections in the Nixon-Ford years, and now with Reagan, Hammerschmidt had been able to funnel a number of pork-barrel projects into the district.

---

* After Jim publicly talked about the matter in the winter of 1997, Susan denied ever having an affair with Clinton.

The Third Congressional District covered all of northwest Arkansas and dipped south, below the underpopulated Ouachita mountain range. A sprawling district with irregular borders, the Third's demographics no longer favored Democrats. The area included Fayetteville, a progressive university town. But Fayetteville's Democratic base was outnumbered by the voters of Fort Smith, the state's second biggest city. Fort Smith was an old military center, with a strong conservative tradition. Moreover, the north Arkansas hills were full of people who had always considered themselves Republicans—old-time descendants of mountaineers who opposed secession and found comfort with the GOP after the Civil War, as well as newcomers to towns like Springdale and Rogers, transplanted Yankees who brought their Republican registration with them. Blacks, the most reliable Democratic constituency in the state, represented only 3 percent of the district voters. And since much of the district was old Faubus country, it was foreboding territory.

The legacy of Cuban refugees at Fort Chaffee hung over my head. Voters in the Third District had not forgiven Carter and Clinton for the chaos. Carter had won only 37 percent of the district's vote in 1980. That was not a propitious number for me as I tried to raise the Democratic banner two years later, but I thought I saw an opening.

Despite Reagan's popularity, I felt times were still hard for the small merchants and farmers, even as Republican fat cats were growing fatter from Reagan's huge tax cut in 1981. The region was in an economic slump, and I thought Reagan could be compared with Herbert Hoover, the president of the Great Depression.

Although I had lived in the district for less than two years, no one could accuse me of being a carpetbagger. My family had been in Arkansas longer than that of anyone else in the race. My political connections in the area were more than twenty years old, dating from my service in statewide campaigns. It was not as if I were a political newcomer.

I had toyed with the idea of running for Little Rock's congressional seat in 1980. Ed Bethune, a Republican, had won the district in a fluke in 1978 after Jim Guy gave up the seat to run for the Senate. At first, it appeared the freshman Bethune might be vulnerable, but I concluded I would rather seek business opportunity in north Arkansas than tackle a Republican incumbent in a year when Democrats were self-destructing across the country. I'd made the right move: Bethune received 79 percent of the vote in the Reagan landslide. Nevertheless, I had never been able to set aside my ambition to go back to Washington as a congressman someday.

Before I ran in 1982, I conferred at length with Steve Smith, who had run Clinton's campaign against Hammerschmidt eight years earlier. Steve urged me to plunge ahead. It might be a long shot, he said, but the odds were not prohibitive.

A few days before the filing deadline, I made a decision to run. Though Susan and I had discussed my political aspirations over the years, I didn't consult her this time. She was working in Augusta and living with my parents. When we talked, it was of family matters and business news. Susan and I were inching our way toward a reconciliation. I happened to be in Little Rock the day I revealed my candidacy. After I finished an interview with a reporter for the *Arkansas Democrat*, I realized I needed to tell Susan. I called her at the savings and loan. She approved of my plan. "Great!" I remember her saying, and she made the hour-and-a-half drive to Little Rock to join me in time to watch the news on local TV.

Steve became my campaign manager and his wife, Julie, served as press secretary, the same positions they once held for Clinton. R. D. Randolph, who drove me to the sale barns on John F. Kennedy's behalf in 1960, handled my scheduling.

At Steve's suggestion, I hired a fellow named Pat Harris, who was interested in getting into politics. Pat was a modest, retiring young man whose family had been active in Democratic affairs in Johnson County. Although he had little political experience himself, I gave him a job as my deputy campaign manager. I liked his enthusiasm.

We had such a good relationship that I later brought him into business with me.

I faced three opponents in the Democratic primary: a seventy-five-year-old former state supreme court justice named Fred Jones; Butch Johnson, whom I suspected of being a Republican cat's-paw drafted to mark me up in the primary—he was constantly calling me a "liberal" and a puppet of organized labor; and a third candidate, a young guy from Fort Smith named Anthony Leding, who didn't scratch.

The *Arkansas Gazette*, a statewide newspaper published in Little Rock, endorsed me in the primary. The editorial described me as the "unmistakable" choice of the candidates: "A banker at Kingston, former professor of political science at Ouachita Baptist University and—best of all—a former aide to the great Arkansas senator J. W. Fulbright." The newspaper said my years with Fulbright gave me "unusual credentials to step right into the Congress with full knowledge of its workings." Dismissing Butch Johnson as a right-winger, the newspaper said, "If he wanted to run for Congress he should have entered the Republican primary."

I never mentioned my Democratic opponents during the primary campaign and concentrated instead on Reagan, describing him as the leader of the vested interests. Although I was confident of prevailing in my own race, the primary became an awkward period. After years of circling each other, Bill Clinton and Jim Guy Tucker were finally locked in a personal duel. Their accusations of incompetency and sniping comments about each other's irresponsibility, made quietly over the past decade, were now being shouted in public forums in the contest for the Democratic gubernatorial nomination. His voice bristling with scorn, Clinton described Tucker as a tool of the "special interests" and a dilettante with a lousy attendance record when he was in Congress. Tucker retaliated by accusing Clinton of commuting the sentences of more than a score of convicted murderers in his last days as governor.

It was a battle in which I had never wanted to take sides. Jim

Guy, a former roommate, was my friend, Clinton my colleague since the Fulbright days. Despite my knowledge of his affair with Susan, I'd never developed any animosity toward him.

At a Democratic dinner in Russellville we were all thrown together. When Susan and I walked into the old armory, teeming with Democratic partisans from Pope County, we spotted both Tucker and Clinton. As I made my way to the front, Susan sat with Jim Guy and Betty. She had always been fond of Betty. I tried to be equally enthusiastic in my greetings to the Tuckers and to Bill, who was holding forth in another corner of the cavernous building. In their speeches, both men were warm in their praise; though reluctant to make an endorsement before the Democratic primary, it seemed obvious I was their favored congressional candidate.

I was the night's closing speaker, and I concentrated on the iniquities of the Republicans, bellowing in my best imitation of "Give 'em hell" Harry Truman when he ran against the odds in 1948. My peroration resounded from the rafters. My microphone squealed. I awoke some of the diners who had been slumbering through much of the earlier oratory, and I thought the night ended on a high note.

Jim Guy's bid failed abysmally. He still couldn't connect with the common folks. He didn't even make it a two-man race. After winning only 23 percent of the primary vote, Jim Guy was left out of the runoff. Clinton's opponent in the second primary was Joe Purcell, a mild-mannered former lieutenant governor who insisted on keeping his campaign on a positive note. Clinton won 54 percent of the vote to set up a rematch with Frank White in the general election.

I was already assured of a place on the Democratic ticket that fall. By claiming more than 52 percent of the vote and eighteen of the twenty counties in the district in the first primary, I avoided a runoff.

In the general election, Clinton and I shared the platform at rallies across northwest Arkansas. He was ever the blithe spirit, never showing a hint of guilt. Campaigning in my district, Bill often arranged to link up with me because he felt I was energizing the Democratic vote. As he scrambled to win back the governor's office, he acknowledged to voters that he had drifted out of touch with them during his first term, and he promised never to lose contact again. Clinton dissociated himself from some of the assistants who'd served him during his failed administration. Several times, speaking on the stump, Clinton hailed me as his former aide and said, "Jim McDougal's the only person I had on my staff who was popular." I would respond, when it was my turn to speak, in more general terms. Unprepared to hail the man who had been running around with my wife as a great American, I preferred to depict Bill as the ideal candidate to restore Democratic principles and common sense to the governor's office.

Quite often, Bill was joined on the campaign trail by his wife, now going by the name of Hillary Clinton. It had taken her a few years in the state, but Hillary had finally realized that many conservative Arkansans were troubled when a married woman insisted on keeping her maiden name. After my run-ins with her over the Whitewater finances, I had become less charitable toward her. I thought of her as "Auxiliary Hillary," the woman who would do anything to advance her husband's cause.

Hillary had her own ideas of how the Democratic campaign should be handled that year, and she was about as helpful to me as a carbuncle. It became clear that she resented my populist rhetoric and disliked the visceral reaction it triggered in audiences. Voters stomped their feet and yelled at my speeches. She felt Arkansas politics should be dignified and issue-oriented. I used Arkansas colloquialisms she didn't understand. When I referred to "box holders" in one speech, she told me afterward to stop using the expression because no one knew what it meant.

She picked at Clinton, too. His inability to stay on schedule drove her crazy. Hillary was the one with the organizational skills. She once told Susan, "I have to kick his ass every morning."

Bill was as thoughtless about time during the campaign as he had been in the governor's office. Once, after he arrived more than an hour late for a rally, one of his aides approached me with some advice. "Jim," he said, "you need to go out and shake some hands."

I felt like punching the guy. "I've been here for an hour and a half," I said, "and I've already met everybody in the goddamned place while we were waiting for you all."

Hillary pushed Bill from rally to rally, but I suspect she felt that Arkansas politics, with our heat and our dusty sale barns, was a demeaning exercise. Wellesley and Yale Law School had not prepared her for the passionate, Baptist oratory of our politicians or the backroom deals necessary for advancement. I'm not sure she ever appreciated the environment of a rural southern state where a small network of personalities controlled events.

One day Susan remarked to Hillary, "Your parents must be awfully proud of you, married to the governor of Arkansas."

Hillary said, "My parents think I should have been United States attorney by now. It's no big deal to be governor of Arkansas."

While Clinton relied on personal magnetism in his quest to regain the governor's office, I made my party a principal element of my campaign. Over the years, many Democratic candidates in the South had become wary of the party label because of the liberal platforms of the national Democratic Party. I was unabashed, and ran a fierce populist campaign.

I led crowds in singing the Democratic anthem, "Happy Days Are Here Again." I inveighed against the evils of aristocratic, Republican policy.

While covering my campaign, Mike Trimble of the *Arkansas Gazette* began a long Sunday piece:

"At a political rally a few weeks ago, Jim McDougal of Kingston, the Democratic nominee for Congress in the Third District, had just delivered a tub-thumping anti-Republican tirade that could have melted the fat off a New York taxi driver's neck.

" 'Nice speech,' commented an observer to McDougal's campaign manager, Steve Smith, who was standing nearby. 'Who wrote it?'

" 'Franklin D. Roosevelt,' Smith replied."

As I traveled around the district, I summoned all the skills I had developed as a boy listening to the speeches of Roosevelt and John L. Lewis, and I drew on the speaking lessons I learned as a young man studying to become a preacher. I found that I could get the audiences crackling with cheers and applause when I turned up the volume.

After mounting the podium and acknowledging the perfunctory clapping from the crowd with a wave, I usually started with a joke. Then I would shift into high gear. "I won't soft-pedal the fact that I'm a Democrat," I yelled. "I wear it as a badge of honor. After all, it's not my party or my party's representative who voted for zero pay increase for Social Security or voted for nothing for the retired veteran or nothing for the civil servant, and then came home to brag about it."

Pointing toward wayward Democrats, the folks who might have forsaken the party for the right-wing platitudes of Reaganism, I reminded them of their roots. "I'm not asking you to do anything radical. I'm just asking you to vote the way your fathers and grandfathers did."

In certain venues, I couldn't afford to dismiss Republicans. While making a speech to the Farm Bureau, one of the most conservative organizations in the state, I told the crowd that no farmer had ever had to beg for a loan from me. "Don't ask the Democrats," I told them. "Ask the Republican farmer. I treat them all the same."

But when my listeners were obviously Democrats, I pounded on Reagan and Hammerschmidt. I emphasized education and was endorsed by the Arkansas Education Association, the teachers organization. I liked to say that the reason Hammerschmidt voted against education was because he didn't have any—although, of course, he did. Politics gives you a license to exaggerate.

I was backed by the AFL-CIO and considered myself a champion of working men and women. Calling for decent wages and a stable Social Security system, I struck the populist themes and whacked the excesses of Reaganomics. The plumbers, the carpenters, all the craft unions were with me.

◆ ◆ ◆

After a quarter century of experience, I considered myself a veteran politician, but I was about to learn another lesson. On a local level, elections are often decided by personalities. But on the federal level, party alignment becomes crucial. Control in Washington means thousands of jobs, from low-level duties in Congress, such as those I held under McClellan, to cabinet members charged with making billion-dollar decisions. In 1982, the GOP held the White House as well as a majority in the Senate. It appointed local postmasters and regional-development commission chairmen; it named new federal judges, U.S. attorneys, and the heads of regulatory agencies. Federal enforcement was in the hands of the Republican Party.

The bank at Kingston was usually inspected in March by federal examiners from Memphis. We enjoyed a good relationship with them, and they seemed favorably impressed with our efforts to bring modern technology to a bank that had had only one telephone line when we bought it. The bank added computers and copying machines, and when it reached its seventieth birthday in 1981, we pitched a party on Kingston's town square with a hot-air balloon and a bluegrass band. We even conducted a "millionaire for a day" contest, where the winner received one day's interest on a million dollars. Steve and I felt that the bank was running smoothly and the townspeople were our friends; deposits had climbed to $8 million.

With no warning in the fall of 1982, as the general election campaign was heating up, a new set of bank examiners showed up. They started giving us unshirted hell. Picking through every piece of paper and faulting every policy, the examiners attacked me for investing in thirty-year bonds; no matter that when the interest rates finally began to fall, these bonds with a fixed rate brought us a big profit. After studying our file of delinquent payments on car loans, the examiners discovered that delinquencies were all the way up to something like $157! The year before, the delinquencies had amounted to a mere $100. They scolded us and said, "Don't you realize this is a fifty percent increase?"

The examiners also described as "unsound" a loan that Madison Bank & Trust had extended to the Whitewater project, raising the first legal caveat for our struggling development.

There was no question in my mind that the bank examiners had been dispatched by Hammerschmidt or one of his Republican agents. Anonymous complaints can trigger formal investigations, but Hammerschmidt had the power of his congressional office to send a referral to the regulatory agencies that would guarantee action. He had an interest in a savings and loan in Harrison, which was in our trade district, putting me in business as well as political competition with the Republican incumbent. With his connections, Hammerschmidt was well placed to cause me trouble.

The bank examiners managed to divert Steve, my campaign manager, and me, for most of the fall. No charges ever came out of the examination, but it was demoralizing and impeded my campaign.

As the underdog, I was probably destined to lose. On election night, Bill Clinton won back the governor's office, but I was defeated. Hammerschmidt nearly doubled my vote: he won 66 percent; I took only 34 percent.

Despite the magnitude of his victory, I learned that Hammerschmidt was not finished with me. I had stung him and his party with my jibes during the campaign, and he planned further retribution. A week or two after the election, I ran into my friend Henry Hamilton, who told me: "Every time I see Hammerschmidt, he's drinking, and he's bragging about how he's going to get you."

11

In the weeks following my clash with the bank examiners, I broke with the government I had served as an Air National Guardsman, a Senate aide, and a citizen. If the federal government could send politically motivated agents to tie up a candidate in the middle of a congressional race, then there was no reason for me to be bound by loyalty to it. I developed an outlaw's mentality.

Bonnie Parker and Clyde Barrow became folk heroes among the people of my region during the Depression by robbing the banks that denied help to the poor. Not ready to rob banks, I was prepared to bend the rules. Looking back, my experience in Kingston became the watershed in my life.

Steve and I had built our little bank by treating our customers with dignity. Steve had known many of these people for years, and he recognized their strong character in adverse situations. We took risks on men and women with shaky credit ratings and were rewarded with rising deposits. Only one of our customers went bankrupt. I believe we created an atmosphere in Kingston that added to the general prosperity of the region. And for our efforts, the federal government harassed us.

It was obvious, long before election night, that the voters of the Third Congressional District did not intend to send me to Washington, so Susan and I made plans to return to Little Rock to rebuild our sagging real estate business. Over the months since her move to Augusta, we had threshed through our personal problems and decided to reunite. Susan seemed particularly enthusiastic about starting anew in Little Rock. With the Whitewater development stalled, she felt there was no way to make money in northern Arkansas. The fields of opportunity lay around Little Rock, we concluded, where we'd enjoyed success before Kingston.

Susan joined me in Fayetteville for the election returns. Eager to get back to Little Rock, we drove part of the way the night following my concession speech. The next day, we checked into a Little Rock motel. Susan began looking for an apartment; I started the paperwork for a subsidiary to our savings and loan association to handle our real estate ventures. Still pleased with the name Madison, I called the company Madison Financial Corporation.

Determined to make the best of things, Susan and I moved into a modest complex called Riviera Apartments. We rented office space in a building owned by Jim Guy Tucker. The investment had not worked out well for him, and Jim Guy was trying to sell the place, floor by floor, as a condominium, but there were few takers. The building had become another cash drain in the period after his political setback, so Susan and I located our offices there as a favor.

After a hiatus of nearly three years, the McDougals were back in Little Rock, and Bill Clinton was back in the governor's office. But our good times would never be rekindled. Much of the cheer characterizing our friendship in the previous decade had evaporated. I felt responsible for drawing the Clintons into the Whitewater investment; instead of quick profits, which Hillary expected, we had sustained losses. The disagreements between Hillary and me were serious, and there was the matter of the telephone call I had overheard.

Things had changed from the time we were a foursome, newlyweds, casually dropping by each other's houses unannounced. In spite of the problems, we maintained contact. After all, we were business partners. I regarded my relationship with Hillary as slightly cool but correct. With Bill, it was impossible to keep a distance. He kept pulling me into his orbit.

Shortly after he regained the governor's office, Bill called and asked if I could serve as his liaison to the Senate again. Even though I wanted to build some momentum for our new businesses, I returned to the capitol for the two-month session, working with Maurice Smith, just as I had in 1979. Maurice and I hung out in the back of the Senate chamber all day, trading stories and bargaining on legislation with the senators, trying to bridge the differences between the governor's interests and their own. But the legislative give-and-take that had enthralled me a quarter century ago was no longer fascinating.

The Marion Hotel had been demolished. Before the workers laid the explosives to bring down the old edifice, someone thoughtfully emptied the tank in the Gar Hole, carried the old fish a few steps to the Arkansas River, and loosed it in the waters. Like the politics of Orval Faubus and Paul Van Dalsem, the gar disappeared into oblivion.

At the capitol, a new breed of legislators had taken up residence. Girded with degrees in political science and lacquered with hairspray to maintain appearances for local TV, these men and women made a study in contrast to the bygone era. Not only were they more urbane, they came from more urban districts. Following the one-man, one-vote decision, Arkansas had reconfigured its legislative map. The rural, sparsely populated counties that once had their own representative in the House were merged into multicounty districts. Meanwhile, Little Rock's strength in the legislature nearly doubled; the Pulaski County delegation to the House swelled overnight from eight to fifteen.

Arkansas also averted the stern supervision of the Voting Rights Act of 1965 by enacting its own election reforms. A constitutional amendment passed by the voters eliminated the poll tax and brought stronger assurances of enfranchisement for African-Americans. Black and brown faces lent fresh color to the ranks of the legislature that had once been uniformly white.

I have few memories of the 1983 legislative session, but I remember one pivotal moment. It is a recollection of Bill Clinton, leaning against a door in the capitol and signing a note for a $25,000 loan from my savings and loan, Madison Guaranty.

The loan was one of a series of transactions we took in the early 1980s to stave off debts from the Whitewater investment.

When the Clintons and Susan and I bought the property in 1978, we borrowed $180,000 from Chris Wade's Citizens Bank and Trust Co. of Flippin. We also took out a $20,000 loan from the Union National Bank of Little Rock to make the 10 percent down payment.

In 1980, when Jim Guy Tucker and I sought financing from the Union bank for an apartment building we wanted to buy in the historic Quapaw district of Little Rock, I was told that my Whitewater down-payment loan needed to be cleared up. To pay off Union, I obtained a $20,000 loan from the Bank of Cherry Valley, where Maurice Smith served as chairman of the board. I took full responsibility for the new loan, thus removing the Clintons from liability for the down payment at a time when Bill was running for re-election.

Sales at Whitewater had been slow, and in some years nonexistent. In 1981, I renewed the larger Citizens Bank loan without calling on the Clintons for further payments. The sale of one prime lot enabled the Whitewater corporation to meet payments that year.

But the next year, the bank examiners raised questions about a

$25,000 loan I had taken in the name of the Whitewater corporation from my bank in Kingston to meet payments at the Flippin bank. The examiners felt I was exceeding my credit limit at Madison Bank & Trust; thus I needed to turn elsewhere when the time came to make the next Whitewater payment.

That occurred early in 1983. I explained the situation to Clinton during a brief conversation in the governor's conference room following a meeting with the statehouse press corps. I said I needed him to sign for a new loan in order to pay off the next Whitewater note. I didn't anticipate any objections; I already had papers made out. Using his name, Clinton would borrow $25,000 from my new savings and loan so our Whitewater company could meet the forthcoming payment. Clinton simply said, "Hey, okay." He leaned back on the door jamb and signed the note.

Within a few months, I had second thoughts about the arrangement. After my experience in Kingston, I anticipated that savings and loan examiners would soon be poking through Madison Guaranty's books. Clinton would be facing re-election again in 1984—the governor's term was only two years at this time—and I didn't want his name to show up. Anytime a public official's name appears in a lending company's records, it automatically raises a red flag for examiners. The loan could cause political problems for Clinton and create questions for me. As a result, I asked our Marion County realtor, Chris Wade, to take a $25,000 loan from Madison Guaranty to wipe out Clinton's loan.

To pay off Chris's loan, I then used the name of one of our earliest real estate entities, Flowerwood Farms, to take out yet another loan from the Bank of Stephens in Stephens, Arkansas. It was a circuitous sequence, but the various transactions enabled me to escape my loan ceiling at Kingston and to erase Clinton's name from Madison Guaranty's records.

The Clinton-McDougal partnership still existed at Whitewater, but I was increasingly interested in other business pursuits. As soon as the legislative session ended, I turned my attention to the Madison subsidiary I had conceived.

◆ ◆ ◆

Albeit on a small scale, Madison Financial operated on the same principle as General Motors and its finance company, General Motors Acceptance Corporation. Under this concept, the parent company issues money to its subsidiary to arrange financing. Customers borrow from GMAC and drive away with the auto, but GMAC holds the title until the loan is paid off. Madison Financial Corporation, drawing from Madison Guaranty, loaned money to our customers to purchase property but retained title to the land until their debt was erased.

After a modest start at the office we rented from Jim Guy, the Madison enterprises quickly outgrew its quarters. We moved to new offices at a nearby financial center, and within a year, we made two more moves to accommodate a growing number of employees and additional equipment. Once the Little Rock branch of Madison Guaranty won approval from state authorities, in October 1983, we opened new headquarters at 1600 Main Street. Our business restored life to a rundown neighborhood just south of downtown Little Rock, near Interstate 630, the city's east-west highway.

Susan employed her artistic touch, turning an old laundry building into stylish banking quarters with glass blocks and bright colors. My office, which doubled as the boardroom, rested a half flight above the main floor, on top of the old laundry boiler. A spacious room equipped with a conference table, the office was encased in glass so anyone could see me when they walked in the front door. Susan won a design award for the renovation, and the downtrodden neighborhood of burned-out hulls and porno houses gradually took on trendy tones. We provided financial backing for Juanita's, which became Little Rock's best Mexican restaurant, and I believe our presence led other shops to open in the area.

After establishing Madison Financial Corporation, our first big project involved the purchase of more than one thousand acres from

International Paper Co. just south of Little Rock, near the highway to Pine Bluff. We called the development Maple Creek Farms, and put a cluster of three- and five-acre lots on the market. It proved to be a phenomenal success.

When I had discussed the formation of a service corporation for the savings and loan with the federal regulators, they'd suggested I build shopping centers, apartment buildings, and downtown parking decks. I told them I preferred to subdivide land and to sell housing lots to people who wanted to live outside the city. The regulators raised no objections to my plan. I assumed I had their blessing.

To promote the development, Susan took charge of advertising. She starred in several television commercials, sharing the screen with a beautiful, prize-winning horse we rented as her costar. As Susan walked the horse through the bucolic scenery, she said, "Come out to Maple Creek. You'll have the country and tranquillity . . . and maybe even have a horse."

Maple Creek was like a snow-cone franchise on a summer day. We sold the larger tracts and subdivided the rest of the property into smaller lots that were gobbled up. Maple Creek grew into a small, prosperous community.

Susan then turned her talents to another piece of property we were developing near Bradford, a stretch of raw, cheap country land where prospectors had once searched for gold. The hills of White County contained no gold but mounds of iron pyrite, the glittering, worthless "fool's gold." We named our project Goldmine Springs and carved the land into ten-acre tracts for buyers wanting to escape the congestion of Little Rock. Susan played on the history of the area in our advertising campaign: "There's no gold in Goldmine Springs," she said. But, she promised, "It's a beautiful place."

Our real estate operation was rewarding, but we encountered stress at Madison Guaranty as deposits at the savings and loan soared from near insolvency to $50 million in two years. I had read that at the outset of the Civil War, Abraham Lincoln's chief of staff warned it would take three years to build an army, so I understood that the expansion of any organization would be accompanied by growing pains.

Slowly, I assembled a management team. I had left the Madison Bank & Trust in Kingston in the hands of Gary Bunch. I only went back for meetings of the bank's board of directors. To run Madison Guaranty in Little Rock, I hired John Latham. A certified public accountant who had obtained a law degree at night school, John impressed me with his intelligence and earnestness. Even though he was only thirty and had no experience in banking, I felt confident putting him in charge of the savings and loan so I could devote my energies to the real estate division. After hiring him in 1983, I said, "Once we get to a certain figure, I'm walking out of here and you're going to be in complete control." He was chairman of the Madison Guaranty board by the next year.

Business boomed, creating so many jobs that I felt I was running an employment agency. I persuaded my old friend Henry Hamilton, one of the mischievous twins from Madison County, to join me. Henry not only took a job at Madison, he moved into an apartment in the same complex on East Capital Street where Susan and I lived. I hired Don Denton, a hot-tempered redhead who had handled a number of loans for me at Union National Bank, and I put a few guys I knew through Alcoholics Anonymous on the payroll. It was like a class reunion. Tempering my wrath at the government examiners, I even hired one of them, Sarah Hawkins, as a compliance officer. I thought it best to find someone else to handle regulations.

It seemed as though half the Henley family came to work with me. Three of Susan's brothers, as well as her sister and her brother-in-law, eventually took jobs with Madison. One of her brothers, Bill, had been elected to represent the Camden district in the state Senate in 1982, but he spent so much time in Little Rock working for us as a real estate salesman that his constituents decided he had neglected them. They turned him out of office in the next election.

Just as Steve Smith and I had catered to the poor farmers around

Kingston, Madison Guaranty reached out to the minority community in Little Rock. Many of our customers were black, and half of our board was composed of African-Americans. When Daisy Bates, who'd led the effort to integrate Central High School as state president of the NAACP, faced foreclosure on her house, Hugh Patterson, publisher of the *Arkansas Gazette*, asked me, "Can you make her a loan? Nobody else will do it." Madison made the loan, and I personally guaranteed her note.

My business practices took place in the realm of "creative financing." We relied on innovation, and it paid dividends. It also attracted the attention of the savings and loan examiners. Although profits from the Maple Creek Farms subdivision had helped keep Madison Guaranty afloat, the examiners objected to our bookkeeping. They said the property needed to be secured with formal deeds rather than purchase agreements. I traveled to Dallas to meet with a Federal Home Loan Bank Board supervisor, and I offered a simple solution: "What if we issue warranty deeds and retain the land?" The supervisor seemed distracted by the press of other cases. "Oh, that will take care of it," he assured me. The savings and loan examiners were overwhelmed with serious problems arising in hundreds of other thrifts all over the country. Madison Guaranty appeared to be the least of their worries.

In 1983, I spotted an advertisement in the *Wall Street Journal* offering forty-four hundred acres of land for sale on Campobello Island. Campobello had been Franklin D. Roosevelt's summer retreat, and the musical name of the New Brunswick island belonged to Roosevelt history. Though he died before I was five, I have a memory of listening to FDR's radio speeches with Uncle Bert, mesmerized by their smooth, comforting quality. My favorite movie about FDR, featuring the elegant Ralph Bellamy as the president, was called *Sunrise at Campobello*. Magic seemed to be associated with the place.

From the ad, I realized that Campobello was accessible from the

Roosevelt International Bridge linking the island to the coast of Maine. Much of the property looked out upon the Bay of Fundy—an added attraction because the only water view that had failed me was Whitewater. The price for the land at Campobello was about $1.6 million, roughly $400 an acre. I asked John Latham, our new chairman at Madison Guaranty, if we were in a position to make a bid. With his assurance, I decided to go take a look.

As I prepared to fly to Campobello, Chris Wade and his wife, Rosalee, walked into my sales office at Maple Creek. They had come down from Marion County to conduct some business in Little Rock and were stopping in to see me before going back. The visit turned into a major shopping excursion. Not only did I value Chris's judgment of property values, I wanted company. My health was not great, and I didn't feel like climbing through island underbrush by myself. On the spur of the moment, I asked Chris to accompany me. Within a day or so, we were examining the property on Campobello and discovering it had thirteen miles of ocean frontage.

I thought: God, people are dying to own an ocean view. It's a finite resource in heavy demand along the East Coast. Here were thirteen miles of the cheapest ocean frontage to be found anywhere. The spectacular views took in the rugged coastline east of Maine and the legendary high tides produced by the Bay of Fundy. The land offered privacy, too. The beachfront was free of the clutter of souvenir shops, chintzy motels, and ugly condominiums. Inland, the unspoiled property harbored bird sanctuaries and forests. Only a day's drive from the population centers in the Northeast, Campobello could lure the same kind of Bostonians and New Yorkers who made the islands of Martha's Vineyard and Nantucket their vacation homes. I envisioned Campobello as the biggest business venture of my life. I figured there was potential here to make twenty to thirty million dollars.

I signed an agreement to buy the land before leaving Campobello, freezing the property while I raised the capital. Negotiations spilled over into 1984. By this time, I had reached Madison Guaranty's 6 percent limit on investments that could be put into my side businesses. Campobello had become more than I could swallow alone, so I turned to other sources.

Deciding to put together an Arkansas consortium, I compiled a list of local men who might have the daring and wherewithal to invest in Campobello. I thought of Sheffield Nelson. I'd had virtually no dealings with him since my cabal of Young Democrats had torpedoed plans by the Faubus crowd to elect Nelson as state YD president in 1965. In the intervening years, he had become head of Arkansas Louisiana Gas Co. as well as an important player in the growing Republican Party in Arkansas. But putting politics aside, I respected Nelson's business acumen.

When I called Nelson, he was as cordial as if we had been friends and allies down through the years. The Arkla offices were only a couple of blocks from my place, so I walked over to meet with him. Nelson also invited Jerry Jones, the Arkansas millionaire who later bought the Dallas Cowboys. An oil and gas wildcatter, Jones liked to take risks. As we sat in Nelson's office, I made my presentation, laying out for them the attributes of the Canadian island and the prospect of a handsome return on investment. Nelson and Jones agreed to buy a quarter interest in the Campobello project, sight unseen.

Chris Wade also invested in the development. He wanted to handle sales there, but found it too difficult to split his time between Campobello and his business interests in Arkansas. My real estate company eventually bought him out, and Susan and I wound up owning three-quarters of the property.

The next time I went to Campobello, during a brutal cold snap in the winter of 1984, I asked Jim Guy to come along. Since he was my lawyer, I wanted him to see the lay of the land. Trooping through the woods, we stumbled upon an old lodge. Closed for years, the building had once been a fancy summer home for a wealthy family. When we inquired, we discovered the lodge was owned by the New Brunswick provincial government. The authorities were happy to lease their white elephant to me, and I converted the place into a sales office and a model home.

The Campobello project perked along. Since the island was made of granite, we were able to lay down a network of rudimentary roads fairly easily. We developed a television pitch to the people of Boston and northern New England, inviting prospective buyers to come to Campobello and spend a free weekend at the lodge, offering comfortable sleeping accommodations, a reception area, a cocktail lounge, and a dining room with good home-cooked food. In our advertisements, we promised there would be no high-pressure selling. We kept business low-key and hired local people to show the clients around the island.

Dozens of lots sold. Most of the ocean-view lots were an acre in size and priced at $25,000—a bargain for an ocean view on the eastern seaboard. Before making improvements on the land, we had paid only $400 an acre. I thought FDR's Campobello would become the flagship of Jim McDougal's empire.

Beyond the Campobello project and the growing Madison operation in Little Rock, I dreamed of expansion in northern Arkansas. With Henry Hamilton, I talked of establishing a branch of our savings and loan in his hometown of Harrison. Henry encouraged me to think even bigger. We discussed the possibility of moving into other northwest Arkansas counties—Searcy, Newton, Marion (the home of Whitewater), and Madison, where I had bought the bank. I hoped to merge the Kingston bank with my savings and loan.

To accomplish these goals, we realized we needed friends in key positions in state government. Congressman Hammerschmidt had an interest in a savings and loan in the region, and he would be sure to object to our plans on the federal level.

Although Henry was technically my employee, he often lectured me like an older brother, providing insight into the world of Arkansas business and politics. Henry and his twin brother, Joe, were products of the old school, and they knew tactics I never taught in my government courses at Ouachita. Cut from the crude terrain of the Ozarks, the Hamilton brothers had a knack for the outrageous. Joe had been an irreverent legislator; he'd played jokes on his colleagues and even insulted Fulbright. Once Joe had told him, "Senator, your speeches are so bad you couldn't talk a dog off a meat wagon." I'd cringed, but Fulbright had laughed. Henry also specialized in backwoods humor and the politics of the hill country. Whenever we traveled through the Ozarks, the senator told me to bring the Hamilton boys along.

Joe died in 1984. His weak heart, diagnosed at the twins' birth, gave out. Henry and I grew closer. We had apartments in the same building and often ate dinner together. He broached the subject of a proposal one night as we dined at the Black Eyed Pea. "You need to give the boy a little spending money," he told me, referring to Clinton. As I sat there, picking at my chicken-fried steak, Henry explored a dark zone of Arkansas politics, an area where I had little familiarity. An old hand at the practice, he explained the need to give money to important officials. It was a necessary evil, he said, to seal essential friendships and to get things done. The Hamiltons had always known how votes were bought and sold—by entire families who promised to vote the straight Democratic ticket at the ballot box, by lobbyists seeking legislative relief, and by state representatives swapping votes on the floor of the legislature.

I suppose I was naive. Never having seen money change hands at the capitol or the Marion Hotel, I suspected quid pro quos, but thought deals were handled more subtly.

I recalled an experience when I'd worked for Clinton during his first administration. Steve Smith and I lunched regularly with the Little Rock financier Witt Stephens. My differences with Mr. Stephens had been set aside. He controlled the state's biggest securities operation, and I represented the governor's interests in the banking community. It was important that we get along.

Mr. Stephens enjoyed presiding over lunch. He held court at

an elaborate business suite in a downtown high-rise, complete with a kitchen and a cook who plied us with cornbread, fried chicken, and string beans. We used the occasions to talk over political rumors and banking affairs, maintaining a line of communication between the governor and the most powerful private citizen in Arkansas. Mr. Stephens never asked for any extraordinary favors. Once he said he'd like to establish a commercial loan bank with $50 million in capital. "Fantastic," I said. Mr. Stephens and I both liked the idea of competition in the banking industry, and the new institution he mentioned would put more money in circulation in Arkansas.

One day at lunch, Mr. Stephens said he was considering the purchase of some property in Camden, and he asked me to take a look at it the next time I was in the vicinity. I did, and later I casually told him how much I thought the land was worth. When Steve and I next had lunch with Mr. Stephens, his secretary handed me an envelope. After I returned to my own office, I opened it and found a one-thousand-dollar check. On the "For" line at the bottom of the check, next to his signature, Mr. Stephens had written "appraisal."

Uncomfortable, I sent the check back with a short note to Mr. Stephens. I wrote that I didn't charge friends for appraisals. "Besides," I added, "with all the good cornbread and string beans I've eaten with you, I probably owe you money."

Through all my years in Arkansas politics, I had never given or received an illicit payment. Aside from routine political contributions, Clinton had never hit me up for money. There seemed to be no venal side to his politics. Clinton never seemed to care much about money, or to have money on hand. Affection was Bill's aphrodisiac—not just sex, but the political love he won with his charm. He struck me as the ideal candidate for the talk-show age. Instead of sticking out his hand for clandestine payments, Bill held out his arms for an embrace. He projected the air of a vulnerable fellow who has known hurt in his life, and who understood the sufferings of others. Long before he was elected president, he used that approach: "I can feel your pain," he seemed to be crying. "Can you feel my pain? Can we get through this together?"

It never occurred to me that Bill Clinton would reach for money. But Henry insisted that under-the-table payments would solidify our connections in state government. At the request of Jim Guy Tucker, I had already called Clinton and asked him to appoint Beverly Bassett securities commissioner. Beverly had been a partner in Jim Guy's law firm, specializing in banking and finance. I didn't know her, but I agreed to recommend her for the job. Taking my advice, Clinton overlooked his animosity toward Tucker and appointed Bassett.

To ensure that my future recommendations would be favorably received, Henry said, I needed to see that some "pocket change" made its way to the governor's office.

We developed a system to pass money to Clinton. I considered it just another way of helping to take care of Bill. A contractor agreed to pad my monthly construction bill by $2,000. The contractor put the figure on his invoice as a cost for gravel or culvert work. After I paid the full amount on the invoice, the contractor reimbursed me the $2,000. I turned the money over to Henry to give to Clinton.

We were looking for control of the savings and loan board, and I arranged several appointments there, including one for John Latham. Clinton seemed amenable to my suggestions for appointments at all the agencies overseeing financial institutions in the state. Sometimes I sent him memos recommending names. Other times I would mention my choices in casual conversations. There was never an explicit agreement, just a general understanding: if I kept up my connection with Clinton, I would never encounter any bureaucratic roadblocks.

When I had a grievance with the Health Department after a state inspector refused to grant septic tank permits to our subcontractor at the Maple Creek development, I asked for a meeting with health officials. Clinton sat in on the meeting and made it clear he was sympathetic with our case. The subcontractor obtained the permits and the inspector was transferred.

"That's the way the world works," Henry told me.

Once, after I handed Henry his latest consignment of twenty hundred-dollar bills to relay to the governor's office, he turned the bills over and over in one hand, like a magician. Henry grinned. "You know," he said, "Caesar had his Brutus, Charles the First had Cromwell. Clinton could profit from these examples if he crosses us."

12

At the height of summer, it's a southern practice to go to work early, before the sun turns the countryside into a furnace. I was in my office about 6:30 one morning in August 1984, when Bill Clinton dropped by. There was nothing unusual about the hour or his visit. The governor's mansion was only a few blocks from Madison Guaranty's office, and Bill occasionally stopped in to shoot the breeze after he had been jogging.

For all of his leadership abilities, brilliance, and exposure to celebrity, Bill enjoyed everyday talk about ordinary topics, carrying on conversations on anything from last Saturday's Arkansas game to the latest best-seller.

I remember his visit clearly because Bill was dripping with sweat from his run, and he plopped down in a new orthopedic chair Susan had given me to ease my lower-back pains. That was Bill's style. Since he assumed his hosts were always glad to see him, he never thought about things like sweating on a new leather chair. Colored oxblood, the surface of the chair turned a dark umber.

Having never run a business in his life or shown a capacity for discipline, it didn't occur to Bill that he had interrupted me in the middle of my own work. I grunted, but set aside the titles and abstracts on my desk to listen.

Bill usually had an exuberant manner, but this morning he wore a hangdog expression. He was distressed, he said, about Hillary's problems at Rose Law Firm. She had been told she was not generating enough business and she felt under pressure to bring more clients on board.

The oldest law firm west of the Mississippi River, Rose was one of the most high-powered operations in the state. The partners were well paid—I expect Hillary was making far more than the governor's salary—and the client list included Arkansas's wealthy triumvirate: the Stephens's financial interests, the Tyson chicken industry, and the Waltons, founders of Wal-Mart.

I had one previous experience with the Rose firm, and it had not been altogether satisfactory. In 1981, when Steve Smith, Jim Guy Tucker, and I made an attempt to establish a branch of the Madison Bank & Trust in Huntsville, we retained Rose Law Firm to represent us. One of their better young attorneys, Vince Foster, handled our case in chancery court. Vince had grown up with Clinton and he became Hillary's close friend at the firm. He was a sober, studious man, and even though we lost in the first round of our case, we felt Vince presented our arguments effectively. For our appeal, the Rose firm sent a young, inexperienced lawyer to represent us. Unprepared, he failed badly. Steve felt the firm had treated us cavalierly and withheld payment of their fee.

At the time of Clinton's early-morning visit, our savings and loan operation already retained Tucker as our local lawyer. Yet I was so anxious to get back to the papers on my desk that I asked Bill, "Would it help if we gave her some business?" I made the offer simply to get him out of my office. Bill brightened and said, "Oh, yeah."

I told him I'd put Hillary on a retainer, stood up, and said, "Glad you dropped by." I was trying tactfully to dismiss him. He left, saying Hillary would be in touch with me. After Clinton departed, Susan's brother Bill stuck his head in my office. I gestured toward the chair just abandoned by the governor and told him, "I don't mind supporting the guy, but I wish he'd keep his wet butt out of my new chair."

Within two hours, Hillary arrived. It was as though my office had become a stage set for a play with comic entrances and exits. It was still early, before our business office opened. Months had passed since I had seen Hillary. She was wearing a stylish suit, and I was pleased to see that she sat in the soggy chair.

"Bill asked me to come by," she said. "What am I supposed to do?" In Hillary's oblique manner, the question was quite disingenuous, as if she did not know why she had been asked to stop by.

Speaking vaguely of intermittent legal problems we faced, I told Hillary the Madison operation would be willing to pay the Rose firm a two-thousand-dollar-a-month retainer. There would not be much work involved on our account, but I'd concluded that we could afford another legal retainer.

I said nothing to Hillary, but I saw her retainer as a way to legalize my monthly two-thousand-dollar subsidy to Clinton. In the months since Henry Hamilton had convinced me of the importance of giving to political friends, I'd tried to think of the payoff as an insurance premium rather than a form of bribery. Bill never said anything to me, and I never raised the subject when suggesting an appointment. With the same amount of money going to Hillary at Rose Law Firm instead of the governor's office, the payments would take place over the table.

Hillary seemed happy with the arrangement, and she left smiling. "Bye, Jim, I'll see you," she said. It would be the last time I ever saw her.

Nearly six years had passed since the Clintons and the McDougals purchased the Whitewater property, and setbacks at the unsuccessful enterprise had created tension between Hillary and me. One involved a project that became known as "Hillary's house."

To encourage sales at Whitewater, I built a model home on one of the lots. Even though people say they want "to live at the end of the road," they really don't. They want company. To give our development an inhabited appearance, I hired a builder to erect a two-bedroom fabricated house on a Whitewater lot. At the time, the Whitewater company was not self-sufficient, and I made a short-term loan to the corporation through one of my real estate entities to make the original payment on the new house.

After it became apparent that I had reached my limit for loans in my own name at Madison Bank & Trust, some refinancing was necessary. We arranged a $28,000 loan in Hillary's name to take over the house payments. Although Hillary was personally liable, it cost her nothing. We sold the house to a fellow named Hilman Logan. His payments to the Whitewater corporation were tailored to be the same amount necessary to amortize Hillary's loan.

A couple of years later, due to a clerical error at the bank, Hillary received a form letter saying the incoming payments were insufficient to cover the amount due. She responded with a curt letter telling the bank to speak with Susan or me about the discrepancy.

After the bank examiners raised questions about loans between Madison Bank & Trust and the Whitewater project in the fall of 1982, we were not in a position to renew Hillary's loan. The examiners declared Whitewater out of the Kingston bank's territory. To satisfy the bureaucrats, the loan was moved to a bank in Paragould—on the other side of the state and even farther from Whitewater than Kingston. Bill took out a $20,000 loan in his name from the Security Bank of Paragould. By this time, Bill was governor again, and the former chairman of the Paragould bank, Marlin Jackson, had been appointed bank commissioner. The $20,000 was applied to Hillary's loan at Kingston; I made up the balance to retire her loan there. The transactions were merely paperwork and cost the Clintons nothing, but Hillary seemed irritated.

◆ ◆ ◆

Another problem developed. Under our program for selling lots at Whitewater, we took promissory notes and held title to the property until the notes were paid off. The contracts required the buyers to pay taxes on the land. In 1985, someone failed to pay taxes. When the local newspaper published a list of delinquent taxpayers on the Marion County tax rolls, Whitewater Development Company was included.

Clinton was known to be a partner in Whitewater, and the governor erupted when he heard the news. Though it didn't constitute a legal problem—there was time to pay the taxes—the notice in the newspaper carried the potential for a public relations disaster. And another election year was rolling around.

Clinton called me up, yelling that the tax delinquency posed problems for him, adding that Hillary was "mad as hell." I tried to assure Bill that annual real estate taxes are often overlooked; the system allows property owners a couple of years to make payments. Property taxes were as abstract to Bill as the theory of relativity.

Weary of dealing with the Clintons, especially Hillary, I suggested to Bill that he and Hillary should simply extricate themselves from Whitewater. I had borne most of the financial burden. In the end, by my accounting, Whitewater cost the McDougals about $140,000 and the Clintons about $13,500. I told Bill he could resolve the issue without further loss of family money or political face by turning their shares over to me. I would assume all the remaining liabilities, and Whitewater would no longer be a political albatross.

Clinton said that suited him fine, but asked me to "run it by Hillary." I had no interest in running it by Hillary.

Instead, I prepared a stock transfer certificate and asked Susan to take it to Hillary. Susan was in a bubbly mood when she delivered the papers to the Rose Law Firm. The transfer would relieve us from worry about the Clintons' finances, and it would free the Clintons from their Whitewater woes.

According to Susan, Hillary looked at the certificate and frowned. In hostile tones, she demanded to know what Susan thought she was doing. Hillary's reaction stunned Susan. Although she did not know all the details, Susan explained that Bill and I had agreed on this course of action to spare the Clintons further problems from Whitewater.

Hillary refused to sign the stock transfer. She told Susan, "Jim promised that Whitewater was going to pay for Chelsea's education."

When Susan reported her exchange with Hillary to me, I was amazed. I had never told Hillary any such thing about Chelsea's education.

Despite my differences with Hillary, my bond with Bill remained unbroken. Our ties had evolved, over the years, from an early friendship to a business partnership to a relationship involving mutual political interests.

In the spring of 1985, Maurice Smith approached me about holding a reception to help Clinton retire a debt left over from his re-election campaign the year before. The campaign still had a deficit of $35,000, I was told. Bill and Hillary had signed a note in that amount at Maurice's Bank of Cherry Valley, and both Maurice and the Clintons wanted to settle the account.

Fund-raising had never been my forte in politics. Though I made modest contributions to friends, such as Clinton and Tucker, I had never held a fund-raiser. But I felt obligated to Maurice, because of our friendship over the years, and I saw this as another opportunity to strengthen the ties between the governor's office and the Madison enterprises.

I told Maurice I thought we could raise enough money to take care of the campaign debt in one evening. I said I would contribute three thousand dollars, the legal limit, and issued invitations to a late-afternoon event at Madison Guaranty's offices.

The reception took place in early April, as daylight lengthened past the closing hours for business. Dozens of guests arrived at our Main Street office, where tables for cocktails and hors d'oeuvres were set up in the lobby. The governor and his retinue of statehouse aides mingled with the guests. Bill even exchanged pleasantries with Jim Guy Tucker, whose presence surprised me. I had persuaded Jim Guy to make a thousand-dollar contribution to the Clinton affair; I thought it would show gratitude for Beverly Bassett's appointment as securities commissioner, but I didn't expect him to appear at the reception.

As the voices of cocktail chatter swelled to a din in the lobby, Maurice and I sought quiet in my glassed-in office, poised above the ground level. Neither of us drank, and we spent the rest of the early evening talking politics. By nightfall, the reception ended. It was not a particularly memorable affair, but we raised the $35,000 and Bill and Maurice went away content.

On the business front, the Campobello project appeared to be off to a profitable start, and I looked for new horizons. Madison Guaranty, our savings and loan that represented the source of funds for Madison Financial, our real estate operation, needed to raise additional capital. With my own investment limited, I sought new options. One possibility involved a sale of preferred stock to new investors. I thought it was a good time to use connections.

The Rose Law Firm was already on retainer, and doing damned little to justify the expense. I didn't want to deal with Hillary myself, so I suggested to John Latham that he ask her to make inquiries on our behalf to the securities commission regarding the preferred stock plan. Beverly Bassett, of course, was in charge of that department.

In late April, Hillary contacted Bassett about our proposal.

Bassett responded within two weeks with an opinion that the preferred stock plan "is not inconsistent with Arkansas law." As it turned out, I decided not to pursue the preferred stock issue. But I took up another venture that provided additional business for the Rose firm.

I had been considering the purchase of a tract of land owned by International Paper south of Little Rock, but I faced a problem. There was no access to the property from the highway. The path was blocked by an old industrial park.

In an effort to obtain an easement, I asked one of my employees, Seth Ward, to meet with the park owners, several elderly members of established Little Rock families. As a local figure of some prominence, Seth was on equal footing with them. He had recently retired, a wealthy man, after developing a successful parking-meter company, and he'd taken a job with my real estate company to stay busy. His son-in-law Webster Hubbell had been mayor of Little Rock. Seth knew most of the movers and shakers in the city.

Seth returned from his meeting to report that the owners were unwilling to grant me an easement. However, Seth said, they were willing to sell the land for $12 million.

"Oh, Seth, that's out of the question. There's no way we can do that."

But I didn't give up on the idea. The property, roughly a thousand acres with an existing water and sewer system, was more attractive than the tract I originally had my eye on. I entered into negotiations with the owners and wound up buying the land for $1.7 million.

We intended to subdivide the property into residential lots. Within an easy commute of downtown Little Rock, it promised to be our most ambitious undertaking in Arkansas. I decided to call it Castle Grande.

Webb Hubbell was one of the Rose partners, so Seth turned Castle Grande's paperwork over to him. We had no further dealings with Hillary, other than to ask her to contact another state agency, the Alcohol Beverage Control board, to see if it would be permissible to build a microbrewery on the site.

I pushed my financial limits, developing land, dealing lots, and reinvesting in new property elsewhere. Whitewater had been the biggest loser, though we continued to sell lots there sporadically. In 1985, Chris Wade agreed to take over the unsold lots at the Whitewater development. In exchange for the land, Chris gave me an airplane, which I sold immediately to pay down the principal on the old loan. Chris assumed half of the remaining debt. The other half was covered by regular payments from individuals who had purchased lots earlier. Whitewater was actually operating with a slight surplus. The only debt remaining involved the $25,000 Bank of Stephens loan I had taken out during my manipulations to remove Clinton's name from the 1983 Madison Guaranty loan. Overall, I had lost more than $100,000 on the venture, but I thought I was free of it at last.

Susan and I had a steady flow of income. She specialized in advertising and drew commissions for the television and radio commercials arranged by her own firm, Madison Marketing.

She was a conscientious business partner. After her Maple Creek commercials had become the talk of the town, I'd encouraged her to run for the Little Rock city board of directors. She filed as a candidate, but her grandmother became ill in Belgium, and Susan and her mother spent much of the campaign overseas. Like my run for Congress, her first race for public office failed.

In spite of our genuine affection for each other, our marriage continued to founder. She seemed distant and depressed. One night, when we were talking at our apartment, Susan spoke of going to Dallas to take a course in advertising.

"Why don't you do that?" I said. "Maybe it will cheer you up." I didn't think her temporary absence would make me miss her.

Susan went to Dallas in May 1985, ten years from the day we'd met outside Jim Ranchino's office. She rented an apartment there, and signed up for some classes. We talked regularly on the telephone. I later learned that Pat Harris was flying to Dallas every week to be with her. He was the young fellow I'd hired as my assistant campaign manager in 1982 and had brought into business with me in Little Rock.

Susan stayed in Dallas through the summer, then moved back to Little Rock. She didn't return to our place at the Riviera. Though we would remain business partners and good friends, we would never live together again. Susan chose to rent a place at Quapaw Tower, a fashionable apartment building off MacArthur Park, within walking distance of the governor's mansion and our headquarters at 1600 Main. Several state officials lived at Quapaw Tower, as did a nightclub singer named Gennifer Flowers.

As 1985 ended, I moved into a manic high. Deposits were growing at the savings and loan, and I held out the hope of branching into northwest Arkansas. Sales picked up at my real estate ventures. My difficult personal relationship with Susan had been resolved. And Whitewater, I thought, was behind me.

The first symptom of the problems that would engulf me showed up early in 1986. The savings and loan examiners were back, exuding hostility. A new set of examiners had taken over from the regular team from Dallas, and they disapproved of our policies and criticized the level of loans from Madison Guaranty to me and my businesses. I had lost none of the animosity from my experiences with the examiners in 1982, and my reactions were counterproductive. I suspected that Congressman Hammerschmidt was to blame again because he knew Henry Hamilton was working with me to establish a Madison branch in their home town, Harrison, and that made me angry. I was uncooperative with the examiners, responding to their questions with scorn and ridicule. They challenged our unorthodox transactions, but they failed to intimidate me. I knew the government relied on unusual accounting measures to salvage failing savings and loan associations elsewhere, and I was indignant that they faulted our policies.

Our savings and loan had been saved by liberal initiatives. When we bought the operation in 1982, the little thrift in Augusta had been practically mismanaged out of existence. Woodruff County Savings and Loan was paying about 15 percent interest on deposits and getting an average of 9 percent on their mortgage loans. They had it backward. Around the time that we took it over, I received a letter from the state savings and loan supervisor warning that the association had losses of $39,000 in the first four months of the year, and a net worth of $40,000. If we could not find additional capital for the institution, it would be insolvent in four months. Susan and I scrambled to save it by expanding the operation into Little Rock.

The examiners were unimpressed by our growing deposits; instead, they were critical of the loans made to support my operations at Madison Financial. I had carried my borrowing power to the limit, but I remained convinced I had done nothing illegal. Nevertheless, it was apparent that I was tapped out at Madison Guaranty. The savings and loan was given a cease-and-desist order. There would be no more loans to me from my own institution.

Undeterred by these events, Susan and I still hoped to buy the International Paper tract that had once needed the easement through the industrial park. We wanted to turn it into a residential development to rival the success of nearby Maple Creek. I planned to call the development Lowrance Heights; that was an inside joke, since it was one of the flattest areas around. With the old industrial park in my hands, an easement was no longer a problem. But a bigger obstacle lay in our way. We needed a substantial loan to buy it. Since we could no longer go to Madison Guaranty, we had to look elsewhere.

Jim Guy Tucker suggested that we ask David Hale about a loan. I had known David slightly at the university, where we were both members of the Acacia fraternity. Though he and his brother had been active in the Young Democrats, I lost track of him over the years.

David's boyhood home was the hills, and even though he had a college education, he still pronounced "Mrs." as "Miseries" in the hillbilly manner. He was a country boy who'd made it to the city, and he knew how to ingratiate himself with the local crowd. As a member of the Jaycees, a gung-ho civic organization, David strived for recognition. He wound up national president of the Jaycees. He held a part-time position as a traffic court judge in Little Rock, an appointment he received from Clinton, and he had experience as an entrepreneur as well. He had accumulated a bit of money and had started a small-business investment company called Capital Management Services, Inc.

My only recent contact with David involved a deal at Castle Grande. He and Jim Guy bought forty acres from us with the intention of putting up a shopping center. I was enthusiastic about their plan; a shopping center would serve as an amenity to attract buyers for our lots. It turned out that I had had another business connection with David. Madison Guaranty had given an $825,000 loan to a fellow named Dean Paul, a partner of Hale's. Paul, I learned, was a straw figure, obtaining the loan for one purpose and using the money for another. The $825,000 was handed over to Hale to provide capital for Hale's new investment company.

Not long after Jim Guy mentioned Hale as a source for a loan, Susan and I ran into David at the Black Eyed Pea, the same restaurant where a chance encounter with the Clintons in 1978 had produced Whitewater. In the informal fashion of the family diner, David, Susan, and I sat down together. Aside from his shopping center at Castle Grande, I was interested in the possibility of a loan. I had already asked one of the officers at Madison Guaranty if there was any rule against one banker loaning another money, and they said it was okay. I thought David might hold the key to Lowrance Heights, and I had done some homework.

Capital Management Services was licensed by the Small Business Administration and authorized to make loans to disadvantaged businesses owned by women and members of minority groups. Despite that limitation, I discovered that Arkansas fell within a wide Appalachian-like territory the federal government called the Delta Development Region. Anyone in the region could claim to be disadvantaged.

At dinner, we asked David about the possibility of a loan to Susan's advertising agency, which theoretically qualified—as a woman's enterprise—for a small-business loan. In fact, we intended to use the money to buy Lowrance Heights and to pay off the last $25,000 note left over from Whitewater.

Hale said he didn't think it would be a problem.

I went back to the office and typed up a proposal on my word processor. In the document, Susan officially asked for a loan to expand her agency and declared the money would be deposited in an operating account. She took the proposal to Hale's office the next day.

A few days later, I became apprehensive. We were preparing, quite consciously, to break the law. I had been creative in the past, but had kept within the rules. This venture would take me over the edge. After mulling it over, I typed up a second application, which stated that the loan would be used to finance Lowrance Heights. I took it to Hale and he tore up his copy of the original proposal. Too late. I would learn several years later that Hale had already sent the application to the Small Business Administration.

While Susan's loan application was pending, David met with me at the Castle Grande development to check on the land where he and Jim Guy planned to build their shopping center. I had been working at the development's sales office because the examiners had taken over my personal office in town.

Our meeting took place in a double-wide modular home we used for our sales staff. Castle Grande was a remote location, south of Little Rock and about eight hundred feet off the freeway, a suburb in the making. A few houses had been built in the development, but it was a lonely place, and we usually closed the office before it became dark.

When David and I finished our meeting, daylight was fading. We closed the office. One of Susan's brothers, Jim Henley, who was working at Castle Grande, locked the front door. The three of us walked a few feet down the sidewalk, past a picket fence, and headed toward the parking lot. In the gloaming, Clinton appeared. Castle Grande was an incongruous place to run into the governor of Arkansas, particularly at twilight. It was quite natural for Clinton to drop in at our downtown office, but this was too far for him to have jogged. Besides, he was dressed for business. He must have driven to the site.

Always gregarious, Bill engaged us in a couple of minutes of small talk, standing on the sidewalk outside the sales office.

I was tired and ready to go home, so I said to Hale: "Well, I guess we're through, aren't we?"

Bill interjected, "Did you discuss Susan's loan?"

David said, "That's been taken care of."

Instead of accepting David's assurance, Bill blurted, "There's some land up in Marion County that can be used as collateral."

I remember thinking: But, Bill, all the lots at Whitewater have been sold. Then I remembered that he was never on top of the situation there.

Our conversation petered out. There wasn't much more to say. That was the essence of Bill's exchange with David Hale. I heard it, and so did Jim Henley.

I thought nothing more about Clinton's appearance until I got back to my apartment that evening. Then it hit me like a thunderclap. How did Bill know about Susan's loan? Why did he care about the loan? And how did he know that I would be meeting with David Hale at Castle Grande at that precise hour?

I had talked with Susan several times during the course of the business day. It was clear that she knew I was seeing David. No one else knew. And no one else was involved in the loan application.

I sat down in a chair in my living room, utterly alone, pondering the questions. There could be only one conclusion: Susan and Bill had resumed their affair, and she had asked him to make it clear to David Hale, the man he had appointed judge, that the governor was interested in Susan's loan application.

13

My health began to fail long before my finances. As early as 1983, I had problems with dizziness and blurred vision. Driving home from the Maple Creek development one evening, I felt ill. A dark shade seemed to come over my eyes, and after I reached my apartment, I passed out altogether. When I regained consciousness, I realized I had fallen and cut my head. A physician I saw believed my blackout was related to a heart condition and instructed me to wear a device to monitor my heart for forty-eight hours. I walked around for a couple of days with his gadget strapped to my chest, but after I returned the monitor to the doctor, he discovered the batteries were dead and nothing had been recorded. I said forget it.

I developed numbness in my extremities. The sensation seemed to strike me in the evenings. After eating dinner at a cafe, Henry Hamilton and I would often drive to a shopping mall to stroll for exercise, and I would lose feeling in my hands. I told Henry I was worried about my condition; I seemed weaker than usual. He suggested that I slow my pace. I began to take midafternoon breaks. I'd go home and lie down for a nap before going back to close the office.

My father's health was failing, too. He began to suffer heart attacks, and after each seizure my mother would call me, frantic and crying. Rushing to Bradford to be with them, I was often hit with sensations of vertigo. I would have to pull my car off the highway and wait until the dizziness passed. I didn't know it at the time, but these were symptoms that my carotid arteries were clogged, diminishing the flow of blood to my brain.

My father died on New Year's Day 1984. He was seventy-six years old, and his own depressions had lifted by the end of his life. But he suffered from what they call in the country a "slow heart." After his body's electrical system broke down, he was given a pacemaker, but it did no good. When he felt the surge of his last attack, he went into the bathroom to be by himself, and he died there.

His death floored me. I drifted into a depressive cycle, discouraged by sad dreams about my father, dreams in which I was a child again, misbehaving and provoking his wrath. They were vivid, sorrowful dreams. My father had rarely rebuked me as a child, and after I'd sobered up and become a political figure in the state, he'd expressed great pride in me. Thrashing in my sleep, I suddenly felt that our lives had passed before we could become close. I would be washed with grief and wake unrelieved. Not only was my spirit troubled, I could feel my body giving out.

The timing of the examiners was always exquisite. They'd descended on me at the Madison Bank in 1982, when I was running for Congress, and they'd arrived at Madison Guaranty in 1984, a few days after my father's death. When they returned in 1986, with their questions and admonitions about the way we did business, I was near the end of my patience.

Flying back and forth between Arkansas and Campobello added

to my exhaustion, and I labored feverishly, seven days a week, to get sales at the Castle Grande project moving in order to keep up the cash flow. Meanwhile, the examiners were combing the savings and loan books, expressing disapproval of negative balances in the Madison Financial accounts.

I had falsified applications to obtain the loan from David Hale, and I had funneled money illegally to Bill Clinton, but I'd never plundered the savings and loan, and I resented the examiners' insinuations.

I retreated to my last sanctuary, my apartment at the Riviera building, mentally and physically beaten.

When the board of directors of the savings and loan was summoned to the Federal Home Loan Bank Board offices in Dallas in early July, I was too ill to attend. Jim Guy Tucker had referred our case to John Selig, an attorney specializing in financial affairs in Tucker's law firm. Selig represented Madison's interests in the Dallas hearing. Beverly Bassett, the securities commissioner, also attended. Following the meeting, Selig called to tell me I would have to give up my role in the Madison operation.

The examiners had put a halt to funding for my projects from the savings and loan. I could do no more financing. Inasmuch as my projects depended on a ready supply of money, I was out of business. The psychological impact was enormous, and the nightmares returned. In one dream my father left the door to his store open, and townspeople wandered in from the street to carry away his inventory. Devastated as I was by my reversals, my dreams reflected the guilt I felt. My take-it-to-the-limit practices had led to this moment. In a throwback to my remorseful days as a drunk, I thought: My God, I deserve this.

I recognized it was time to quit. I called Steve Cuffman, an attorney who had been working with Madison Financial. I told him to take over the operation. He came to the apartment and I gave him my letter of resignation, effective July 31. I also handed over the keys to a Jaguar sedan. Always a lover of flashy cars, I had been using the Jag, one of a fleet of cars Madison had bought for Henry Hamilton's leasing program targeted at young doctors.

Within a little more than a year, my health had failed, my marriage had fallen apart, and the business I had conceived and developed had passed from my control.

About ten days after the ultimatum from Dallas, on a sweltering July day, Susan stopped by to discuss the situation. Beyond my recollection of Susan's arrival and an intense pain, my memory of the day is poor. According to Susan, I suddenly went berserk. In the middle of a conversation, I leaped from my chair and dashed barefooted from the second-floor apartment down the fire escape to the street below. The pavement was blisteringly hot and burned the bottoms of my feet. Susan screamed and telephoned the police as well as Jim Guy Tucker.

When I regained my senses, I was standing at the door to the Riviera, talking with the police. Though I assured them I felt fine, I was dazed and disoriented. Susan called an ambulance and climbed inside to ride with me to the hospital.

Jim Guy and John Latham, who had been severely criticized by the savings and loan examiners, were waiting at the hospital when I arrived. After they helped settle me into a room, I remember saying to John, "I let everybody down." I feared that the entire Madison operation was going under. Not only had Jim McDougal's dreams unwound, I thought all the people I had hired would be thrown out of work.

The doctors determined that I had survived a stroke, a manifestation of the blackouts I had been experiencing for three years because of the loss of blood to my brain. While neurosurgeons studied my physical deterioration, my erratic behavior prompted Jim Guy to ask a psychiatrist to take me as his patient. I submitted to a number of tests. The psychiatrist diagnosed me as manic-depressive; the physician found I had blocked carotid arteries.

My friend and one-time business partner Dr. C. E. Ransom had been hinting for years that I was manic-depressive, suffering from my father's and grandfather's illness. He had prescribed a drug, but the medication pushed me deeper into depression. Until my hospitalization in Little Rock, I hadn't realized the full extent of my problems. I had never even heard of carotid arteries.

Discharged from the hospital after a month, I moved to a little house. My behavior seemed comparable to the grim period thirty years earlier when I'd witnessed my father moping around our home, doing nothing for months.

While I was convalescing, Jim Guy came by my house. He had been helpful as my lawyer and as my friend, and I trusted him as much as any man I had ever known. After we chatted a bit, he asked, "Can I do anything for you?"

I admitted I needed money. I told him that no bank would give me a loan. The newspapers had reported my abrupt resignation from the Madison operation, and it was common knowledge that my business had collapsed. Nevertheless, I said, Susan and I still held $109,000 worth of promissory notes from our Flowerwood Farms project. I asked if he could use the notes to get me a loan.

"Sure," he said.

Despite my impaired condition, I remember clearly the details of our agreement. I would sign the notes over to Jim Guy, and he would arrange a $50,000 loan in his name. He would turn the money over to me. After the regular income from the notes—it was $1,754 a month—paid off the $50,000 loan in a few years, Susan and I would get back from Jim Guy the remaining principle of $59,000. In the meantime, the $50,000 would be like a transfusion to a hemorrhaging patient.

The money was a godsend. Susan hired a woman to help care for me. Meals were brought to the house. I stayed inside, brooding. Susan visited every day, trying to bolster my morale. We discussed our business interests, especially the Lowrance Heights project, which we had bought with the money from David Hale. It represented the last vestige of the McDougal enterprises, and I wanted desperately to believe that Lowrance Heights might deliver us from our troubles. Every afternoon Susan came with her paperwork, and sat for hours in my living room to keep me company.

I drifted there for nearly eight months, through another dreary Arkansas winter of early darkness, cold rain, wind, and sleet. Jim McDougal, the bon vivant, had become a hermit.

The following spring, I thought it might help to move to California, the state of sun, growth, and opportunity. California had attracted the Joads of *The Grapes of Wrath* and thousands of real-life Okies and Arkansans, and I, too, felt its pull. My Uncle Willie had his dreams realized there, and lived out his last years in the comfort that had escaped him in rural Arkansas. All things seemed possible in California.

After scouting locations in southern California, I settled in San Diego, still depressed and unable to perform any kind of work. Although I had been unemployed for nearly a year, I had a nest egg for rent payments and living expenses. Susan and I filed a joint tax return for 1986—a year in which I worked only for six months—and reported income of $358,000. We were not yet paupers. Aside from the $50,000 Tucker had provided, Susan and I had monthly checks arriving from other promissory notes we held from earlier ventures, before the savings and loan experiment. We turned over our Madison Guaranty stock to Hale to pay off the $300,000 loan and sold our interest in the Madison Bank & Trust Co. in Kingston. Expenses were devouring much of our net worth, but I didn't require a lot of money to maintain my lifestyle. I slept much of the time and listened to the radio. Sometimes, I sat in a park alone.

Susan telephoned regularly, reporting on how she and her brother David were progressing on Lowrance Heights. She kept me abreast of Arkansas news. Even though we were estranged, she was my link to home.

While I was in California, Hillary Clinton began agitating Susan. She demanded the records from Whitewater. Corporate tax returns had not been filed for a couple of years, and she wanted to clear the books before Bill's next campaign. Bill was actually planning to run for the 1988 Democratic presidential nomination, but he abandoned the idea in the summer of 1987. According to rumors in Little Rock, he was dissuaded by the prospect of ugly questions regarding his private life. Adultery had become a public issue following Gary Hart's departure from the presidential race earlier that year, and Bill, it was said, didn't want to be part of the debate.

Susan said Hillary had grown vicious with her, and she described Hillary as unsympathetic toward me. Hillary mocked my flight to California. "Jim McDougal's out there being Jim McDougal," she told Susan.

Actually, Jim McDougal was in California trying to escape Jim McDougal.

Before Christmas of 1987, my money finally ran out. I couldn't pay my rent, and I couldn't work. Subsisting on cheap sandwiches, I felt my situation had become hopeless. If I tried to stay in California, I knew I would end up on the street. Defeated, I returned to Arkansas.

After my father's death, my mother had moved to Little Rock, and I stayed a few days with her. Then I made arrangements with my old friends the Rileys, of Arkadelphia, to move back to their cottage where I had enjoyed better times, teaching at Ouachita and courting Susan. I was not sure how I was going to support myself, but the Rileys were always willing to help.

Following a spell of unbroken bad luck, I was rescued—ironically, by a check from the same government that I felt had broken me. At the end of 1987, I was told my application for permanent disability had been approved by the Social Security Administration. A check for $6,000 appeared in the mail, representing retroactive payment to cover my illness. The government action put an official imprimatur on the time my trouble began: July 1986, the same month that I'd surrendered my position with the Madison enterprises and suffered my stroke. The Social Security decision also ensured monthly disability checks. It was, I thought, a miracle.

My holiday joy was short-lived. I fell back into depression in Arkadelphia, sitting in the little house at the foot of the hill on the Rileys' property, chain-smoking and listening to the radio. I rarely watched television and seldom bothered to open the mail, which piled up on a table in a vacant room. Every now and then, Claudia Riley peeked inside to make sure I was alive.

Shortly after I returned to Arkansas, Susan moved to California, hoping to start over herself. Other than my mother and the Rileys, there seemed to be no one left for me in Arkansas.

The years of 1988 and 1989 are largely blurs. John Paul Hammerschmidt's pal George Bush was elected president, but the event barely registered on my consciousness. The Berlin Wall was demolished and eastern Europe escaped the shackles of communism, yet I have little memory of the news from overseas.

My personal quandary deepened. I learned I was being investigated in connection with irregularities at the Madison enterprises.

John Selig, the lawyer I'd retained at Jim Guy's suggestion, had done me no favors. He'd hired a Memphis accounting firm to inspect Madison's books, and the accountants had charged Madison about $250,000 for a report that would be used to implicate their own clients. The report was turned over to the new U.S. Attorney, Charles Banks, a loyal Republican who had been recommended for the position by Hammerschmidt.

It didn't take Banks long to develop accusations that I had wrecked my company. I believe I was the first person in Arkansas his office investigated. In the summer of 1989, I was indicted, along with two of Susan's brothers, David and Jim Henley, on charges of fraud. We were prepared to fight the charges, but the investigation claimed one victim. John Latham pleaded guilty to a relatively minor offense.

I didn't fully understand the charges, and I was in no position to defend myself. At Jim Guy's suggestion, I accepted a young lawyer named Sam Heuer as my court-appointed attorney. Sam was from Batesville, Arkansas, a graduate of the University of Mississippi and the University of Arkansas Law School, where he had studied under Bill Clinton. He had worked briefly in Tucker's firm before setting out on his own in Little Rock. After I learned that Sam had recently bought the Tuckers' old house, I surmised that Jim Guy wanted Sam to pick up enough money from my case to support his mortgage payments. Another Arkansas connection.

I was not much help to my own lawyer. I couldn't recall details or think clearly for any length of time. My memory was so poor that I checked myself into a psychiatric hospital in Little Rock. I thought I was losing my mind. For the second time in my life, I heard the term: carotid arteries. An artery to my brain was blocked. Unless it could be cleared, I would suffer another stroke and die. I didn't need therapy at a psychiatric hospital, I was told; I needed surgery.

As a measure of my incapacity, I returned to Arkadelphia to pack and put my suitcase in front of the door so I wouldn't forget it. Leaving, I must have stepped over the bag on the way out. When I arrived at the North Little Rock hospital, I realized I had to make a 150-mile round-trip to retrieve my clothes.

The surgery provided some relief, but I was still unable to prepare for my trial. Sam suggested a plea of "diminished capacity," and the court sent me to a federal psychiatric center in Springfield, Missouri, for evaluation. After forty-seven days, the psychiatrists made their diagnosis, a finding that was accepted by the court. I was manic-depressive, but in command of my faculties. In other words, I had problems, but I was sane, sober, qualified, and capable of standing trial, the only Whitewater figure fully certified by the government as sane.

My victory and my vindication came in federal court in Little Rock in the spring of 1990.

I was charged with thirteen counts altogether, including eight counts of fraud—the government is very good at working up multiple counts of wrongdoing—in connection with two transactions at Castle Grande. I suspect the prosecutors could have brought specious charges against anyone involved with the development, but they didn't bother my old friend Senator Fulbright, who'd bought a tract at Castle Grande for $770,000 as a long-term investment for his family. Nor did they charge Jim Guy Tucker, who was elected lieutenant governor that year. Jim Guy had not only bought a tract at Castle Grande with David Hale, he had purchased a water and sewer system as well.

Instead, the U.S. Attorney's office concentrated on the powerless, bringing charges against Susan's brothers. The government accused me—a political irritant to Republicans—of selling property through straws in order to plow money back into Madison Financial.

In one case, a guy named Davis Fitzhugh, who owned a broker's license and worked with the savings and loan, bought a piece of Castle Grande where a building once used by the Levi Strauss Co. was located. The building itself rented for five thousand dollars a month, assuring the owner a steady income if occupied.

While Fitzhugh was handling the property for us as a salesman, he came by my office with an observation. "You know, I think we may be too high on the price," he said. "But at five hundred thousand dollars, it will carry itself because it has sixty thousand a year in rental income."

I said, "Well, why don't you buy it if it's such a good deal?"

"Do you care?" he asked.

"Hell, no," I said.

I was in business to make sales. He bought the property, and as a salesman, he got a commission, which he used for the down payment. It was the same as if a car salesman at an Oldsmobile dealership bought an Olds; he had to pay for it, but he got a commission on the sale. Nothing illegal to it.

A similar proposition governed the second case. The Henley

brothers, both salesmen at Castle Grande, and R. D. Randolph, who was handling construction projects at the development, bought property there. David and Jim took commissions on the sale and used the money to make the down payment.

The transactions enhanced the cash flow at Castle Grande, but there was no need for funny business. The project had already produced sales of more than $3 million on a $1.7 million investment.

Nevertheless, the accountants flagged the deals involving the Castle Grande salesmen, and four years later, I found myself in court. It was a time when public reaction against savings and loan excesses had triggered a series of prosecutions around the country. Though convinced of my innocence, I held out little hope of acquittal.

Even after the charges against David Henley were thrown out before the case went to the jury, I remained pessimistic and bewildered. I never understood the charges, and neither, I believe, did the jury. I had muddled through Sam's attempts to prepare a defense.

Then, on June 5, I took the stand, and I experienced a mental breakthrough. As I began my testimony, I regained some of the composure and logic that had been missing for several years.

As Sam walked me through his direct examination, I told how the savings and loan regulators had first suggested a service corporation to build shopping centers and marinas, and how I had asked them, "Don't you think it would be safer if we just subdivide the land and sold people some land so they could live out in the country?" They had agreed, and Madison Financial Corporation was born.

I told how we had built Madison Guaranty from the ashes of the old Woodruff County savings and loan. When Sam asked if I was the boss, I answered: "Well, down at that grocery store, when Daddy walked in he was the boss. You know, he owned it." I was the boss, I explained, but I didn't understand everything that went on. Once, I said, when I tried to pinch-hit at a teller's window, the employees told me if I ever came in there again, they'd kill me.

I tried to be folksy and self-effacing while I waited for the prosecutor's cross-examination. I told of Senator Fulbright's investment in the property, and added, "I don't believe he thinks it's a sham." I vouched for the honesty of the other politician involved in the project, Jim Guy Tucker.

My overall dream for Castle Grande, I testified, was to give "the kind of people they called 'working people' when I was growing up, the people who work for a salary, a chance to be outside the city, but where they just immediately get on the freeway and go to work."

I pointed out that John Selig, among others, had given me legal advice assuring me that our salesmen could receive commissions on the real estate they bought for themselves.

When the U.S. prosecutor, a well-dressed and obviously well-trained man named Ken Stoll, began his cross-examination, I was ready. All of the self-doubts that had clouded my thinking for the past four years seemed to be lifting.

Stoll was not bombastic, but he resorted to cheap tricks. He pitched a red herring into the proceedings by asking about the Jaguar. The question didn't bother me. It had been a used car, I told him, and I had put further use on it.

He asked me about the bonuses I paid myself.

Stoll: "I think the Burrod and Huggins report indicates from 1983 to October of '86 the salary and bonuses you got over that period of time was $373,000. Do you recall that?"

McDougal: "I wouldn't argue with it."

I told him I had invested $400,000 in all. "So I went in the hole. I worked four years for nothing and lost everything I had."

Stoll suggested that Susan and I were "collecting a substantial amount of money."

"Almost as good as being assistant United States attorney, working thirty hours a week making $70,000 a year, isn't it, Mr. Stoll?" I replied.

"Do you want to go back to my question?"

"Your question is entirely pejorative, you know it is," I shot back. "It's inflammatory. What do you want me to say?"

He didn't seem to understand that Susan was paid through her own advertising agency commissions. And when he expressed incredulity that we sometimes sold property at less than the appraised value, I told him:

"This is going to be difficult to teach to a man that's never been in business, Mr. Stoll. But the people that hold out for the top dollar are the people who go broke. We paid about $1,750,000 for this. It didn't take me ninety days to recover that. I wanted the rest of the profit as quickly as I could get it to capitalize this business."

When the prosecutor continued along this line, I added: "We were in business to make a profit. We're capitalists, not communists."

When he suggested that the Madison operation was bankrupt, I told him, "It was not then bankrupt and it is not now bankrupt."

Stoll had 220 questions he had wanted to ask me. I know, because I saw he had tallied them on a legal pad. Discouraged by my testimony, he stopped far short of number 220.

Jim Henley and I were acquitted. David's charges had already been thrown out. When it was over, I declared to the Arkansas reporters covering the trial that it had been a "political show trial that would do Joe Stalin proud."

The *Wall Street Journal* reported that in 1989, the year we had been indicted, the government brought formal charges against 247 people associated with savings and loans. Only three were cleared or found not guilty: David Henley, Jim Henley, and Jim McDougal.

I made a copy of a single sheet from the court records, the page stating that I had been acquitted. I took the document home to Arkadelphia, had it framed, and hung it on the wall of the Rileys' cottage, where I was preparing to resume my life.

My long nightmare, I thought, was over.

14

           he Whitewater case unfolded because I wanted Bill
Clinton to feel my pain. Bill, and especially Hillary,
surely caused me pain. But the deterioration in my
friendship with the Clintons was nothing compared to the betrayal
by one of my best friends, Jim Guy Tucker.

It was Tucker's refusal to return $59,000 worth of promissory
notes that drove me to take my grievances with Tucker and the
Clintons to Sheffield Nelson, my one-time business partner and one
of the top Republicans in the state. It was Nelson who passed the
information on to Jeff Gerth, an investigative reporter for the *New
York Times*. It was Gerth's story that first described the troubles of
the Whitewater development and raised questions about the propri-
ety of the Clintons' involvement in the project. And it was subsequent stories that dug into Whitewater and other Arkansas business
connections that loomed over the president of the United States
from the day he took office and later convicted Tucker, the governor of Arkansas.

The genie was unleashed in January 1992, when I decided to seek
legal advice from Nelson.

Although we had not seen much of each other in the years since we were partners in Campobello, I felt comfortable in taking my case to Nelson. He and Jerry Jones had received a good return on their investment in the island when they sold their interest in 1988, around the time Madison enterprises shut down its sales office there. I was out of the business by then, but I understood that Nelson and Jones made a $275,000 profit on their $400,000 stake. Campobello was now in the hands of the Resolution Trust Corporation, which took over the project after Madison Guaranty finally failed, several years after I left, a collapse that I was told cost taxpayers an estimated $60 million dollars (God only knows where that inflated figure came from). Nelson never complained about my stewardship of Campobello, and he went out of his way to be solicitous one night when Susan and I bumped into him at the Black Eyed Pea shortly after I was acquitted. Nelson congratulated me for my court victory and inquired about my health. Afterward, I told Susan, "I hadn't seen the fellow in years, and he's more genuinely concerned about me than some of my friends."

Other than our background at Campobello, Nelson and I had another thing in common. We had both been humiliated by Bill Clinton.

In 1990, when Nelson challenged Clinton as the Republican candidate for governor, Clinton dredged up old allegations of a sweetheart deal between Nelson and Jones. The case that came under scrutiny involved connections between Arkansas buddies, but no wrongdoing was ever proved.

Nelson had been head of Arkla, the giant Arkansas utility, in the early 1980s, when there was a shortage of natural gas reserves. To expand Arkla's supplies, he struck a deal with Jones, the wildcatter who had parlayed his willingness to take risks in the gas and oil fields into a personal fortune. Jones wagered $50 million on his bid to produce the gas for Arkla; in return, Arkla gave Jones favorable terms on the price of the gas. If Jones's wildcat operation, Arkoma Production Co., failed, he stood to lose his $50 million investment.

Instead, Arkoma successfully tapped into a rich gas vein in one of its basins in the Southwest, and Arkla eventually bought Jones's company for $175 million. By the time Arkla agreed to pay the huge sum to acquire Arkoma, Nelson had resigned from the utility, replaced by Thomas F. "Mack" McLarty, one of Clinton's closest boyhood friends.

As the 1990 campaign approached, Clinton appointed a panel of his political allies to review the transaction for the state's Public Service Commission. Critics publicly called the Arkla-Arkoma agreement a "crooked, sleazy deal to rip off the ratepayers." Clinton assailed the Nelson-Jones arrangement from the stump, hissing the term "Arkla-Arkoma" as if it were a dread disease. Clinton's handpicked panel found no evidence of legal or ethical misconduct by Nelson, but it never stopped a whispering campaign against the Republican.

Clinton, of course, prevailed in the election, but he and Nelson became enemies for life.

When I first went to see Nelson, I was smarting from a variety of insulting actions by the Clintons that had accumulated in the years following my breakdown. At one point, Hillary refused to provide a financial disclosure statement we needed to renew our Whitewater loan at Citizens Bank, the loan supported by payments from the promissory notes. After she took charge of the Whitewater affairs, Hillary demanded that Susan turn over all the records of the company. Bill tried to take the edge off Hillary's request with a softer approach. He simply asked Susan nicely: Would you mind letting Hillary look at the documents?

At the time, I was in no shape to object; Whitewater was the least of my worries. Susan collected bank statements, check stubs, corporate records, deeds, mortgages, and notes related to the Whitewater company and put them in a banker's box. I heard later that Pat Harris, Susan's lover, prevented her from personally taking the

documents to the governor's mansion. He knew Clinton's reputation around women; perhaps he suspected that Susan and Bill were
more than just friends. At any rate, Pat told Susan he didn't want
her "within a mile of Bill Clinton." Bill Henley, Susan's brother,
delivered the box to the governor's mansion.

Later, it became apparent that as far as Hillary was concerned,
Susan and Jim McDougal had fallen off the face of the earth. When
she sought our signatures for a routine corporate transaction, she
couldn't locate us. She didn't realize I had moved back to Arkansas
from California; nor did she know Susan had moved to California.

With Bill's presidential campaign cranking up in 1991, Hillary
wanted to clear the decks of Whitewater. She called upon Susan
and me to grant her power of attorney in connection with the
business. I refused. Hillary eventually reached Susan in California. I believe Pat Harris must have signed Susan's name to Hillary's document. I feel certain Susan never signed it. In a
telephone conversation, I strongly advised Susan not to acquiesce
to Hillary's demands.

Hillary kept up her offensive. Bill never bothered to get too
deeply involved; he still wanted to be everybody's buddy. But he,
too, had aggravated me after my collapse in 1986.

Following my return from California, he had called me to come
to his office. I think Susan must have asked him to see me. I was ill,
broke, and needed help. When I sat down with Bill at the capitol, in
the room where I had once regaled him with imitations of Churchill,
he asked if I wanted a job in his administration. Fumbling to avoid
the appearance of a pitiful supplicant, I said I knew of no specific
job. But I added, "If Maurice Smith has an opening in the Highway
Department, I think my background might qualify me for a job
there." Bill nodded. When I left, I thought Clinton was prepared to
put me on my feet. I never heard back from him.

A couple of years later, a day or two after my acquittal, Bill
called. He reached me at the Rileys' home in Arkadelphia. When
Claudia told me the governor was on the line, I assumed he had

telephoned to congratulate me. He did that, but something else was on his mind. I could hear a television clearly in the background, and at one point, Bill broke off the conversation to walk into another room and ask someone to turn down the TV. I realized Hillary was listening on an extension. When Bill got back on the line, he told me he and Hillary had incurred about $3,000 in expenses since taking over the Whitewater records. He asked if I could reimburse them. I couldn't believe it. I was living on a Social Security disability check, and the governor of Arkansas and his wife wanted another $3,000 from me. I told him it would be impossible.

In the days that followed my trial, I had tried to put back together some of the pieces of my life. I spent about six weeks in Arkadelphia, simply resting from the ordeal. Then I began visiting some old friends in Little Rock. I stopped to see Betty and Jim Guy Tucker at their home. Jim Guy brewed a pot of coffee for me in the kitchen, then we went into the family room, where Betty was playing with their two daughters, Anna and Sara. I had always given mints to the girls when they were younger. Though I had not seen them in several years, one of the girls approached me and asked, "Do you still have peppermints?" I laughed. It was good to be remembered favorably, and it made me think that the Tuckers had not talked about my troubles at the family dinner table.

Jim Guy and I discussed a business deal, a piece of farmland we might buy together, but I noticed Betty growing tense. There was a look of apprehension in her eyes, as if she wanted to convey a warning to back off the subject.

I knew Jim Guy was holding my promissory notes worth $59,000. According to my calculations, the $50,000 loan he had arranged for me would be paid off by the end of the summer of 1991. At that time, he was supposed to return the balance left from the $109,000 in notes I had given to him in 1986. I didn't mention the money to the Tuckers during my visit. I considered it a social call, and I felt uncomfortable discussing the notes in front of Betty and the girls.

After I left the Tuckers, I drove to north Arkansas to see Chris Wade and to explore the feasibility of new real estate ventures there. The Whitewater experience had not discouraged me from making more investments in the area. I anticipated a big payment from Jim Guy, and I thought it was still possible to use the money to carve a fortune out of the Ozarks.

Then blindness—the same condition that hobbled two of the best men in my life, Uncle Bert and Bob Riley—struck my mother. She lost her sight in January 1991, following an adverse reaction to tests she was taking prior to an operation. I moved Mother into a little housing development called Caddo Valley near Arkadelphia so I could care for her, and my plans to renew my real estate operations were set back. I suffered another loss when my good friend and business associate Henry Hamilton died. Heart failure claimed the last of the Hamilton twins. Saddled with grief and debt, I filed for bankruptcy. I had debts of $700,000—much of it owed in back taxes—and about the only assets I could claim were my clothes. I was beginning to think that the biblical character Job had it easy compared to my own vicissitudes.

Mother and I lived humbly in Caddo Valley, left with little more than our recollections of better days. She cherished her memories of my association with Clinton. She was one of the governor's greatest supporters, glorying in the times he had singled out the McDougal family with expressions of gratitude for our friendship in his life. Bill had always been thoughtful to his elders. A natural politician, he had the personal touch, winning over the mothers and fathers of his friends with sentimental remarks.

Even though Susan and I were moving toward a divorce, Mother maintained a fondness for her. It was at Susan's suggestion, I believe, that Clinton telephoned our house to commiserate with my mother following her loss of sight. Mother was thrilled by the call from the governor. He said he was sorry about the troubles that had beset us, and he promised her that he had an important job for me in his administration.

When my mother told me about the conversation, she wept with joy. She was relieved. I was her only child, and she worried for me. She had her own health problems, but I believe she cared more about my rehabilitation. A job with Clinton, she told me, would restore my reputation.

But Clinton, by then, was preparing to run for the Democratic nomination for president, and neither my mother nor I heard from him again.

I was disappointed. But my mother's dismay seemed far more cruel. Almost every day she asked me, "Has Bill called you yet?"

My treatment at the hands of the Clintons was painful, but my break with Jim Guy Tucker was even more traumatic. Three decades of friendship were wiped out in 1991, the year after Jim Guy was elected lieutenant governor on a Democratic ticket headed by Clinton. The promissory notes Jim Guy was supposed to be holding represented the last vestige of worth in my family's estate. I had been living on my disability check and some of my mother's funds, and as my money ran out I assigned the remaining assets of Flowerwood Farms—the promissory notes—to my mother.

Late in the summer of 1991, at a time when my old $50,000 loan had been paid off, I wrote Jim Guy about the remaining notes. When he didn't respond, I wrote again. After several attempts, I finally reached him by telephone at the lieutenant governor's office. Jim Guy was evasive; he offered me a lot of doubletalk about how I had sold him the notes. He claimed not to understand my position. In my duress, he insisted, I had sold him all of the notes for $50,000. I couldn't believe Jim Guy was claiming that the remaining $59,000 belonged to him.

As I talked with him, a sinking sensation overcame me. I realized my good friend had concluded that no one would believe my version. Ill, bankrupt, and once indicted, I had little credibility compared to the lieutenant governor of Arkansas.

He suggested that my understanding of the deal was skewed by my memory loss. I'd had gaps in my memory in recent years, but I could recall our 1986 arrangement precisely. It was clear that Jim Guy intended to cheat me. Terribly disappointed and discouraged, I told him, "I suspect this is the last conversation we'll ever have." Then I hung up.

When I investigated the matter, I found that instead of taking out a $50,000 loan, Jim Guy made papers for $55,000. He put the extra $5,000 in his pocket as a "legal fee." I had been suspicious of Jim Guy's law partner John Selig after the Madison tailspin. Selig had charged the Madison enterprises huge legal fees and arranged the audit that resulted in my trial. Even though I had problems with Selig, I always trusted Jim Guy.

His claim on the notes upset Susan and me more than any other setback. It was punishing to both of us. More than money, it involved friendship and familial connections. I was fond of Jim Guy's mother and father; Jim Guy's sister, Carol, had been a special friend. During some rough patches in Jim Guy's career, I had assisted him financially. Now in our time of trouble, Jim Guy had deserted us. Susan was devastated by the behavior of her best friend's husband. "I can't believe it," Susan wailed to me over the phone.

At the beginning of 1992, the golden boys of Arkansas, the dashing fellows with Ivy League educations, were riding high. Bill Clinton led a weak Democratic field in the race for the presidential nomination, and Jim Guy Tucker, as lieutenant governor, was poised for a higher position.

I was bitter. My old friends had abandoned me to my troubles, while pursuing their own fame with a show of sanctimony that damn near nauseated me. The Clintons had left me to pay a disproportionate share of the Whitewater losses and Tucker had taken $59,000 in notes.

I was prepared to sue Jim Guy, but knew I couldn't ask Sam

Heuer, my lawyer in the 1990 trial, to represent me, because of his relationship with Tucker. Other Democratic lawyers in Little Rock would be reluctant to take a case against Tucker, who seemed to be moving inexorably toward the governor's office as Clinton's stock rose nationally.

As a result, I turned to Sheffield Nelson. Roughed up by Clinton on the Arkla-Arkoma charges, Nelson fought back with his own negative campaign in 1990. One of Sheffield's supporters, a former state employee named Larry Nichols, filed a suit against the governor in the midst of the campaign, complaining that he had been wrongfully dismissed from his job on the Arkansas Development Finance Authority in 1988. Nichols had been sacked for making hundreds of dollars' worth of calls in support of the right-wing Nicaraguan group the Contras on a state telephone. When Nichols's lawsuit failed to gain much attention, he called a press conference on the capitol steps and passed out a press release identifying five women with whom, Nichols claimed, Clinton conducted affairs while drawing from a state slush fund to finance out-of-town rendezvous.

A statehouse reporter felt obligated to ask Clinton about the women. As he read each name from the list, Clinton issued a denial. When the reporter reached Gennifer Flowers's name, the governor paused, then wisecracked, "God, I kind of hate to deny her." She was an attractive blond, a singer well known on the Little Rock cocktail lounge circuit. But Clinton denied having an affair with her, too, and the story blew over without much impact.

But the 1990 campaign left a residue of bad blood between Nelson and Clinton. I thought of taking Nelson as my counsel as a marriage of convenience, like an alliance between England and France.

In a preliminary discussion with Nelson about my dispute with Tucker, I told him of the Clintons' role in the Whitewater project. I explained that Hillary had been claiming deductions on the Clintons' personal income tax returns for payments made by the Whitewater corporation.

Nelson was gleeful. He wanted me to talk with Gerth, the *New*

York Times reporter who had written a long, investigative article about the Stephenses extensive connections in Arkansas a few years earlier. Gerth had been sent back to Arkansas to snoop around on the Clintons' finances, and Nelson's office had been one of the first stops on the reporter's schedule.

Gerth contacted me, and I agreed to see him. He drove down to Arkadelphia, and we met at the Western Sizzlin', my favorite cafe in town. After we helped ourselves to a buffet featuring steaks and salads, we settled down to talk. Gerth already knew some of the bare bones of Whitewater, and I filled in some blanks. I felt the Clintons had taken advantage of me, I told him. It was the first of several conversations we had, both in person and on the phone.

Although Hillary had possession of most of the Whitewater documents, I still had a few papers that stayed with me providentially. After my 1990 trial, I cleaned my house of the detritus left from my business years and began burning the junk in a trash pile. A few pieces of paper swirled out of the fire. When I retrieved them, I saw they were old check stubs from the Whitewater Development Company. The documents showed that various McDougal entities had made substantial deposits into the Whitewater account over the years, at a time when the Clintons were contributing nothing.

I gave the check stubs to Gerth, and they became his ace in the hole. When Clinton's representatives lied to Gerth early the 1992 campaign, claiming the Clintons had made equal payments to the project, he produced my papers. Suddenly Clinton's aides began to find some of the documents they originally said they couldn't locate. After Gerth was able to see the Clintons' tax returns, he discovered that they had, indeed, taken personal deductions for payments made by the company.

While combing the files of the state Securities Department, Gerth also found records of the 1985 communications between Hillary and Beverly Bassett, the securities commissioner, in connection with Madison Guaranty's preferred stock proposal. The investigative reporter was closing in on the Clintons.

After my meeting with Gerth, I arranged to see Sheffield Nelson again. The meeting took place in Nelson's tastefully appointed law office, high in the TCBY building—named for one of Little Rock's nouveau concerns, The Country's Best Yogurt. I was armed with some of my own documents as well as the contents of a mysterious manila envelope recently mailed to "Jim McDougal, Soldier of Fortune, Arkadelphia, Ark."

I spent the first few minutes explaining the transactions involving the model home at Whitewater that became known as "Hillary's house." The $28,000 loan made in the Clintons' name was actually a corporation debt. "All payments of the loan, from its inception to its retirement, were made from assets of the corporation," I told Nelson. "At the time the Clintons assumed control of the corporation, the loan had been paid down to about $13,000. They sold a corporate asset—the modular home and the land it was situated on—and used the proceeds to retire the note."

I told him I was sure the Clintons had claimed the corporation's interest payments to whittle down their personal taxes on Hillary's commodities windfall.

But I was more interested in describing Tucker's activities.

As I laid out details of Tucker's scheme involving the promissory notes, Nelson recorded our conversation. I described how Tucker had submitted an exaggerated, fraudulent financial statement when he obtained a loan from Madison Guaranty, and how he used much of the money for purposes other than those spelled out in the application.

Tucker and his partner John Selig, the erstwhile lawyers for Madison, had found no problem with Tucker's loan, but they had skewered me for my own loans. "I realize now I was so screwed then. All the self-serving shit," I told Nelson.

Tucker had obtained a $260,000 loan from Madison Guaranty, ostensibly to buy a forty-acre tract at the Castle Grande development in order to build the shopping mall. The land cost $125,000. He said he needed the rest of the money for improvements. Instead, he apparently took the remaining $135,000 and used it to pay off a mortgage he had guaranteed that was in default.

"He never used the money the way he told them?" Nelson asked.

No, I said, no work had been done on the land. "Hell, it's laying there right now, it's raw land and hasn't been touched."

"Who owns that land now, by the way?" Nelson asked. "Tucker?"

"Well, we are going to get to that in a minute," I said. "This is what is really going to appear strange."

Then I pulled a memo from the manila envelope. The four-page document, written by Tucker and addressed to David Hale and R. D. Randolph, spelled out the terms of a partnership between the three of them for the Castle Grande shopping mall. Luring David and R.D. into the agreement, Tucker told them the land had cost $260,000. I knew that was the size of the loan, not the cost of the land. He was screwing them, too.

"When Jim Guy was doing all of this sort of thing, it was back before he really had any money, isn't it?" Nelson asked.

"Oh, he was into everything. Everything was terribly inflated. He didn't have anything. He was in the hole. He needed money. He had big campaign debts, and he was pumping everything at that point," I said.

"I imagine if he could reconstruct history just like Clinton today, he would go back and redo all of that and not have taken advantage of those situations, because he has exposure," Nelson said.

"Oh yeah," I said. "It's easy to be a Christian when you got money."

After I spread my documentation across a table, Nelson's secretary grinned. "You ever worry that somebody's going to knock you off at night?" she asked.

"Naw," I answered, with a touch of bravado.

Nelson sorted through the material I gave him. I said I wanted to sue Tucker. He raised the possibility of filing criminal charges against the lieutenant governor. Referring to the Republican U.S. attorney who had targeted me, Nelson said, "I would imagine that Chuck Banks would come unglued on some of this stuff, wouldn't you?"

We talked about the prospect that I could face new charges myself. "Let me tell you something, Sheffield, there ain't nothing in my life that they haven't seen," I said. I believed if the federal agents had failed to find incriminating evidence for the 1990 trial, they never would. "But they would like to get Tucker," I added. "That FBI agent really wanted to get him. There's a whole bunch of work already done. They're just too dumb to know how to use it."

"Do you think we probably have enough here?" Nelson asked.

"Yes, I think so. He and Hale were just trading back and forth, looting the place and looting my savings and loan."

Nelson was delighted to have this information. He could pass it to Gerth and hobble the 1992 Democratic presidential campaign. And he could deliver it to the Republican U.S. attorney's office and set in motion the events that could bring down Jim Guy Tucker.

By the time Gerth's first article appeared on the front page of the *New York Times* on Sunday, March 8—two days before the Super Tuesday primaries in several southern states—the Clinton campaign had already been fighting off more sensational charges. Gennifer Flowers used a supermarket tabloid to claim that she and Clinton had been involved in a long-running affair. Just when that story seemed to be winding down, the *Wall Street Journal* published details of how Clinton had escaped the draft.

By comparison, Gerth's Whitewater story was tame. It was a long and sometimes incomprehensible piece that began, "Bill Clinton and his wife were business partners with the owner of a failing savings and loan association that was subject to state regulation early in his tenure as governor of Arkansas, records show."

Although the article failed to produce the same sort of frenzied reaction as Gennifer Flowers and the draft story, the Clinton campaign went ballistic. They devised a strategy to deal with follow-up stories, and they asked Jim Blair to silence me. They could not have made a worse choice.

Blair called my lawyer, Sam Heuer, a good Democrat, to raise hell about my cooperation with the *New York Times*. It had to stop, he said. I believe Sam, who was younger and less established in legal circles, wanted to be cooperative. He had been Clinton's law student, and perhaps he thought Blair could throw some Tyson Foods business his way.

Sam agreed to issue a statement: "As the attorney for James McDougal," his press release said, "I am appalled and affronted by the allegations and reckless disregard of the facts by the *New York Times* and its reporter Jeff Gerth." Sam asserted that the suggestion that I had used money from the savings and loan to subsidize the real estate venture "is not only false but probably actionable by Mr. McDougal against the *New York Times*."

Blair suggested that I sue the *Times* for $10 million.

Blair also asked Sam to set up a meeting in Little Rock. In the meantime, Blair dispatched my old pal R. D. Randolph to quiet me down. R.D. had a job with the state and was in no position to refuse a request from the Clinton camp. He drove down to Arkadelphia to see me, and he seemed embarrassed by his mission. We went to the Western Sizzlin' for dinner, and he never mentioned the story as we worked our way through a couple of plates of ribs. Instead, we reminisced about our travels to the sale barns on behalf of John F. Kennedy thirty years earlier. Then, as we left the diner and walked to the car, he finally got around to telling me, "Somebody came through and said you're talking to a reporter from New York, and it's got them really scared up in Little Rock." The headquarters for Clinton's campaign was in Little Rock. R.D. seemed almost apologetic about conveying the message.

I knew what he was trying to say. "Go back to Little Rock and tell them not to sweat it," I replied.

When a reporter from the Associated Press contacted me shortly afterward, I told him: "I've never done anything illegal, and as far as I know Bill Clinton has never done anything illegal or unethical." That was the truth, as far as the Whitewater story was concerned.

At that point, neither the Clintons nor I had done anything illegal at Whitewater.

I was willing to assert Clinton's innocence, but I refused to be intimidated by Jim Blair.

When I later met with Blair at Sam's office, Blair asked me to speak with Jim Lyons, a lawyer from Denver who had volunteered to help the Clinton campaign. Lyons was preparing a report on Whitewater.

"I don't have time to waste talking to him," I told Blair. "I could explain it to him and he wouldn't understand it."

Blair didn't understand Whitewater either. He said I had taken money out of the Whitewater company, and he claimed the Clintons' contributions to the project had been about equal to mine. My anger against Blair, an emotion that had been building for years, exploded.

"I'll tell you one fucking thing," I yelled. "The Clintons have put in the grand total of about thirteen thousand dollars and Susan and I have lost more than a hundred thousand. Do you want me to tell the press about that? Do you want me to tell the press about the time Bill Clinton came to my office and asked about getting Hillary business? Do you want me to tell that fucking story to the press?"

Blair looked as if someone had kicked him in the stomach.

Our meeting ended, but Blair pursued the theme. After returning to northern Arkansas, he wrote Sam a letter, a veiled threat. He observed that the statute of limitations may not have expired on the Whitewater affair and implied that the Clintons might have both civil and criminal claims against me.

I instructed Sam to tell Blair to take his evidence to the prosecutor in Little Rock. Then, for good measure, I called up Gerth and told him about my exchange with Blair.

Whitewater receded as an issue as the Clinton campaign gathered momentum during the year. Political reporters following the candidate were more interested in polls, the choice of his running mate, the decline of President Bush, and the ups and downs of Ross Perot than the minutiae of Whitewater.

Although I knew I had stung Clinton by going public with the story, I had no further interest in trying to sabotage his campaign. As a Yellow Dog Democrat, I had no desire to help a Republican get elected president. There seemed little more to say about the issue, anyway. Whitewater was merely a poor investment, not a crime.

Yet the Clintons considered Whitewater a liability, and they wanted to eliminate any association with the venture following Bill's election. Seven years after I first recommended to the Clintons that it would be smart politics for them to get out of the Whitewater company—a suggestion Hillary had rejected vehemently—Sam Heuer called to say that they were "frantic" to settle up. I said, "Fine."

To put a formal end to the partnership, Sam arranged a meeting at his office on December 22. Clinton, due to be inaugurated in less than a month, was still immersed with the task of choosing his cabinet and could not attend. Hillary had other duties, too. They would be represented by Jim Blair.

Unenthusiastic over the prospect of seeing Blair and discouraged by the wintry conditions, I left Arkadelphia late. I drove slowly to Little Rock and arrived an hour late, deliberately. Ordinarily, I wouldn't pull a petty stunt like that, and I'm sorry now I did. Blair's plane had been fogged in upstate and he couldn't make it to Little Rock. Vince Foster, looking morose, had been sent to represent the Clintons.

Well acquainted with stages of depression, I could tell Vince had severe problems. To pass the time, Vince and I talked about personal ailments that develop as one grows older. Trying to be amiable, he talked about losing his hair and his eyesight, but there was little humor in his plaint. I suspected he was on some kind of medication. As a Rose Law Firm associate of Hillary's, he was going to Washington as a deputy White House counsel, and the Clintons were already piling responsibilities on him. His office would become the repository of the Whitewater records, but before he even made it to Washington his hands were soiled by the case.

An odd, almost ghostly atmosphere prevailed in the large conference room. Just the three of us were there, and no one else seemed to be coming or going in the office suite. It was three days before Christmas, and both Sam and Vince appeared to be under pressure from the Clintons to wind this up before the holiday.

After reviewing some of the papers, Sam decided he needed to call Blair. We moved to Sam's private office, where he reached Blair on the speakerphone. With little introductory comment, Blair began giving Vince directions, as if Foster were some kind of lackey. Hearing Blair's voice made me cantankerous. When he asked me to sign something, I asked Vince, "Would you tell your client to do that?"

"I'm just the messenger," Vince said, his voice full of gloom.

The Clintons were prepared to transfer their Whitewater interests to me. There would be an official consideration of $1,000. I paid them nothing. I understand Blair gave them the sum and claimed it represented a loan to me to make the final settlement.

Before our meeting broke up, I told Blair that since I was now the sole owner of the Whitewater Development Company, I wanted the corporate records back from Hillary.

Blair assured me the papers would be sent within thirty days.

"With all due regard," I said, "I know lawyers can never get anything done in thirty days. Just make it ninety days, but make sure I get the records back."

"I'll give you my word," Blair said.

"No offense, Jim, but I want it in writing," I added.

I was in Arkadelphia the day Clinton was inaugurated, and I couldn't have cared less. I didn't bother to watch the event on TV. My mother's health was failing, and I felt ill myself.

Neither Hillary nor Blair produced the Whitewater records. After waiting exactly six months, I called Vince Foster at the White House. The date was June 21, 1993. I didn't reach Vince, but I explained to his secretary that Vince had some old company records I needed.

White House records show that Vince called Blair the same day. He had a request: I don't want Jim McDougal calling me at the White House. Blair, I understand, said he would take care of it.

Within a couple of days, a Washington accounting firm sent me a Whitewater corporate tax return for 1992, the last year of joint Clinton-McDougal ownership. Like other documents that originated with Hillary, it bore dates out of sequence. I noticed that the letter of transmittal from the accountant was dated oddly—before the date on the tax return. I refused to sign the return until I received all the Whitewater documents. If Hillary attempted to stonewall me, I was prepared to pester her.

One month later, in the third week of July, I heard the news: Poor Vince Foster, deputy counsel to the White House and keeper of the Whitewater records, had committed suicide.

15

A few weeks after Foster's death, David Hale paid me a strange visit. He arrived in the early evening, unannounced, at the mobile home at Caddo Valley I shared with my mother. It was Mother's bedtime. In poor health, she needed rest, and I needed David's visit like a bull needs teats. We had been involved in business together, but our interests had never blossomed into close friendship.

Without displaying a great deal of graciousness, I invited David into the living room. Mother stayed in her bedroom, but the house was so small she could hear much of the conversation. The office of Capital Management Services, his firm that loaned Susan $300,000 in 1986, had been raided by the FBI—coincidentally the day after Vince died—and David realized he was in big trouble.

The FBI was investigating several loans he had made, including the one to Susan, as well as the $825,000 loan that Madison Guaranty had made to Dean Paul, one of David's associates. The agents were trying to develop a pattern of loans back and forth between

Capital Management and Madison in order to establish a conspiracy to defraud the government.

David said he was going to be indicted, and he predicted Susan and I would be charged as well. He spoke awkwardly and seemed determined to extract some kind of admission from me by asking several leading questions about a meeting between the two of us and Bill Clinton at the Castle Grande sales office in early 1986. He wanted me to confirm that Clinton had appealed for Susan's loan and to corroborate other details involving Clinton.

David's version of the "meeting" did not square with my own recollection. I recalled clearly that Clinton had showed up after a meeting I had with David and mentioned Susan's loan in passing, but I had no intention of providing David any information. It was obvious he wanted to implicate Clinton. With a new Democratic U.S. attorney, Paula Casey, in charge of the case, I supposed David felt he would have leverage if he could involve the president.

I responded to his questions with noncommittal grunts and *hmmm*s and *uh-huh*s. He asked about events that occurred just before my stroke, and I told him I didn't remember much, which was not entirely true.

Instead of helping him with Clinton, I informed David that he had a greater problem with Jim Guy Tucker, by now the governor of Arkansas. Jim Guy had screwed me out of $59,000, I said, and he had been working a larger con on David and R. D. Randolph in their land deal at Castle Grande.

David squirmed in his seat. Near the end of our conversation, he rose suddenly and said he needed to put his coat in the car. Though I said nothing to him, I realized David had been secretly trying to tape me with a recorder in his coat pocket.

As it turned out, the tape proved crude and useless to David's efforts to drag Clinton into the case. He failed to set me up as a witness, but he succeeded in upsetting my mother. After David left that night, she was distressed. She cried and asked if I was really going to be indicted again.

◆ ◆ ◆

We struggled to lift our spirits. On a day near the end of September, I asked the Rileys' daughter Megen to stay with Mother while I went to get her lunch at Western Sizzlin'. When I returned, Mother seemed to be in a good mood. The last thing I remember her saying to me was, "There's the big man with the big lunch." I went back to my room to lie down. After a few minutes, I heard Mother coughing, followed by the sound of her groping down the narrow hallway toward me. I rose to meet her just as she collapsed. Megen helped me move Mother to her bed. "Time to be with Leo," she said, as she died in Megen's arms.

More than the specter of new investigations, this loss devastated me. Mother had nurtured me as a child, made sacrifices for me, and had always tried to impart to me her Christian verities. She was a good and strong woman, and her devotion never faded in the face of all my troubles. She was the last of the family from her genera-tion. All my relatives—my grandparents, my parents, my uncles and aunts and cousins who'd gathered that sunny day outside Little Rock when Susan and I were married—were dead, except an an-cient aunt. Susan and I were divorced. I was the last McDougal in my bloodline.

A few months later, Bob Riley died. It seemed my sorrows would never end.

David Hale took other steps to snare Clinton. He sought strategic help from Justice Jim Johnson. David's decision smacked of my own approach to Sheffield Nelson—a Democrat with Clinton con-nections seeking assistance from a Republican convert who loathed Clinton. But I had gone to Nelson to sue Jim Guy Tucker and em-barrass Clinton. David was out to save his own skin.

Although the elderly Johnson had moved to the peaceful college town of Conway, a short drive from Little Rock, he was still capable of producing thunder. During the 1992 campaign, he helped uncover an old letter Clinton wrote to an ROTC commander, thanking the officer for saving him from the draft; the disclosure rocked the Clinton effort. The following year, at a conservative rally in Washington, Johnson described the new president from his home state as a "queer-mongering, whore-hopping adulterer." If one were seeking to find ways to dump on Clinton, Justice Jim seemed a natural resource for advice. David apparently told Johnson some of the details of Clinton's query about Susan's loan, and Johnson turned the information over to his conservative allies in Washington. Soon stories of the president's involvement in an illegal loan were appearing in the press.

Hale was indicted the same week that Mother died. On the day of her burial, I went to see Sam Heuer. He had called to warn me, "It looks like they're going to open all this stuff up again." I was not in a conciliatory mood. I told Sam to tell the U.S. attorney: By God, come ahead, investigate McDougal all you want. I felt I had beaten back the best they could throw at me in the 1990 trial, at a time when I was mentally woozy, and I was confident I could defy them again. I was determined not to be the fall guy this time, a lonely defendant against the might of the United States government. I warned Sam that if they went after me, other government officials would suffer. Clinton would be tarred by an investigation, and if it led to my indictment again, I said, I was prepared to turn the case into grand theater and take down the governor of Arkansas, Jim Guy Tucker, with me.

The White House, of course, was in a state of panic that criminal charges were being turned up in Arkansas like worms in a compost heap. While Justice Jim worked to plant Clinton in the case, national reporters returned to Little Rock, sifting through rumors that not only Clinton but also Tucker were targets of the investigation.

Bruce Lindsey, one of Clinton's closest friends on the White House staff, was put in charge of efforts to ride herd on the story. From Washington, he reached out by phone to associates in Arkansas for information. I knew Bruce slightly from his days as a Little Rock lawyer, and I remembered he was extremely defensive about any criticism of Clinton. He began developing a network of Arkansas attorneys loyal to Clinton, a group, I later learned, that included my own lawyer, Sam Heuer. Sam was in regular contact with Jim Blair, who had become Lindsey's chief damage-control operative in the state.

During my discussions with Sam, I told him of Hale's visit to my home. Without my knowledge or consent, Sam told Blair and Blair told Lindsey. So much for lawyer-client confidentiality.

With a storm gathering, Tucker met privately with Clinton at the White House on October 6, a couple of weeks after Hale's indictment. Clinton's counsel, Lloyd Cutler, claimed Tucker was there to discuss a finance center for a military installation in North Little Rock. I said to someone, If you believe that, I've got a piece of land in the Ozarks to sell you.

The case the press kept calling Whitewater had heated up again. For the first time in a year, I was getting calls from reporters from all over the country. I insisted to them that Clinton had done nothing illegal.

One fellow who phoned was Chris Vlasto from ABC News in New York. Many of the Yankee reporters had a brash, aggressive manner. Chris was pleasant and sounded quite knowledgeable about the case. I figured he was either a damned good con artist—a type I had come to know well—or a warmhearted guy.

When he asked me if Clinton had done anything illegal, I said, "Hell, son, come on down to Little Rock. You can set up a lie-detector test and we can exonerate Bill Clinton forever." He called back to say that his bosses weren't ready to underwrite another trip to Little Rock. But they eventually sent him to Arkansas, and he hit pay dirt. We wound up spending a great deal of time together. Though Chris had the lean and hungry look of a young journalist, his manner was that of a scholar. I discovered that the man belonging to the gentle voice on the phone had the cunning of a con artist but the soul of a true friend. I soon trusted Chris more than my own lawyer.

Other journalists were not as reassuring. During the fall of 1993, I didn't have time to mourn my mother properly. It seemed that Sue Schmidt from the *Washington Post* was calling every five minutes to ask, "Have you been indicted yet?" I tried to explain to her that the legal process was slow and nothing was going to happen for a while. It didn't stop her calls.

Finally, I packed my bags and drove to Galveston, Texas. In a way, I was making a sentimental journey. Galveston had been the destination for our high school's senior trip, and I had always liked the place. I checked into the Sea View Motel, a clean, inexpensive place along the water. Galveston gave me a sense of escape and I spent several weeks there, incognito. Back in Arkansas, it was said that Jim McDougal had gone underground.

Just as I prepared to move into a comfortable bed-and-breakfast inn located in a historic district known in Galveston as the Strand, I was ambushed outside a restaurant by a crew from the TV-tabloid show *Hard Copy*. Irritated at first, I soon saw that the young woman trying to interview me seemed frightened by the confrontation with the dastardly godfather of Whitewater. I told her, "Honey, I'm not going to hurt you." I made a few wisecracks about Republican jerks, and the guys on her camera crew started laughing. Once we loosened up, I found I enjoyed jawing with them. "You know, I hate these damned Republicans," I said, and they captured my remarks on camera. That's the way they pitched their show: McDougal versus Republicans.

After the interview ended, I thought to myself: Nobody is ever going to leave me alone. The press is after me and the federal investigators are going to make another run at me. These guys might be out to kill me, but I didn't have to whimper and wait to be tracked down. I decided to have as much fun with this case as possible. I felt I had nothing left to lose. Maybe it was another manic phase kicking in, but as soon as I finished with the *Hard Copy* crew I went back to the motel, packed my clothes, and drove back to Arkansas, into the maw of the Whitewater storm.

The Clintons had their own Christmas spoiled by new allegations of Bill's night-crawling by a couple of disgruntled Arkansas state troopers from his old security detail at the governor's mansion. The troopers claimed that Clinton, with their connivance, often sneaked away at night to visit other women, and that his return would be heralded by Hillary's angry shouts and the clatter of flying pots and pans in the kitchen.

The troopers' tales soon led to Paula Corbin Jones's sexual harassment lawsuit against the president, a tawdry action based on her claim that Clinton, while governor, had lured her to a hotel room in Little Rock and invited her to engage in oral sex.

After years of living with the L'il Abner stigma, many Arkansans had thought our state's image would be enhanced by the personable Rhodes scholar in the White House. Instead, we were subjected to commentary about a white-trash culture involving "big-haired women" and life in the trailer parks.

Little Rock teemed with reporters and camera crews from around the world, and when the story they tagged "Troopergate" died down, they turned back to Whitewater. At ABC's Chris Vlasto's urging, I decided to use television to speak to the Clintons, but I didn't tell Sam Heuer because I suspected he would alert Jim Blair and set in motion an effort by the White House to silence me. ABC put me up at the Essex Hotel, a swanky old skyscraper overlooking Central Park. My simple message to Bill and Hillary was: Stop lying about Whitewater. I didn't accuse the Clintons of any crime, but I showed ABC how the Clintons' claim of contributing more than $60,000 to Whitewater was bullshit. The $28,000 loan in Hillary's name to build the model home had actually been repaid by the company, I explained, and a $20,000 payment by Clinton to the bank in Kingston involved a loan for his mother's house and had nothing to do with Whitewater. I urged the television guys to go down to Arkansas and see for themselves, and I told them where to look. Chris made a quick trip and returned with the check proving Clinton's $20,000 payment was not intended for Whitewater. Inasmuch as the White House had been disputing my accounts, the check gave me instant credibility with ABC.

Clinton admitted at a subsequent White House press conference that his check, indeed, had been written to repay a loan for his mother. He even said he had never known Jim McDougal to do anything wrong.

The president's expression of support made me even more ornery with the federal investigators. By this time, Whitewater had been taken out of the office of the U.S. attorney and turned over to an independent counsel, Robert Fiske. A special investigative unit had been set up in Little Rock, and after officially informing me that I was a target, a succession of FBI agents began appearing at my door in Arkadelphia. My tolerance for their questions and demands was low. After I dubbed a pair of the agents Beavis and Butt-Head, it tickled me to hear that the nicknames caught on in FBI circles in Little Rock.

In spite of intensifying pressure, I was still determined to enjoy myself. I called Al Norris, one of the agents assigned to my case. Holding the phone far from my mouth, I shouted, "Can you hear me, Al?"

"Just barely, Mr. McDougal."

"Well, Al, I'm down in Peru to do a little surfing and I just wanted you to know my whereabouts."

"Oh Lord, Mr. McDougal," he said. "You can't do that."

After I was subpoenaed to come to Little Rock to give handwriting samples, I decided to turn my appearance into the first act of the dramatic performance I'd promised when they started digging into the case. Dressed in my Sunday finest, a nice blue cord suit and tie, I donned a Panama hat, which would become my trademark, and carried a cane, which added to my air of flamboyance. Actually,

I needed the cane because I was having severe pains in my legs from recent surgery, but the rest of my wardrobe was for effect.

When I arrived at the independent counsel's office, a gaggle of reporters, photographers, and camera crews waited outside. I had made a modest proposal to the investigators: I would talk freely with them if the press could sit in on the interviews. I knew my offer was as outrageous as Jonathan Swift's suggestion that the English use the children of the troublesome Irish as appetizers, but I thought it might arouse a bit of attention.

Standing at the door to the independent counsel's office, I invited the press to come inside with me. When a receptionist unlocked the door, I used my best southern manners to hold it open for the gang pushing behind me. Disconcerted, the legal staff shooed the press outside, as though ridding the building of a Mongol horde. Nothing like a bit of mischief to brighten the day.

While the agents took samples of my handwriting, I coughed and acted as though I was going into a swoon. The investigators went into another swivet, troubled that I might expire on their watch. They agreed that my future encounters with the FBI could take place at my home.

The FBI visited Arkadelphia regularly. During one of their fishing expeditions, I could tell they were trolling for Jim Guy Tucker. I made a crack. "Tucker's like any lawyer," I said. "He'll steal anything that's not nailed down." The agent put that line in his notebook.

I didn't confine my comments to the FBI. Giving an interview to the *Arkansas Democrat-Gazette*—the surviving Little Rock daily after the old *Gazette* folded—I said, "If they send me to prison it will improve my standard of living. I live in a house trailer and I expect the government has a lot better house trailers than I do." The paper didn't have much news that day, so they gave big play to my comments.

Like Mencken, I was throwing dead cats into the sanctuary. I was achieving celebrity status, part John Dean, the Watergate confessor, part Jay Leno. I went on TV shows with David Brinkley and Larry King, spicing the dry explanations of Whitewater with humor and literary allusions. People began to recognize me when I walked through airports. Total strangers would shake my hand and wish me luck. Others would call out, "Right on!" or "Keep the faith!" I was having so much fun I decided to run for Congress again.

Part of my motivation was a legal ruse. I figured the feds wouldn't dare indict me if I was a congressional candidate. Moreover, running for Congress could be a pleasure this time instead of an arduous ordeal—a homecoming, where I could travel the area and see old friends and bask in my notoriety. Instead of trying to raise tens of thousands of dollars, I spurned contributions. I called my committee, somewhat tongue in cheek, the Committee to Support the President. I got a tape of Clinton's assertion that Jim McDougal was an honest man, and turned it into a commercial, in which I used that portion of his press conference and concluded with the words "Thank you, Mr. President!"

I was having a hell of a good time. In the three-man race for the Democratic nomination, Jay Bradford, a well-known legislator, raised about $300,000 in a serious bid to win. I was just a gadfly, bopping around the district, making a few speeches.

Jay took my rivalry good naturedly. We made joint appearances and never criticized each other. While I spoke, Jay would fetch me a Coke to wet my whistle. I thought I might get fifteen hundred votes. In the end, I received a respectable vote and finished second. Bradford won the nomination, but he lost to a Republican, Jay Dickey, in the general election.

I gave up my forum as a candidate, but my performance went on. With Congress conducting Whitewater hearings, I wanted to be called as a witness. Jim Leach, an Iowa Republican and chairman of the House Banking Committee, had been making hay out of old charges by Jean Lewis, a right-wing investigator from the

Resolution Trust Corporation. She hated Clinton and had seized on Whitewater and the Madison Guaranty case, exaggerating the problems and misstating the facts in an attempt to torpedo his 1992 campaign. Though eventually discredited, she inflicted a lot of damage.

Democrats were howling about the partisan handling of the Whitewater case by Senator Al D'Amato of New York, Leach's equivalent in the Senate, but I felt Leach was worse. Leach cultivated the appearance of a midwestern moderate, but he used Jean Lewis and other radical right-wing extremists working hand in glove with Justice Jim Johnson. Leach exuded self-righteousness, I thought, and I wanted to debate the savings and loan affair with him. But neither the House nor the Senate committees dared call me as a witness. So I threw a dead cat into their sanctuary.

CBS invited me to Washington. Feeling rundown from all of my activity, I asked if my buddy Tamara Meacham could come along to assist me. The network obliged with two plane tickets and two rooms at a Washington hotel.

Tamara was a student at Ouachita Baptist University and worked at the Western Sizzlin'. As the restaurant's loyal customer, I had gotten to know her during the many meals I ate there, and we developed a good, platonic friendship. I've always enjoyed the company of women, and Tamara was bright and interested in my case. Blond and attractive, she stood out in a crowd. With so much TV exposure, so did I.

After I finished a CBS radio call-in show, I thought it might be fun to drop by Leach's hearing. We stood in line outside the committee room, like ordinary tourists, and were finally seated in the middle of the afternoon session. Clinton's counsel, Lloyd Cutler, was droning away as a witness when we sat down. In no time, I was recognized by the photographers kneeling at Cutler's feet. Tamara's presence added to the sensation. The photographers came scrambling our way, shooting pictures of Tamara and me. The whirring of their camera shutters sounded like a covey of doves spooked from the brush. We created quite a commotion, and soon the committee members were murmuring to one another about their uninvited guest.

After listening to about an hour of Leach's questions and Cutler's testimony, I concluded it was pure Washington rhetoric and, as Harry Truman said of General MacArthur's farewell speech to Congress, "a bunch of damn bullshit." When we left, we were surrounded by reporters. I was asked what I had hoped to accomplish by showing up at the hearing.

"I don't have to accomplish anything," I said. "Breathing is all I'm really interested in right now."

It seemed that every journalist in America had become a Whitewater junkie, seeking me out for a fix. I appeared on ABC's *Nightline* with Ted Koppel and assured him of Clinton's innocence in the Whitewater affair. When he rephrased the question and asked if I could give the same assurance about Hillary, I suggested that he move on to the next question.

I would go to bat for Bill, but not Hillary. She had been high-handed with me and discourteous to Susan, and she still refused to give up the Whitewater company documents.

When I appeared on another TV show, I looked straight at the camera and said, as plaintively as possible: "Hillary, I really need those records back."

She finally had her flunkies return part of the Whitewater records. There were some old tax returns and worthless papers, but I noticed that the bank statements and check stubs—the documents that would undermine her claims about the case—were missing.

From the beginning, Hillary had been treacherous. It was interesting that the Rose Law Firm worksheets itemizing the billing fees of their attorneys were printed out on February 21, 1992, the day after Gerth discovered Hillary had contacted the Securities Department on Madison Guaranty's behalf.

Hillary's association with Madison seemed to put her in a dilemma. She could either claim, as she did at one point, that she had done little work for the McDougals' notorious enterprise. Or she had to take credit for the sixty hours work the Rose firm allegedly performed for Madison to prove she earned her two-thousand-dollar-a-month retainer. She tried to have it both ways, and the discrepancies in the Clintons' various stories are obvious.

During the course of addressing Whitewater questions, the president denied he ever asked me to channel business to Hillary. That didn't surprise me, but I was amazed when Hillary claimed her visit to my office took place on April 23, 1985—eight months after the actual meeting. And she said she saw me because another Rose lawyer asked her to contact me about work the firm might do for Madison Guaranty. Lies, lies, lies.

In a written interrogatory made during the Resolution Trust Corporation investigation of Madison Guaranty, Hillary asserted that the Rose Law Firm didn't want me as a client "until he paid his bill." She was referring to the dispute that arose after Steve Smith refused to pay the firm for work in the 1981 case involving our attempt to establish a branch bank in Huntsville. Steve negotiated with the Rose firm, settled for a slightly reduced fee, and paid the bill long before 1985. During the Whitewater investigation, a curious document turned up, a $5,893 bill from Rose Law Firm to Madison dated December 23, 1981. Despite the date, the paper refers to "legal service and professional advice through May 15, 1982."

Strange things happened to Rose documents. After the firm's worksheets—documents that Hillary and Vince Foster carried to Washington—were subpoenaed, the evidence disappeared. Some two years later, the worksheets magically materialized in the Clintons' living quarters in the White House. They showed Hillary had billed Madison for about sixty hours. She appeared to be claiming the hours Webb Hubbell put in for the Rose firm in connection with his work for his father-in-law, Seth Ward, on our Castle Grande project. The only two chores Hillary handled for Madison involved the correspondence with the Securities Department and the call to the Alcoholic Beverage Control board concerning a microbrewery at Castle Grande.

Now, as I inspected the Whitewater company records, it appeared Hillary had withheld several critical documents. Links were missing, but the papers weren't entirely worthless. Sam and I came up with a scheme to sell official sets of the Whitewater records for a thousand dollars each to the journalists clamoring for any Whitewater-related document they could get their hands on. The funds would go to the McDougal Defense Fund. Sam sorely needed the money because he was making little on my case.

I thought it was an inspired move, but the reporters reacted as if we were calling for the abolition of the First Amendment. They wailed at a press conference, complaining that the thousand-dollar fee was highway robbery. I said, "Hey look, you guys, your bosses pay six dollars for every shot of whiskey you drink at the hotel bar down here, what's wrong with paying a thousand dollars for legitimate documents?" They muttered and fumed, and I should have known they would figure out some way to screw me. The big news organizations pooled their money and bought one set, to reproduce and share among themselves.

So much for Sam's legal fees. Eventually I wearied of his complaints about money. I told Sam he had my permission to withdraw from the case. I had little money to pay him, and no interest in becoming a burden. If I actually had to stand trial, I figured, I might have enough from my mother's inheritance to pay for my defense.

I was uneasy over Sam's relationship with Jim Blair anyway, and unhappy with the tone of his correspondence with the investigators. Instead of taking an adversarial position, Sam addressed them informally. He seemed eager to cooperate. I told Sam he was being too responsive to what "they"—the White House and the investigators—wanted, and that he no longer seemed to have my interests in mind.

I concluded I would be better off handling my own defense. Sam raised no objections. After I relieved him of his responsibilities, I called the independent counsel's office and told my case officer to send all further communications to me instead of Sam.

I became fatalistic about my situation. Fiske, the independent counsel, had been replaced by Kenneth Starr, a deep-dyed conservative Republican who appeared hell-bent on investigating the Clintons and anyone with connections to the president.

Starr's lieutenants were badgering Susan in California, and that bothered me. But when they subpoenaed Claudia Riley, it sent me over the edge. Bob and Claudia Riley had helped care for me for years, through all sorts of hardships, and they had been honorable friends. Claudia was sixty-seven, a widow, living a quiet life in Arkadelphia, and the investigators treated her like Lizzie Borden. The independent counsel's office summoned her to Little Rock to appear before a grand jury, demanding that she bring all sorts of documents.

She responded to the subpoena. Gathering every paper that might be considered relevant, she filled a big pasteboard box with documents and struggled to carry it into the Federal Building without help. I was indignant and called a press conference at the Capital Hotel.

I called the Whitewater investigators "a bunch of thugs," and I was just warming up. "That these despicable little men would summon the widow of a blind war hero who is respected by everyone who knows her in an attempt to intimidate my supporters is really the most disgusting and reprehensible thing that has occurred in this whole melancholy endeavor," I declared.

I assumed the public posture of an aggrieved citizen, but privately I knew I was exposed to criminal charges on the $300,000 loan from David Hale.

The case closed in on me.

Hale had begun plea-bargaining early. He pleaded guilty to two counts of defrauding the Small Business Administration and started cooperating with the prosecutors before beginning his twenty-eight-month sentence.

Chris Wade was caught in the net. He pleaded guilty to bankruptcy fraud and a charge of submitting false applications to a financial institution. Neither count involved Whitewater directly, but he was an associate. Chris was sentenced to fifteen months.

My friend and former partner Steve Smith pleaded guilty in June 1995 to a misdemeanor charge in connection with the misapplication of funds from a loan from Hale's firm.

Larry Kuca, who'd worked on the Campobello project, pleaded guilty to a misdemeanor charge of conspiracy involving another loan from Hale. In exchange for his agreement to testify against Susan, Jim Guy, and me, Kuca escaped prison and was put on probation for two years.

There had been a lot of false signals from the independent counsel. It seemed to me they were concentrating on Tucker. I suspected they might indict me as payback for all the grief I had caused them. But I saw no reason for them to indict Susan.

In August 1995, well into the third year of Clinton's presidency, Susan, Jim Guy, and I were indicted. The independent counsel assembled nineteen felony counts against me, and if convicted of all of them I could be sent away for nearly one hundred years. For a man with a medicine cabinet filled with prescription drugs, even ten years was a laugh.

I learned of my indictment late in the afternoon, and I accepted the news calmly at my home. After taking about three dozen telephone calls from various members of the press, I went to bed and had a good sleep.

At six o'clock the next morning, I'll be damned if I wasn't awakened by another telephone call. This time it was Sam Heuer. "If you don't mind," he said, "I'd like to get back into this thing."

16

The trial began early in March 1996 during a bleak period when winter had waned in central Arkansas but not yet yielded to spring. I had little reason for optimism. My health was poor and my case shaky. Not only did the government have possession of records demonstrating that we'd never opened a bank account for Master Marketing, the name of the firm Susan created to receive the $300,000 loan from David Hale, but investigators had seized a computer disk from my old word processor that still contained our original, fraudulent application to Hale. Instead of using the money for Susan's firm, we'd spent it to pay off some debts, including the last Whitewater loan, and to acquire some land. I knew we were guilty of misrepresenting the purpose of the loan, and I was further troubled by the knowledge that several of my former associates were prepared to testify for the government.

There were other irritants. I was a codefendant with Jim Guy Tucker, and we had not spoken since our dispute over the promissory notes. Susan's presence as the other codefendant complicated the situation. A victim of my scheme and the independent counsel's zeal to convict anyone with the remotest connection to Bill Clinton, Susan had been dragged into the case. Meanwhile, I was put in a position where I might have to lie to protect the president concerning his interest in the $300,000 loan.

To prepare for the case, I had invested in no less than five lie-detector tests, administered by a couple of Little Rock firms, to see if there was a way to wiggle out of a question regarding the "meeting" with Clinton and Hale. In each instance, I passed all the routine questions, but failed on the topic of our 1986 encounter at Castle Grande. Because it was not really a meeting, I felt I could get by with a denial—as I had in earlier interviews with the press—but the lie detector trapped me each time. The point is, I couldn't lie convincingly to protect Clinton.

I had also lost faith in my lawyer. By the time the trial opened, seven months after my indictment, I concluded that Sam's early-morning offer to represent me again came from a request by Jim Blair rather than the goodness of Sam's heart.

In the years since we had been allies in the Young Democrats and Fulbright's final campaign, Blair and I had developed an enmity for each other. I believed he was a weak and vain man who weaseled his way into Democratic circles; I know he felt I had sullied Clinton. In his role as the president's damage-control agent in Arkansas, it was important for Blair to stay on top of the Whitewater case. Knowing I would give him no cooperation, he established a back channel through Sam.

My suspicions were confirmed by Blair's deposition to the Senate Whitewater Committee in November 1995.

When he was asked about his relationship with Heuer, Blair said, "He has at one time asked my help in trying to get a job and then decided he didn't want the job, and I have referred cases to him that were small cases that the big firms wouldn't handle."

How many cases?

"I would say that it's less than five, but more than two."

When was the last referral?

"Oh, it's been within the last three months."

And the one before that?

"Oh, maybe nine months, a year ago."

As general counsel for the giant Arkansas chicken producer Tyson Foods, Blair said he never sent Sam any Tyson business. He only passed on clients he described as "petty."

Had Blair had conversations with Heuer about David Hale?

"Yes. One of them was that Hale had supposedly been to see McDougal and tried to get McDougal to lie about various things that Hale wanted to claim was [sic] reality."

Had Blair passed Heuer's information to Bruce Lindsey at the White House?

"Not specifically. I mean, I occasionally passed on what I would call almost street gossip."

What about conversations with Heuer concerning McDougal's indictment?

"It was just in generalities and just a gossipy-type conversation."

Did you report the conversations to the White House?

"I don't have any recollection of that. I'm not saying if I didn't hear something interesting, I might not have passed it on to Bruce Lindsey."

Did you discuss a legal defense fund for McDougal?

"I think that I have maybe heard some conversation about a proposal to try to raise money for McDougal . . . I think it may have been more of a joke-type thing."

Blair said Sam "was whining about how he didn't see how he could continue to represent McDougal and not get paid." Blair added that a McDougal Defense Fund was "a highly crazy idea" because "McDougal is not a sympathetic character. You've got to have a woman who's got polio or crippled or something. I mean, you've got to have some kind of sympathy to create a defense."

As the trial opened, I had little defense. Since I was paying Sam nothing, I suppose you could say I was getting my money's worth, but I grew angry that again Sam spent more time discussing the case with Blair than with me.

I complained to one reporter that Blair was so eager to get involved in the case that he was "like a mad dog in a meat house."

After we attended the first pretrial hearing, Blair rode down in the elevator with Sam and me. He smirked and said, "Like a mad dog in the meat store, huh?"

"No, Jim," I said. "You got it wrong again. It's like a mad dog in a meat house."

When we reached street level, Blair walked away. I turned and said to Sam, "If that son of a bitch is ever in court again, I'm leaving. So you deal with it."

Blair did not attend any further trial sessions, but reporters who met with Sam in the evenings after court recess told me he was still in constant contact with Blair by telephone.

As a procession of prosecution witnesses weaved a tapestry of my guilt, I found it difficult to keep a positive frame of mind. In my 1990 trial, when I was imbued with a sense of innocence, I rallied with righteous indignation. This time, I realized I couldn't do an effective job of defending myself and I should never have testified. Stuck with the task of justifying my various land deals and money transfers, I still felt an obligation to keep Clinton out of harm's way. My feelings toward the president were ambivalent. Though irritated by Hillary, I continued to harbor some odd loyalty to Bill. After all these years, Bill remained, in my eyes, the younger sidekick, constantly in some kind of jam. More importantly, he was a Democratic president, running for re-election. I saw myself as some sort of good party soldier, taking the heat in an election year.

The tension of the trial sapped my energy. Although I dressed in my dapper clothes—referred to by the press as my Savile Row suits and my trademark Panama hats—to maintain appearances as I went off to court each day, I felt like hell and was not in shape to conduct my defense, especially with Blair's Heuer in my corner. At one pretrial hearing, Dr. Bob Gale testified that I had been ravaged by illness and medications. He said my use of the anti-anxiety drug Xanax—prescribed when I was first diagnosed as manic-depressive—had damaged my memory. I was now taking a combination of two other powerful antidepressant drugs, lithium and Prozac, and suffered not only from the bipolar disorder of manic-depression, but from vascular blockades in my carotid arteries. Dr. Gale had first examined me before my 1990 trial and again in the months leading up to the new trial. In spite of my problems, he declared me mentally competent to stand trial. Maybe so, but I was no longer sure I had the physical stamina. Like several others, I should have copped a plea.

At one point during the trial, I collapsed. Susan helped me out of the courtroom, and I returned the next day. But I suffered another relapse and missed a couple of sessions. After doctors discovered I had suffered a mild heart attack, they boosted my prescription from short-term nitroglycerin to long-term pills. I moved through the trial as though underwater. Even the prosecuting attorneys seemed solicitous of my health, but the trial, and my performance, had to go on.

The government spent more than a month building its case against Jim Guy, Susan, and me. Sometimes the prosecutors found strands of a conspiracy where none existed. But they were presenting a formidable body of evidence.

It was awkward sitting at the same defense table with Jim Guy. I had neither seen nor talked with him in the five years since he'd claimed the promissory notes for himself. When I saw him at our first appearance in court, I merely looked at him, shook his hand, and said, "Good luck, pal." The courtroom was small, people were watching, and I didn't want to show my hostility. Division would weaken our case further. Yet as the trial progressed, I found myself losing my anger, and I began to feel sorry for Jim Guy. He, too, was ill, suffering from a liver ailment, and he acted sheepish and defensive around me. Taking the initiative to paper over our differences, I began sharing notes and observations with him at the defense table. He warmed a bit, and sometimes we talked during recesses. But it could never be like old times.

After we were indicted, Jim Guy's press secretary, Max Parker, had become my public scold. She blamed the governor's problems on me. A former press aide to Clinton before he went to Washington, Max knew many of the national reporters from the 1992 campaign. From my own talks with the reporters, I knew she had suggested to them that I was a home-grown Arkansas kook. With the local press, Max took a different tack. She advised them not to bother trying to talk to me because I only dealt with the national press. Despite Max's admonition, a young Arkansas reporter timidly approached me following court one day. After I talked with her, she expressed amazement. She had been told, she said, that I was crazy and inaccessible. In fact, I enjoyed the banter. During breaks in the trial, I liked to spend time with the reporters covering the story.

With Blair missing from the courtroom, I noticed Sam spending more and more of his recess time chatting with Max Parker. A few months after the trial ended, my attorney married my nemesis. I thought of it as just another ironic Arkansas connection.

During the trial, I stayed at the Legacy Hotel, an aging pink building redolent of the period between the two world wars. Susan kept a room there, too, with Claudia Riley. I used the dwindling inheritance from my mother to pay for both rooms. We were an odd couple, no longer married yet still affectionate. During my 1990 trial, Susan had been in the spectators' gallery every day in a gesture of support. Six years later, we were in the dock together in the same courtroom. In the mornings, we walked across West Capital Street together, from the Legacy to the Federal Building, a stolid fortress of stone and marble where, over the years, I had placed myself in the hands of Alcoholics Anonymous, toiled for Fulbright, met my first wife, and fought off prison.

Pausing in front of a group of reporters gathered at the Federal Building entrance, I burnished my reputation as an eccentric. One morning, I posed dramatically with my walking cane and recited from *The Tempest*:

"O brave new world, that has such people in it."

Paul Greenberg and Kane Webb, editorial writers for the *Arkansas Democrat-Gazette*, appreciated my performance. They began a series of long editorials in which they characterized me as the Promoter and critiqued my style:

"Before he steps from the elevator, Jim McDougal extends a hand to let a lady go first. Ah, the Southern gentleman. Then he glides towards the front door. For James McDougal does not walk, he sidles, allowing plenty of time for entertaining. He never looks for a side exit. He knows what awaits and he seems to approach it with both relish and a sense of duty. Like a good teacher heading towards a rowdy class. Cameras and microphones love James McDougal, and one senses the feeling is mutual. After all, he needs them as much as they need him. Codependency, thy name is the press. . . .

"What other defendant greets a horde of reporters, microphones and television cameras every morning with a smile, a precise and juicy quote and sometimes a little literary protein? Like he's been warming up in front of the bathroom mirror. And this entertainer is considerate of inky wretches, as if he understands that both newsmen and promoters are in the same line from time to time: showbiz."

Although I had quoted Miranda, the editorialists compared me to another character in the Shakespearean drama. Like Prospero, they wrote, McDougal "has whipped up his own tempest and once again, is caught in the middle of it." Obviously my manic bravado was not helping my case.

◆ ◆ ◆

On the last weekend of April, when it seemed as though every flower in Washington had burst into color and every tree throbbed with fresh life, the scene shifted to the nation's capital. I felt a bit cheered.

I had called the president as a witness in the trial, and his testimony would be recorded on videotape at an extraordinary session in the White House on a Sunday morning.

Susan and I arrived on Saturday and checked into adjoining rooms at the Guest Quarters Hotel on Pennsylvania Avenue, ten blocks west of the White House. Welcomed as VIPs by the hotel personnel, we encountered similiar treatment outside. Pedestrians pointed and waved. Photographers followed us when we walked down the street.

Susan and I met with ABC's Chris Vlasto and Lloyd Grove, a reporter for the *Washington Post*'s Style section, for drinks at the luxurious Four Seasons Hotel on the edge of Georgetown. Although I drank sparkling water, I felt flushed with encouragement, as if I had downed a couple of cocktails.

"Susan will not be convicted no matter what happens. That's out of the question," I assured our hosts. "She's a throwaway defendant they put in there thinking it would pressure me into giving in. Little did they know."

Susan was even more outspoken. "I hate the prosecutors and I hate the FBI," she said. "I really hate them." She said the investigators had picked on me at a time when I was ill and defenseless, and she voiced her hope that Starr, the independent counsel, would have "a payday someday."

Rising to Susan's defense, I said the investigators had been "especially brutal with women. As a southerner, I'm more outraged at what they're doing to the women than what they're doing to me."

Following drinks, Susan left for another appointment, and Chris and Lloyd took me to dinner at Citronelle, a fashionable restaurant

in the cellar of another hotel just down the street. I had dealt with
Chris for nearly four years, but I was not yet at ease with Lloyd, a
stranger assigned to write an article about our visit to Washington. I
told Lloyd I would talk, but complained that his *Washington Post*
colleague Sue Schmidt had worn me out with her Whitewater questions. When I told him, "I have cast her into the outer darkness," he
thought that was funny as hell.

He asked about Hillary. "Who?" I responded.

I said it would be poor manners to have critical remarks about
Hillary appear in the *Post* on the same day her husband was to
testify, ostensibly on my behalf.

"Oh, come on, Jim," Chris said. He knew how I felt about Hillary
and chided me for being uncharacteristically diplomatic. After
Lloyd assured me that my comments would not appear until after
Clinton's testimony, I sounded off.

"What really irritates me the most, as a Roosevelt Democrat," I
declared, "is this constant self-comparison with Eleanor Roosevelt.
We didn't get any Eleanor. But we got a lot of Evita."

Egged on by Chris and Lloyd's appreciative laughter, I pronounced Hillary's newspaper column "boring as hell." The First
Lady was a phony and a pseudo-intellectual, I said. "Here's what is,
shall we say, infuriating. We don't mind people being one-dimen-
sional. We don't mind people having an IQ of seventy-four, right?
Everybody's got their own baggage to carry or not carry. But when
they get so goddamned sanctimonious, and want to parade themselves as intellectuals, that makes you want to get down and choke
them."

The next morning, Susan and I arrived with our defense team at
1600 Pennsylvania Avenue. Jim Guy had chosen not to come. After
clearing security, we were ushered into a fancy room, furnished
with cherry chairs and tables and decorated with plates of Chinese
pottery. The room was ours for the day, to use for private meetings.
Down the hall, a murmur of voices was audible from the Map

Room, where the videotaping would take place. Clinton's private attorney, David Kendall, a partner at the white-shoe Washington firm of Williams & Connolly, chatted with a group of White House lawyers and staff members. With cameras in place, the scene had the aura of a movie set. The Map Room was filled. Spectators peered from doorways and halls outside the room.

I was given a seat just inside the main entrance. Looking about the Map Room, I saw we were congregated in rows of straight-back chairs, like so many schoolchildren. I spotted Hickman Ewing, one of the members of the independent counsel's staff. Hickman lived in Memphis and usually went home from Little Rock every weekend to visit his family and attend church. He had a reputation as a serious Christian, and I was a bit surprised to see him in a secular setting on a Sunday morning.

"What are you doing here, Hickman?" I asked.

"I'm interested in this witness," he said.

He was sitting in an anteroom, prepared to follow the proceedings through an open door. I later learned he wanted to watch my reaction when I saw Bill Clinton for the first time in years.

When he entered, the president appeared to be the good ol' Bill I remembered. Four years in the White House had not aged him much. His hair was grayer than the last time I saw him in 1987, but he still projected a youthful enthusiasm. Everyone rose in deference to the chief executive, and he stopped to greet me as soon as he stepped inside the room.

"Hey, good buddy," he said, as though he had run into a pal at a party. He clapped his hand on my shoulder, and stepped back to review my apparel. In the old days, we liked to tease each other about our clothes. I wore a collarless shirt under a dark suit and a cream-colored vest. I had left my white Panama in our waiting room.

"You're looking spiffy without a tie," he said.

I told him, "Thank you, Mr. President." I called him "Mr. President."

He was wearing a tie with a bizarre pattern. Had he been governor, I would have commented on his "crappy-looking" tie, but I held my tongue.

The president had a big smile for everyone. He worked the room like a master politician, shaking hands, telling lawyers from both sides he was glad to see them, making them feel welcome in the White House. Though he acted as a sociable host, showing no sign of worry about the testimony he would soon give, I suspect Bill would rather have been golfing.

After a few preliminaries, Clinton was sworn in and began answering perfunctory questions about our backgrounds together in Arkansas politics. He talked about some of the campaigns in which we had been involved. Sam Heuer, handling the direct examination, asked Clinton to characterize his relationship with Justice Jim Johnson.

"I think a fair characterization would be that it was one of opposition," the president said. "The first campaign I worked in, I supported a candidate for governor who was running against Justice Johnson, that was 1966. In 1968, Justice Johnson ran against Senator Fulbright, and I, along with Mr. McDougal, worked against him then, in that we had severe differences of opinion. I vividly remember his characterization of Senator Fulbright as soft on communism.

"At some point in the 1980s," Clinton continued, "after I became governor, Justice Jim Johnson became a Republican and, therefore, more explicitly opposed to me. Now if you would see him on the street, he would be just as friendly as could be, and you would have a cordial conversation, but I was never under any illusions. He and I were basically polar opposites in terms of what we thought was good for our state."

Considering that Justice Jim had publicly branded Clinton a "queer-mongering, whore-hopping adulterer," I thought the president had perfected his gift for turning away anger.

The polite exchange between Sam and the president appeared to be following a preordained path. Sam had cleared every question with the White House staff, I assumed, and Clinton seemed ready with his answers.

Suddenly, Sam asked Clinton if he had ever borrowed any money from Madison Guaranty. I shifted in my seat, amazed. There was no reason to ask the question. No one other than Clinton and I had known about the old loan, and the president had no reason to lie. Nevertheless, he did.

"No sir," the president said. "I never borrowed any money from Madison Guaranty."

After this curious detour, Sam quickly cut to the heart of David Hale's allegations.

"Were you ever present in Mr. McDougal's office on 145th Street when a discussion occurred about financial assistance from David Hale or his Capital Management Services Company involving any other business that you or Mr. McDougal may have had?"

"No, sir, never."

"Were you ever present at any time for any meeting between Jim McDougal and David Hale?"

"Never, I was never present at any meeting."

So far, I thought, so good with this phase of questioning. There was never a "meeting" in my office to discuss the loan.

"Were you ever present when there was any discussion of getting any kind of loan from David Hale or his SBIC?"

"No."

The president looked sure and serene, but he had just perjured himself again. Knowing that Clinton had locked me into perjury if I denied that he had discussed the loan with Hale, my shoulders slumped. Hickman Ewing, watching me instead of the witness, noticed. The prosecutor told me later that he wrote in his notebook that my gesture was the reaction of a man with a conscience, pulled, like a doomed protagonist in a Greek tragedy, by two conflicting forces.

Clinton's interrogation went on.

"Did you ever tell David Hale that you had property in Marion

County, Arkansas, that you could use as collateral or security for a loan from him?"

"I did not do that, no."

"Did you ever ask David Hale to make you a loan?"

"No."

"Did you ever ask David Hale to make Jim McDougal a loan?"

"No."

"Did you ever ask David Hale to make Susan McDougal a loan?"

"No, I didn't."

"Did you ever ask David Hale to make Jim Guy Tucker a loan?"

"No."

"Did you ever, in any shape, form, or fashion, put any pressure on David Hale for the purpose of obtaining a loan or for the purpose of causing him to make loans through his SBIC?"

"I did not put any pressure on David Hale."

Just as Hillary had laid herself open to charges of perjury with her own denials of involvement in the Whitewater affair, the president had just lied repeatedly, under oath.

It was nearly six o'clock in the evening when Clinton finished his testimony. While small groups milled around in the Map Room for a few moments, the president walked over and tapped my shoulder. He wanted to talk privately. We moved out of earshot of others, next to a wall with a map showing the Allied placements on the last day of the fighting in Europe during World War II. I thought of my old hero, FDR, and how he had guided the nation right to the brink of triumph before he died.

Although the election was still more than six months away, Clinton was well on his way to a second term. His opponent was obviously going to be Bob Dole, weakened by age, with his past allegiance to a stridently conservative agenda, his role as a party chairman doing the bidding of such unsavory Republican characters as Richard Nixon and Spiro Agnew, and his new position as

Senate majority leader in a Congress that had been taken over by radicals in his own party. During the past year, the House Speaker, Newt Gingrich, had led the GOP into a series of confrontations with Clinton in connection with a right-wing "Contract with America," going so far as to shut down the government in a pique. According to polls, the public stood ready to repudiate the Republican leadership.

Compared to Dole, Clinton appeared buoyant, an attractive leader in a time of national prosperity. While Dole responded to questions related to national issues with inarticulate grunts and dismissive words—his favorite seemed to be "whatever"—Clinton offered detailed and precise explanations in his own press conferences. Dole seemed frozen in the regressive, compassionless policies of his party. Clinton, meanwhile, had moved the Democratic Party from a self-defeating, ultraliberal agenda to a more centrist approach. Though he was prepared to endorse an election-year, conservative move to overhaul the welfare system, Clinton's programs still retained many of the important, progressive elements of the New Deal.

Now he was poised to become the first Democrat elected to a second term since Franklin Roosevelt. As we stood by the World War II map, I told Bill of my hope that he would be re-elected, and I suggested another parallel with FDR. I said I believed his leadership in pushing for programs to aid rural areas and to lift the poor would give him a place in history with Roosevelt.

I drew my commentary from my own populist platform of 1982, when Bill and I campaigned together across the Third Congressional District of Arkansas. I offered the same sort of supportive chatter I suppose a lot of visitors extend to a president. After all our misunderstandings and estrangement, even after his failure to follow through on his promise to my mother to give me a job, I still found it impossible to carry a grudge against Bill Clinton. In person, he is an immensely likable figure: hail fellow, well met.

Clinton said he appreciated my remarks, then he touched my

elbow with his hand and moved our conversation to a more personal vein.

"I hope you're doing well," he said.

"We're having a hard time," I said. "This has gone on for years."

"I know."

"My health's shot, and I can't do anything."

He nodded.

I saw an opening for a personal appeal.

"I'm willing to stick with it, but if it doesn't work out, or whatever, can you pardon Susan?"

I knew there was no way in hell he could pardon me without an uproar. But I considered Susan a sympathetic figure. Her role in the case had been minor, and if she was convicted, I believed the public would accept a pardon for her.

"You can depend on that," Clinton said quietly.

I injected a bit of humor. "Like I say with all lawyers, I mean promptly?"

He grinned and nodded. "If you all hang with me, I'll do it."

Clinton never treated me better than he did that day. He was a gracious host, and his face showed the glimmer of an old friend. Before I left, he asked if I wanted to take a tour of the Oval Office. I told him, "No, thanks." I was tired, and besides, I had never enjoyed sightseeing tours.

The trial resumed in Little Rock. After taking two months of pounding from the prosecution, I was ready to get in my licks. I had proud memories of my performance in 1990, when I'd turned the cross-examination by Ken Stoll, the assistant U.S. attorney, into an acquittal. I had hopes I might carry the day again. At least, I thought, I could give substance to the defense, because neither Susan nor Jim Guy intended to present any testimony.

I learned later that we were at a disadvantage because of the presence of Al Capp's son on the jury. The creator of *Li'l Abner*,

Capp had been a staunch right-winger who hated Senator Fulbright and other progressive Democrats in Arkansas. Our accuser, David Hale, had been an investor in the Dogpatch, USA, theme park developed from Capp's comic strip. When asked on the jury form if a member of his family had been convicted of an offense, young Capp had failed to mention that his father pleaded guilty to attempted adultery in 1972 after facing morals charges for jumping a female student in Wisconsin. Maybe our lawyers didn't make the appropriate challenges. In spite of his biases, Capp's son was allowed to sit in judgment on three Democrats in a trial where Hale served as the key prosecution witness.

I thought I showed the flag in my testimony, but my friends say my performance was painful. During cross-examination, I was either caught up in contradictions or unable to offer satisfactory explanations for some of my transactions.

During my testimony, I freely acknowledged that some of my banking and accounting practices were slipshod, but I had an explanation. "I would say we had more of a country system. It was put in as needed."

My testimony also gave me a chance to try to explain my unusual relationship with Susan. Even though we were divorced, I said, "I feel like we love each other very much and that we're very close. . . . My ill health was entirely responsible for our divorce because a man who has had a stroke is extremely irritable and has no judgment; she was better off to get away from me, the shape I was in."

It was more difficult to put an affectionate cast to my feelings about Jim Guy Tucker. "Like all relationships, it's been a little bumpy. I think that I've been furious with him," I said, mad enough "to hit him over the head with my walking cane if I could catch him." But I added, "Whatever differences we have, have been resolved." I testified that I had "nothing but the warmest personal feelings for Jim Guy today."

The perils of my decision to take the stand were demonstrated the next day when the prosecutors brought up my remark to the FBI:

"Mr. McDougal, isn't it a fact that on June 30, 1995, you told Special Agent Norris that Mr. Tucker was a, quote, 'Thief who would steal anything that wasn't nailed down' end quote."

I thought for a moment and tried to mitigate my statement.

"I don't think that's exactly what I said," I testified. "I think I said, 'Like most lawyers, he would steal anything that wasn't nailed down.' "

To ridicule lawyers, I thought, might be a smart tactic with the jury.

When the lead prosecutor, Ray Jahn, asked me, sarcastically, if I were an attorney, I answered, "No, sir. Thank God."

I tried to convince the jury that Susan should not be held accountable. "My opinion is Susan McDougal never did anything illegal, immoral, or unethical in her life that I know about," I said. "If the jury thinks there's something illegal there, charge it to me."

I even vouched for Jim Guy's innocence. "I know of nothing he's ever done illegal," I said. And I told other lies.

Sam asked me, "Did you ever meet with David Hale at the Castle Grande sales office and Bill Clinton for the purpose of discussing a loan that would be funded in the name of Susan McDougal?"

"Oh, no, sir."

When Sam asked about the application for the loan in the name of Master Marketing, I answered:

"I have no awareness of how that was prepared."

At least I had fun when Jim Blair's name came up.

The prosecutor asked me if I recalled talking to Blair in March 1992, when the Whitewater story first broke.

"You mean the chicken man Jim Blair?" I asked.

Later in the cross-examination, Jahn picked up on my sarcasm. He, too, referred to Blair as "the chicken man."

Much of my testimony, I must confess, did not go well for me. The government had me cornered by their evidence, and my codefendants offered nothing to refute the independent counsel's case.

After my third day of testimony, I stepped down like a beaten man. With my attorney's help I had made a mess of things.

Three weeks later, after protracted closing arguments and lengthy deliberations, the jury reached a verdict.

Jim Guy Tucker was convicted of two felony counts. He announced his resignation as governor that afternoon.

Although a conspiracy charge against Susan had been thrown out, she was convicted on four other felony counts.

And Jim McDougal, the promoter of Whitewater, was convicted on eighteen of the nineteen counts he faced.

17

More than two months passed after our convictions, and Bill Clinton gave no indication that he intended to fulfill his promise to pardon Susan. It shouldn't have been surprising, considering how he failed to stand up for other old friends. During his climb to political power, he collected names the way some people collect baseball cards. He put them in a file called "Friends of Bill"—FOB for short. They were like a crop he tended. He drew on these friends for money, support, and introductions to other valuable contacts; he milked them for what they were worth, and when their usefulness wore out, he disposed of them.

Bill's path is strewn with the names of friends he abandoned, from "the Beards" who served him during his first term as governor to supporters who helped elect him president. Peter Edelman, a prominent Washington lawyer whom I knew from our Air National Guard days, had become close to the Clintons over the years; his wife, Marian Wright Edelman, headed the Children's Defense Fund, one of Hillary's favorite organizations. Clinton intended to nominate

Peter to the federal judiciary, but after conservatives objected to Peter's liberal views, the president flinched. Clinton dropped Peter, just like he washed his hands of a couple of people he brought to Washington from Arkansas. Rather than standing by his surgeon general, Jocelyn Elders, after her advocacy of unorthodox measures in the health field triggered criticism from the religious right, Clinton exiled her. And David Watkins, a White House aide, was forced to return unceremoniously to the Rose Law Firm after taking an unauthorized helicopter ride. When Webb Hubbell, Clinton's golfing partner and Hillary's erstwhile associate, resigned his high Justice Department post after being convicted of bilking clients and fellow attorneys at the Rose Law Firm, the Clintons dumped him. Hillary even claimed she was one of Webb's victims.

Some of the Clintons' friends, such as Hubbell and the McDougals, were found guilty of crimes, but others merely showed poor judgment or held unpopular opinions. The president and his wife were unwilling to jeopardize their political position for the sake of friends. They were takers rather than givers; they showed that trait in the Whitewater venture and they exhibited it throughout their rise to the White House and afterward.

Like many others, I'm sure Susan and I have been moved from the FOB file to a list of outcasts. As I said on NBC's *Dateline* shortly before I went to prison, "I think the Clintons are really sort of like tornadoes moving through people's lives. I'm just one of the people left in the wake of their passing by, but I have no whining or complaining to do because I have lots of company."

While I awaited sentencing, I killed time at the little house on the Rileys' property in Arkadelphia. Reflecting on the events that had altered my life since I was an adventurous entrepreneur with strong Democratic Party connections and a comfortable home, I could trace my wrong turn to 1982. My brush with the banking examiners, which helped spoil my congressional campaign, had so infuriated me that I'd no longer felt an obligation to follow regulations. In a system governed by capricious enforcement, I'd resorted to my own interpretation of the rules, taking my borrowing power to the limit and exceeding those limitations with artful tactics. I was never out to swindle anyone, simply to beat the system. But I had broken the rules and now I faced the consequences. On balance, I thought, I was getting about what I deserved.

I felt more philosophical than mawkish about the prospect of prison. Surprisingly, after seething over my treatment at the hands of federal prosecutors during my first trial, I held little bitterness toward the team from the independent counsel's office. When Amy St. Eve, one of the young prosecutors, called me to ask if she and one of the paralegals on her staff could come visit, I said I'd be happy to see them. During the trial, I had shared some mints with Amy when she had a sore throat, and she later reciprocated by passing a peppermint to me one day when I began coughing.

Amy and her friend arrived, each bearing a copy of James B. Stewart's best-seller on the Whitewater case, *Blood Sport*. They asked me to autograph the books, and I was flattered. We drove to the Western Sizzlin' for lunch. The women chose salads from the buffet, and as I dug into a chicken dish we talked about various personalities at the trial. Even though my visitors had helped send me to prison, I didn't consider them enemies, merely professionals, performing a job. As they prepared to drive back to Little Rock, I sent greetings to their colleagues.

Amy mentioned nothing about my status in the case, but her trip to Arkadelphia was the first feeler by Kenneth Starr's office. Even before her visit, I had begun to consider the possibility of cooperating with the prosecutors. Although I had protected Clinton at my trial, he had done nothing to help Susan and me. Just as he never followed through, as governor, on his promises of a job for me, he gave no indication of taking up Susan's case. Clinton's high-handedness troubled me, and so did the realization that the White House had interfered with my defense.

Chris Vlasto, my friend at ABC, called regularly to discuss developments in the Whitewater case. He tried to cheer me with humorous asides, but one day he raised a theory that caused me to think more seriously about dealing with the prosecutors. We were discussing my failed defense strategy, and Chris reminded me that Sam Heuer talked regularly with Jim Blair. "Sam wasn't representing you," Chris said. "He was representing the Clintons."

As my sentencing approached, Chris came to Arkadelphia to see me. My spirits were low, and I radiated despair as we talked over dinner at the Western Sizzlin'. I told Chris that I'd spent nearly seven weeks at a federal hospital for a psychiatric examination prior to my first trial, and I was not sure I could handle another confinement. Not only was I despondent, I felt weak and feeble. "I'm not going to last a year," I said. "I'm going to die in jail."

"Listen, Jim," Chris said, "you don't have to go out this way. If you walk in to see Ken Starr, he'll greet you with open arms."

He recommended that I at least talk with the independent counsel. That night, I decided to make a move. Approaching my fifty-sixth birthday, occupying a body described as suitable for someone twenty years older, I faced a sentence that would keep me imprisoned for the remainder of my life.

The next day, I sent word to Starr that I would be interested in talking with him.

Starr responded promptly with a letter, saying he would like to come to Arkadelphia. I understand he sent a letter to Sam, too, though Sam never told me about it. He was probably too busy telling Jim Blair.

The independent counsel arrived in a two-car caravan, with Amy, Ray Jahn, and a couple of FBI agents. I invited them into my house; once we were inside, it was crowded. My place had a bedroom, a bath, a kitchen area, and a small living room furnished with a reclining chair and a couch I'd bought secondhand from David Henley when he was my brother-in-law. The FBI men seemed accustomed to a background position. They pulled up a couple of plastic chairs I had gotten from Wal-Mart and joined the circle. Our gathering reminded me of a newcomers' social, where strangers get together for the first time.

I had shaken hands with Starr at my arraignment a year earlier, but that was the extent of our acquaintance. To break the ice, we talked about a local shoe store that offered bargains to senior citizens. On sale days, it was possible to buy three pair of imported shoes for ninety dollars, I said. Starr snorted. He said he bought only American-made shoes.

I thought Starr had a trustworthy look, with the same determined glint I once saw in the eyes of my early political patrons, Wilbur Mills and John McClellan. The resemblance made me feel easier about dealing with him. Though he was not demonstrative, I could see he was a man of some power.

Afterward, as my guests were leaving, Amy asked us to pose for a picture. We formed a group on my porch. When I smiled for the camera, Amy said, "Look serious!" So I put on a menacing scowl and glared at Starr as if I intended to knock his head off. Everyone laughed.

The next day, Amy and Ray returned. They said they wanted to make a deal. I said I was prepared to negotiate. In exchange for my cooperation, they said they could delay my sentencing and give me latitude in choosing the prison where I would serve my time. Most importantly, they said they would put in a good word for me at my sentencing, which would reduce my prison term substantially.

Sam Heuer helped prepare my proffer, which established the bounds of my cooperation, and he signed off on my formal agreement with the prosecutors. He did nothing to try to stop me. But our relationship ended with my decision to cooperate. I did all my negotiating, ensuring that Jim Blair would no longer have any inside knowledge of my case.

There were a number of things I could tell the prosecutors, but I didn't want to give away all of my information at first. For starters, I told them that Clinton had, indeed, mentioned Susan's loan to David Hale. For verification, I suggested they look at the results of a series of lie-detector tests I had taken to prepare for the trial. On every question regarding Clinton's interest in the loan, the lie detectors had picked up the impulse that I was untruthful in my answers relating to Clinton.

Within hours of my revelation to Amy and Ray, the FBI visited the lie-detector examiners and seized the results. When the prosecutors reviewed the tests, they knew we were in business.

The prosecutors found me an apartment in Little Rock, and I spent several days each week there, talking with the independent counsel's staff and the FBI. I found the discussions less grueling than my earlier encounters with the bank examiners. We carried on talks with mutual respect, and I gave away pieces of information as the weeks passed. I told the prosecutors about the loan from Madison Guaranty that Clinton denied taking. After scouring through two hundred boxes of documents, they found the original records of the loan. It took them weeks, but they located the paper that proves Clinton lied in his White House testimony.

I told them Jim Henley had witnessed the exchange between Clinton and David Hale that evening at Castle Grande. As far as I know, he has not corroborated my story. In the months after I agreed to cooperate with the prosecutors, members of the Henley family became increasingly hostile.

They lashed out at me, as though I were some Svengali holding evil power over Susan. As a result, I no longer felt much kinship with them. They represented another set of ruptured friendships in the rubble of Whitewater. I concluded that the Henleys were the real-life equivalent to William Faulkner's Snopes family, the gang of rapacious relatives who took over Will Varner's store when he married into the family in *The Hamlet*.

During the course of my talks with the FBI, I learned that the investigators were interested in the sources of new business suddenly flowing to enterprises run by Jim and Bill Henley, just as the FBI was exploring lucrative contracts steered to Webb Hubbell by Clinton's friends after he came under investigation. The investigators suspected that a lot of hush money was being thrown around.

As the interrogation continued, I told the prosecutors how I promised Bill Clinton, on the morning he sweated in my chair, that I would send business to Hillary, and I recalled how Hillary showed up a couple of hours later to close the deal with Madison Guaranty.

I told how Hillary lied about her work with the savings and loan, first minimizing her connections, then claiming credit on the Rose Law Firm worksheets for the hours that Hubbell and others actually spent on our jobs. I even told them how Henry Hamilton and I passed cash to Clinton while he was governor.

I never told them that Clinton agreed to pardon Susan, because no one asked me.

I tried to make my own arrangements for Susan. The prosecutors assured me that if she agreed to cooperate, she could escape with probation and serve no time in prison. I had four or five telephone conversations with her, explaining the agreement. She kept vacillating. Susan had a visceral dislike for the prosecutors, but at the same time she was appalled by the prospect of prison. She desperately wanted probation, but feared that her lawyer, Bobby McDaniel, would no longer represent her if she cooperated.

Susan sounded as though she was torn by conflict. From her family, she heard condemnation of the prosecutors. Her mother was comparing the independent counsel's operation to the Nazis' occupation of her home country of Belgium. I believe Susan wanted to cooperate, but she was too confused.

In my last conversation with Susan, I said, "It looks like we're at loggerheads. You need to make up your mind. You've got probation if you want it. Just let me know." She never called back.

I had no way to read Susan's mind, but it seemed apparent she was subjected to pressures to hang tough. A week before she was to be sentenced, she went to New York for an interview on ABC. She was prepared to talk about her relationship with Clinton and his intervention on her behalf in connection with the loan. But on the morning that the program was taped, her brother Bill and her boyfriend, Pat Harris, appeared in the Manhattan studio with her and apparently changed her mind. I heard that each time a sensitive question was raised about Clinton in the interview, her brother Bill and Pat interrupted Susan off camera, instructing her not to discuss the president.

I think they constructed a fairy tale for themselves, believing in a happy ending where Susan would be freed at her sentencing. They planned to tell the judge about her innocent hopes and dreams and her plans to marry Pat and live peacefully for the rest of her days in the sunlight of California. Pat spoiled that strategy when he testified as a character witness and was forced to admit that he started his affair with Susan back in 1984, when he was working for me, at a time when Susan was married and living with me.

My sentencing was postponed for several months while I dealt with the prosecutors. Jim Guy Tucker, who pleaded poor health, got off with probation and eighteen months of home detention. After the investigation into his affairs continued, Tucker agreed to cooperate with Starr in February 1998.

Susan received a two-year sentence and a subpoena to appear before the grand jury on the Whitewater case. When she refused to answer questions related to Clinton, she was found in contempt and led away to jail in shackles. She was still there eighteen months later.

When my time came to appear before the grand jury, FBI agents sneaked me through the back door of Little Rock's Federal Building to avoid the press. It was a new experience, testifying in an environment without the tension and confrontation of a trial. My dealings with Starr's staff over the past few months had been civil, and as I sat before the grand jury Ray Jahn guided me through dozens of questions without any rancor.

We sat in a windowless room during the secret proceedings. Much of it was tedious. The foreman of the grand jury sat on a raised dais, and other members of the panel were seated at tables. Some looked as though they were dying from boredom. I tried to keep them awake with occasional wisecracks. When the stenographer asked Jahn, a Texan, and me not to talk so fast, I said, "I'll slow down just as long as you stipulate that we're both southerners."

For seven hours on the first day of testimony, Jahn asked me about the encounter between Clinton, David Hale, and me. He asked about the circumstances of Hillary's hiring by Madison. He asked a number of questions about Jim Blair, leading me to believe that they were looking into a case of obstruction of justice.

When Jahn asked about the details of the Clintons' decision to end their partnership in the Whitewater development in 1992, he suggested that Blair had loaned me one thousand dollars to pay to the Clintons as a token for their interests. I said that was a joke. "Jim Blair is the last guy on this planet I would borrow a thousand dollars from," I said. Most members of the grand jury laughed. They seemed to be quite familiar with Blair.

I don't know what Blair and Heuer testified, but I understand both men were required to appear before the grand jury to explain the handling of my case.

In my second day before the grand jury, I was asked about Clinton's loan from Madison Guaranty, and there were more questions concerning Hillary.

After all of my discussions with the independent counsel's office, I had the impression they wanted to pursue perjury charges against Hillary, but were put off by the politics. Because of the unchartered legal waters, they were reluctant to press criminal charges against the president. Though my talks with Starr's staff took place months before the Monica Lewinsky scandal broke, I had a sense Starr preferred to deal with the president's involvement in the Whitewater case through a report to the House Judiciary Committee, the panel that can initiate impeachment proceedings.

In the spring of 1997, a year after the trial began, I returned to the federal courtroom for sentencing. Ken Starr made an unusual appearance. We shook hands, and I joked that perhaps he could get me a job at Pepperdine University. Earlier, he had announced that he was taking a job as dean of the law school there; he had then changed his mind when he was criticized for his plan to leave the investigation before it was over.

Starr appealed for leniency in my case. He assured the judge that I had provided significant information that had enabled his office to broaden its investigation.

I was sentenced to three years in prison; I hoped to shorten my stay with time off for good behavior and left the courtroom in a reasonably happy frame of mind.

I made a farewell round of interviews and appearances in Washington and New York. I chose *Larry King Live* for my valedictory. The year before, I had appeared on the show. "I lied to you, and for that I apologize," I told King in the first couple of minutes of my return appearance. "I lied to the American people through your program by denying vehemently the story that David Hale was telling about a meeting with the president that Mr. Hale and I had concerning a loan made to Susan McDougal."

I was careful not to be critical of Susan, but I was looking for an opportunity to settle a score with Jim Guy Tucker. His attorneys had portrayed me as a hallucinating witness in the briefs they'd filed to keep Jim Guy out of prison.

Bob Franken, an Arkansas native who covered Whitewater for CNN, had escorted me to the set, and I think he suggested that King ask me about Jim Guy.

King is a low-key interviewer who puts his guests at ease. About halfway through the program, he dropped Tucker's name.

"This all started with you, right? This whole Whitewater thing with you and the suit with Tucker?"

"Yes," I said, "five years ago. . . . It started out that I was willing to sue Governor Tucker because I felt that he had beat my mother out of money."

"Nothing to do with Whitewater?"

"No, nothing. . . . If Tucker hadn't done that, he would still be governor."

"There would be no Whitewater?"

"There would be no Whitewater, and I wouldn't be on the way to jail."

I acknowledged anger at Clinton, but added, "I was incensed with Tucker, who had been the older friend. I was incensed about what he did to my mother, who, by the way, was blind, helpless." Though I had been unable to prevent him from taking our $59,000, I warned, "There is a payday someday."

Near the end of the program, King asked why Clinton had pressured Hale to loan $300,000 to Susan.

"Never understood that," I said. But then I offered an observation. "You have three confidence men involved in this conversation. And a good con man can say more with a wink and a nod than Tolstoy can say in two hundred pages."

King seemed taken aback by my characterization. To make sure he understood correctly, he asked, "Three con men—Hale, McDougal, and Clinton?"

"Right."

Epilogue

Over the last decade of the twentieth century, a stream of journalists, prosecutors, political analysts, and partisan sleuths beat a path
toward Arkansas. They probed our body politic like pathologists
searching for a cancer, and they followed the spoor of a poor real
estate deal in a hunt for scandal.

Some of the visitors came simply to see the zoo, to get a glimpse
of the species *Redneckus americanus*, even though that strain of
Arkansas society vanished years ago. If these people had studied
our history, they would have known that Arkansas went through a
change long before Clinton, professing to be an "agent for change,"
expressed interest in the presidency.

Our cantankerous country politicians, notably Orval Faubus
from Greasy Creek, have gone to dust, just as Dogpatch, USA,
has fallen to ruin, its lonely playground guarded by a ghost, the
abandoned statue of General Jubilation T. Cornpone. After being
suckered to change the name of their pretty Ozark village to
Dogpatch, embarrassed residents petitioned to restore the original
name, Marble Falls.

Gerald L. K. Smith's monument to Jesus Christ still hovers over the Ozarks, but Smith's evangelical right-wing message has been muted by a modern Christian ministry in Arkansas that practices the social gospel instead of the politics of temperance and segregation.

Even Central High School, the brown-brick edifice in the heart of our capital city, stands as a symbol of racial reconciliation and educational achievement, more than forty years after the National Guard refused entrance to nine black schoolchildren.

The Marion Hotel, of course, has passed into history, taking its rowdy clientele with it. In its place, the Capital Hotel across the street has become a stately national landmark where legislators speak in hushed voices when they meet with lobbyists and reporters along the polished mahogany bar. The Grady Manning Hotel is gone, too, its space along the Arkansas River taken by a sleek convention center. Down the street a few blocks, the Clinton Presidential Library will rise in an old warehouse district.

In his own drive to the top, Clinton broke out of the traces of Arkansas politics. Though some Whitewater chroniclers insist on putting him in the same category as Paul Van Dalsem and Sheriff Marlin Hawkins, Clinton was far more sophisticated and calculating than the good ol' boys. While many of us were still wedded to the New Deal, honoring the principles of Franklin Roosevelt as I did in my 1982 campaign, Clinton was already exploring alternate courses. He was a paradigmatic New Democrat, willing to sacrifice some of the old liberal values to win the support of conservatives. A founder of the Democratic Leadership Council, an organization designed to restore power to Southern Democrats by moderating the party's policies, Clinton trimmed his positions the same way bunco men cut deals. After his courageous stands in the 1960s, once he tasted power Clinton found no position important if self-interest could be better served by moving on to something else. He raised manipulation to an art form.

While Clinton became the most successful Arkansas politician in history, other Arkansas leaders before him formed a bridge between the Faubus era and today, men like Win Rockefeller, Dale Bumpers, and David Pryor.

Rockefeller became a Republican governor years before any other Deep South state considered such apostasy. A transplanted Yankee, he won acceptance in Arkansas at a time when other southern states denied their governor's office to anyone other than a native son. Ridiculed as backward, Arkansas was actually ahead of the times. Today, we are surrounded by southern Republican governors in Tennessee, Mississippi, Louisiana, and Texas.

At a time when Clinton served as an apprentice politician, Bumpers was already thought to be presidential timber. Democratic power brokers outside the state encouraged Bumpers to run, but he refused to take the step. After twenty-eight years in the public eye, the original member of the "new generation" of Democrats to win political primacy in Arkansas is retiring this year, opening his Senate seat and raising the possibility that two Republicans might serve Arkansas in the United States Senate. In 1996, Tim Hutchinson, a Baptist minister-congressman from northwest Arkansas, became our first Republican senator since Reconstruction. While Arkansas again gave its electoral votes to Clinton, the state elected Hutchinson to succeed Pryor, once considered a new Arkansas Democrat himself. After thirty years, Pryor got out of politics ahead of Bumpers.

Thus, the generation of Arkansas Democrats that followed Faubus is already passing from the scene, leaving its inheritance to other ambitious, unknown young politicians. Though Bumpers and Pryor were transitional figures, one could say that Arkansas's modern era really started with Bill Fulbright. When the old man finally died in 1995, at the age of eighty-nine, he was eulogized by the president. "If it hadn't been for him I don't think I'd be here today," Clinton said. "He was a great inspiration to thousands and thousands of us who were young when he was a senator."

Arkansas politics emerged from the backwater in the mid-1960s, when reapportionment replaced many rural legislators and racial reforms extended power to blacks. Yet the visitors examining our state seize Whitewater as Exhibit A in an argument to establish Arkansas as an aberrant place where inbreeding produces walleyed progeny as well as crooked, inside business deals and corrupt politics. Everything from Webb Hubbell's bilking of the Rose Law Firm to Vince Foster's suicide has been incorporated into the Whitewater case. Even Monica Lewinsky's allegations of romance in the Oval Office became the property of the Whitewater prosecutor.

Whitewater was merely a business deal that went bad. The McDougals and the Clintons lost money, but no buyers were swindled. Today, I suspect no landowner in the development would be willing to sell a lot for the same price he paid for it. But because the project failed in the 1980s, it became an embarrassment for the Clintons in the 1990s. In their eagerness to disown their parentage in the affair, both Clintons lied and attempted to cover traces of their involvement in Whitewater.

They denied simple associations. When Hillary was asked, under oath, about one of my developments she represented as a lawyer, she said, "I don't believe I knew anything about these real estate projects." In testimony taken under the roof of the White House, the president claimed he had never borrowed money from my savings and loan.

A comic break in the case took place shortly before my first Christmas in prison. Just as some of Hillary's records seemed to appear out of ether, an old canceled check from Madison Guaranty to Bill Clinton turned up in a used car traced to Henry Floyd, a fellow who once ran errands for my mother. The document seemed to corroborate my account of the loan.

There was never any need for the Clintons to have lied about these connections, but they did. And out of Whitewater grew a scandal that not only hounded the Clintons from the day they arrived in Washington, but metastasized into a beast with many heads.

Many Arkansans rue the day Clinton became president. It put us on the map, but it also put us under the microscope. Petty misdeeds were magnified into vast conspiracies. Private citizens saw themselves transformed into infamous celebrities. Reputations were wrecked. Some of us trooped off to prison, others lived constantly under the threat of prosecution. Guileless people were pushed into a punishing spotlight and handled the notoriety with difficulty. In the case of Vince Foster, a life was lost; others were destroyed.

In their zeal to find misconduct in Arkansas, the New Puritans have swooped down upon our latest governor, Mike Huckabee. A Baptist preacher who wrote a book, *Character Is the Issue*, before leaving the pulpit for politics, Huckabee was recently accused by critics of skimming campaign contributions and hiding other sources of outside income. He is a Republican; he moved into the office after Jim Guy Tucker made his ignominious departure.

According to news accounts reaching me in prison, state and federal investigators are also looking "into suspected legislative self-dealing" in which leaders of the Arkansas House face questions that may "force them out of high-paying new state jobs they helped create." This follows indictments of other legislators on charges of insurance fraud, influence peddling, and inside contracts.

Is there something in the water in Arkansas?

Not really. I read the other day that Fife Symington, a former governor of Arizona, would be joining me in the federal penitentiary system following his conviction for fraud. He takes his place with other disgraced sons of Harvard: Arkansas Democrats Jim Guy Tucker and Wilbur Mills, as well as such once-esteemed Republicans as Richard Kleindienst, Nixon's fallen attorney general who copped a plea for lying during Watergate, and Caspar Weinberger, another cabinet member indicted for lying to Congress during the Iran-contra affair and pardoned by President Bush on the eve of his defeat by Clinton.

Most of the modern scandals—Watergate, Abscam, Koreagate, Iran-contra—were grounded in Washington, though Whitewater seemed peculiarly Arkansan.

Our statehouse has its share of knaves, but I believe that the

Arkansas legislature is no more venal than the general assemblies of Massachusetts, New Jersey, and New York, public bodies with histories of corruption.

Just as Clinton could have been elected anywhere, Whitewater could have happened anywhere, in a tiny, incestuous East Coast state like Delaware where zoning decisions affecting private developers have been the grist for scandal for years, or in the huge state of Texas, where its robust politics have always been tinged with calumny and misconduct.

Looking back on the scandal, I'm convinced that Whitewater could have happened anywhere. But it needed a famously protean character, a tainted president, to move it to the nation's center stage.

Index